American Discontent

AMERICAN DISCONTENT

The Rise of Donald Trump
and Decline of the Golden Age

John L. Campbell

OXFORD
UNIVERSITY PRESS

OXFORD
UNIVERSITY PRESS

Oxford University Press is a department of the University of Oxford. It furthers
the University's objective of excellence in research, scholarship, and education
by publishing worldwide. Oxford is a registered trade mark of Oxford University
Press in the UK and certain other countries.

Published in the United States of America by Oxford University Press
198 Madison Avenue, New York, NY 10016, United States of America.

Library of Congress Cataloging-in-Publication Data
Names: Campbell, John L., 1952– author.
Title: American discontent : the rise of Donald Trump and decline of the golden age /
John L. Campbell.
Description: New York, NY, United States of America : Oxford University Press, [2018] |
Includes bibliographical references and index. |
Identifiers: LCCN 2017038024 (print) | LCCN 2018003202 (ebook) |
ISBN 9780190872441 (updf) | ISBN 9780190872458 (epub) |
ISBN 9780190872434 (hardcover : alk. paper)
Subjects: LCSH: United States—Politics and government—2017– | Trump, Donald, 1946– |
Social change—Political aspects—United States—History—21st century. |
Political culture—United States—History—21st century.
Classification: LCC E912 (ebook) | LCC E912 .C38 2018 (print) | DDC 973.933092—dc23
LC record available at https://lccn.loc.gov/2017038024

9 8 7 6 5 4 3 2 1

Printed by Sheridan Books, Inc., United States of America

To Kathy and Jessie

CONTENTS

PREFACE

I began thinking about this book in March 2016, just as I was heading off
to spend a few months at the Copenhagen Business School in Denmark.
I had been making that trek for more than a decade and I knew that my
friends and colleagues there would be asking me about the current presidential primary elections in the United States. Bernie Sanders and Hillary
Clinton were neck and neck in the polls for the Democratic Party nomination. On the Republican side, a large slate of right-wing politicians, including Marco Rubio and Ted Cruz, were vying for their party's nomination.
Among that group was Donald Trump, a billionaire real estate developer,
entrepreneur, and reality television star. Trump was a political upstart who
had never run for public office and seemed to have entered the race on a
whim, peppering his campaign speeches with an alarming number of outrageous comments that had rallied the Republican Party's electoral base.
Initially, almost nobody believed he would win the nomination, let alone
the general election to become the forty-fifth president. But by the time
I got to Copenhagen in late March, Trump was leading the Republican field
with more than 700 delegates in his pocket—more than half of the 1,200
he needed to win the party's nomination. I braced myself for the following
question in Copenhagen: how could a guy like Trump do so well in the
primaries?

In anticipation of that question, I wrote a short paper before I left home
simply to collect my thoughts. I was glad I did because when I arrived, I was
invited to give some seminars and lectures on the subject. More surprising
was that total strangers asked me that question too, including a couple sitting next to me and my wife at a concert one night at Jazzhus Montmartre in
downtown Copenhagen. During the break, they asked if we were Americans,
and when we said yes, they popped the question. People asked me again at
conferences that spring in Germany and Austria. The Austrians quizzed me
about this because they were facing their own right-wing nationalist political movement led by Norbert Hofer's Freedom Party of Austria. Hofer won

the first round of voting that April but without a majority faced a runoff, which he eventually lost by a slim margin. One person warned me, referring to Trump's success in the primaries, that this was how fascism started in Europe in the 1930s. I heard similar concerns in Denmark where the Danish People's Party, founded in 1995, had become an influential presence in Danish politics thanks to its strong anti-immigrant platform. It had helped support the recent Liberal–Conservative coalition government and in 2014 had won the European Parliamentary election in Denmark, garnering 27 percent of the vote in a race with about a half-dozen political parties.

The paper I wrote that spring for the Danes turned out to be the skeleton for this book, although I didn't plan to write a book at the time. After all, there was no way, I thought, that Donald Trump would win. I figured he was just a flash in the pan. But by Election Day in November, things had changed dramatically. Trump had won the Republican nomination and was only about three points behind Clinton in most polls.[1] As luck would have it, I was in Washington, DC that Election Day with a group of high-level Danish civil servants and businesspeople. Reminiscent of my experiences earlier that spring, the Danes wanted to know how Trump had gotten this far and whether he could win the presidency that day. I had some tentative answers to the first question but was emphatic in my answer to the second: "No, I would be shocked if he won." I wasn't the only one of that opinion. We all went to a local restaurant for dinner that evening and watched the election returns come in on CNN. On the way to the restaurant, we passed several busy intersections, each one manned by lots of police astride motorcycles, fully armed, helmeted, wearing bulletproof vests, and just waiting. But for what? Trump had warned repeatedly that the election was rigged against him and that if he lost that night his supporters would riot in the streets. It appeared that the metropolitan police in DC were taking that warning very seriously. They seemed to think Trump might lose too.

At the restaurant, an initial spirit of excitement gave way to nervousness and then disbelief as the returns rolled in and it started to become clear that Trump might win. Dinner broke up at about 10:00 PM and some of us walked back to the hotel in Georgetown. The motorcycle cops were long gone—no riots that night. People had congregated on Pennsylvania Avenue in front of the White House and in Lafayette Square across the street. The mood was somber when we walked by. By the time I went to bed around midnight, the election hadn't been officially called but it was clear who would win. I awoke twice during the night and checked the TV to see if it was officially over. By breakfast time, Trump had declared victory. Just before lunch, Clinton went on national television and delivered a gracious yet impassioned concession speech urging young women never to give up their dreams. That afternoon the Danes and I attended a symposium on the election at the Brookings Institution where both Republicans and Democrats on the dais were nearly at a loss for words trying to explain how it had all happened, and especially in trying to predict what lay ahead. But they all agreed that the next four years could very easily become one of the most serious tests in history of the US Constitution's capacity to check the power of the presidency. After all, Trump would enjoy a Republican-controlled Congress and very likely a conservative Supreme Court once he had a chance to fill the seat vacated by the death several months earlier of Justice Antonin Scalia. By dinnertime, I had decided that the paper I had written earlier that spring should become a book.

Let me be clear from the start—I find Trump's rise to power very disturbing, as do most Democrats. However, so do many Republicans, including some in Congress. The 2016 election was unlike anything in recent memory, and Trump was an extraordinarily different kind of politician than people were used to seeing. His campaign speeches, press releases, and advertisements were loaded with factually incorrect and misleading information. Politicians often play fast and loose with the truth, but Trump's flare for distorting and misrepresenting it, intentionally or not, was astonishing. Moreover, his campaign rhetoric was often offensive. He insulted Mexicans, Muslims, African Americans, immigrants, women, America's military generals, and one war hero, Senator John McCain, who as a navy pilot during the Vietnam War was shot down over Hanoi, captured, tortured, and imprisoned for over five years by the North Vietnamese. However, as Trump put it, "He's not a war hero. He's a war hero because he was captured. I like people that weren't captured."[2] Finally, Trump was the first true outsider to win the White House in over a century—the wealthiest populist the nation had ever seen, a contradiction in terms, to be sure, but one that appealed to millions of voters.[*]

While being an outsider helped him win the election, it was an albatross around his neck once in office—his inexperience very quickly looked like incompetence as things got off to a very rocky start. Consider his first few months in office. He approved a botched military raid in Yemen that killed a Navy Seal. Both Trump and his team issued several falsehoods, including his subsequently discredited Twitter charge that Barack Obama had tapped his phones in Trump Tower during the campaign. He issued a much-publicized executive order banning entry to the United States for people coming from seven predominantly Muslim countries—a move that sparked nationwide protests at airports, and that the courts quickly blocked

---

[*] Even Dwight Eisenhower, who had never held political office prior to the presidency, had served in the military his entire adult life.

as unconstitutional. Several top administrative and cabinet nominees, including Vincent Viola for secretary of the Army and Philip Bilden for secretary of the Navy, withdrew from consideration amid controversy over ethics issues regarding their personal finances. Andrew Puzder, Trump's nominee for secretary of labor, also withdrew when it became clear that several Senate Republicans would not support him due to his antilabor practices as CEO of CKE Restaurants, parent company of the fast-food chains Carl's Jr. and Hardee's. Michael Flynn, Trump's national security adviser, was forced to resign when it was revealed that he had apparently lied to the vice president-elect about his contact with the Russian ambassador during the presidential transition. Committees in both houses of Congress had already launched investigations into possible Russian computer hacking designed to help Trump win the election. They were also looking at possible collusion between the Russians and Trump's associates during the transition, including Flynn and Paul Manafort, Trump's former campaign chairperson. The FBI was looking into it too. It turned out later that Trump had pressured FBI director James Comey to pull back on the bureau's investigation and go easy on Flynn—a move that some thought amounted to obstruction of justice, an impeachable offense. Soon thereafter he fired Comey. As a result, the deputy attorney general appointed a special prosecutor, former FBI director Robert Mueller, to investigate. There were also accusations that Trump was violating the emoluments clause of the US Constitution by benefiting financially from foreign dignitaries staying at his hotels. And then one of Trump's major campaign promises, to "repeal and replace" the Affordable Care Act (ACA), otherwise known as Obamacare, as soon as he took office hit the rocks. It turned out that Trump didn't have a replacement plan after all, so he left it up to Congress to figure out.

Given all this, it wasn't surprising that Trump's approval ratings quickly sank to the lowest level of any new president in modern American history—35 percent by late March in a Gallup survey.[3] According to Steve Schmidt, a long-time Republican strategist and adviser to former vice president Dick Cheney, "No administration has ever been off to a worse 100-day start."[4] Things didn't get much better after that. The Russian collusion scandal deepened, implicating Trump's eldest son, Donald Jr., and son-in-law, Jared Kushner, who now also worked in the White House as a senior adviser. Congress failed spectacularly to repeal the ACA. And several top White House staff were forced to resign, including Press Secretary Sean Spicer, Chief of Staff Reince Priebus, Chief Strategist Steve Bannon, Communications Director Mike Dubke and then his replacement, Anthony Scaramucci, hired by Trump only to be fired ten days later by Trump's new chief of staff. Also departing during the first year were Assistant Press Secretary Michael Short, adviser Sebastian Gorka, Deputy

National Security Adviser K. T. McFarland, Deputy Chief of Staff Katie Walsh, Senior Director for Intelligence at the National Security Council (NSC) Ezra Cohen-Watnick, Deputy Chief of Staff at the NSC Tera Dahl, Middle East adviser at the NSC Derek Harvey, and director in the NSC strategic planning office Rich Higgins. Presidential historians said they had to go all the way back to the nineteenth century to find an administration as crippled with infighting and legislative disarray as Trump's. And Trump's approval ratings remained stuck at historic lows.[5]

It wasn't just the people who voted for Clinton that disapproved of Trump's performance. Some of those who had voted for Trump were beginning to ask themselves if they had made a mistake. My wife and I were sitting at the bar in a local restaurant having dinner one evening about three weeks into Trump's presidency. A local contractor, born and raised in our small New Hampshire town, sat down next to us and the conversation quickly turned to national politics. He confessed that he had voted for Trump and had been willing to give him the benefit of the doubt for a while but was now having second thoughts. He was particularly worried that under Trump's administration he would lose his health insurance, which he said he had received thanks to the ACA. He wasn't alone in his concerns. A special Twitter site was established for disgruntled Trump voters to post their regrets. It was full of complaints, for example, about his appointing more billionaires to high positions than any other president, putting people in top administrative posts who had no experience running large bureaucracies, and nominating people with no policy expertise in the jobs for which they had been chosen. People also grumbled about his kowtowing to the Russians; tweeting ad nauseam in ways unbecoming of the office of the president; and trying to replace the ACA with something that, according to the Congressional Budget Office, would have caused millions of Americans to lose their health insurance.[6] Lots of Trump voters were beginning to suffer from buyer's remorse.

The point is that I am writing this book both for those who supported Trump and for those who did not—Republicans and Democrats. We all need to understand what the forces were that propelled someone like this so rapidly and so unexpectedly to the pinnacle of political power in America. We need to understand that Trump's rise to power was the culmination of deep trends in American society that had been developing for decades. As the saying goes, "Those who fail to learn from history are doomed to repeat it."

In writing this book I have benefited from conversations with and comments from many friends and colleagues. I apologize to those whose names I have inadvertently left out and take sole responsibility for any errors I may have committed—an especially important disclaimer in today's highly charged political climate where alternative facts and fake news permeate the atmosphere. My thanks go to Michael Allen, Geoff Crawford, Christian de Cock, Marc Dixon, Bill Domhoff, Francesco Duina, Niels Fuglsang, Christina Gomez, Lev Grinberg, John Hall, Brooke Harrington, Jason Houle, Larry Isaac, Lars Bo Kaspersen, Claudia Kern, Phil Kern, Mart Laatsat, Kathryn Lively, John McKinley, Ove Pedersen, Chuck Sherman, Kathy Sherrieb, Antje Vetterlein, and Emily Walton. Eddie Ashbee provided an especially helpful sounding board, often challenging my arguments and forcing me to improve them. I also received many helpful comments when I presented versions of the argument in seminars at Copenhagen University, Copenhagen Business School, the University of Southern Denmark, and Dartmouth College. Finally, three anonymous reviewers from Oxford University Press also provided invaluable suggestions, as did James Cook, my editor.

My wife, Kathy Sherrieb, and daughter, Jessica Sherrieb, were among the hundreds of thousands of protestors in Washington, DC on January 21, 2016, a day after the inauguration, demanding that the new Trump administration show tolerance and respect for the law and women's rights. Their activism was a major inspiration for this book.

John Campbell
Lyme, New Hampshire
September 2017

A NOTE ON SOURCES, ALTERNATIVE FACTS, AND FAKE NEWS

"Then I'll get down on my knees and pray,
We don't get fooled again!"[1]

In his best-selling book *The Art of the Deal*, Donald Trump wrote that one of his favorite rhetorical tools is what he called "truthful hyperbole." He maintained that this was an innocent form of exaggeration and a very useful marketing strategy that he first developed for Trump Tower on Fifth Avenue in New York City. The building has a large ground-floor atrium and then nineteen commercial floors above it before the residential floors begin. However, the first residential floor is numbered the thirtieth floor, not the twentieth. Why skip ten floors when numbering them? According to Trump, it makes the building sound bigger than it is—sixty-eight rather than fifty-eight floors. Moreover, people are willing to pay more for apartments on higher floors, which have higher status in the world of luxury condominiums. This proved to be a very successful marketing strategy that he and other real estate developers have used many times since.[2]

In fact, the phrase "truthful hyperbole" is a contradiction in terms. You cannot be truthful while engaging in hyperbole, which according to the *Oxford English Dictionary* is an extravagant statement used to express strong feeling or produce a strong impression, and that people should not take literally. Often on the campaign trail Trump would say things—perhaps as truthful hyperbole—that fact checkers and others would criticize later for being inaccurate. This became so common that people began saying that we had entered a "posttruth" world where down was up and up was down. This continued after the election—even from his staff. Sean Spicer, Trump's press secretary, announced that Trump's was the largest crowd ever to gather on the mall and watch a presidential inauguration, a claim that was soon debunked by official crowd estimates and aerial photography. When questioned about this a few days later by a television reporter on NBC's *Meet the Press*, Trump's senior adviser, Kellyanne Conway, defended the claim, saying that Spicer was simply reporting "alternative facts."

As I was writing this book, I was invited to a one-day conference on fake news and alternative facts held at Harvard Law School.[3] It was the most disturbing conference I have ever attended. Fake news is fabricated or misleading news often coming from professional-looking websites that are run by people who do not subscribe to the normal standards of professional journalism. They distort the facts, make lots of stuff up, and pass it off as being true and newsworthy. There were three panels at the conference composed of respected academics from around the country and professionals from the BBC, Microsoft Research, FactCheck.org, and Twitter. One panel was about why people believe what they believe; one was about how fake news is disseminated; and one was about what we can do to combat fake news. I learned two very important lessons at the conference.

First, we tend to believe things that we hear repeatedly, especially if we hear them from people we know or trust—even if they don't have the faintest idea what they're talking about and what they say makes little sense. Many psychologists and political scientists have documented this empirically over the years, including some people on the Harvard panels. But I suspect that there is more to it than that.

My hunch is that Americans also tend to believe much of what they hear or read repeatedly for two additional reasons. One is the American educational system. As one panelist at the conference put it, our school system does a lousy job of teaching students how to think critically about what they read and hear. Indeed, many people worry that American students are mediocre by international standards when it comes to reading, math, and science, and that in some of these areas American kids are falling behind their peers in other countries.[4] Without critical thinking, alternative facts and fake news pass unquestioned. Of course, not all our students are mediocre. But the vast inequality in school systems across the country means that some students are much more likely to learn critical thinking skills than others are. Economist Peter Temin argues that we have a "dual education system" in America where, due to a lack of resources, schools in lower-income neighborhoods are failing students, while those at the other end of the spectrum with more resources do better.[5] Let me be clear on this. I am not arguing that poor people are less intelligent than rich people, or that Trump supporters are stupid. There is a difference between *intelligence*, which is the ability to grasp and understand facts, and *critical thinking*, which is the capacity to contemplate and evaluate those facts, and to imagine alternative explanations and scenarios for them. Whether our educational system encourages and enhances critical thinking rather than just intelligent understanding has been in question for a long time.[6]

There is also an emotional reason we tend to believe things without question, especially when it comes to politics. As sociologist Arlie Russell Hochschild found in her conversations about politics with downtrodden working-class conservatives in Louisiana—folks that were likely Trump fans—people tend to believe what makes them feel good. And what makes them feel good is often what resonates with and affirms what they already believe. She found that people often disregard facts if they contradict their feelings and beliefs, which may be one reason they vote against their interests.[7] For example, many of the people she interviewed were deeply religious. Their belief in God made them feel good because it gave them great emotional comfort and moral strength to endure the economic and other hardships they suffered. Pulitzer Prize–winning historian Richard Hofstadter showed that in America, religious beliefs have often been at odds with critical thinking.[8] After all, believing in God is a matter of faith, not fact. It makes sense, then, that when politicians, Tea Party activists, or Fox News commentators appeal to people's beliefs in God, or for that matter any emotional issue, as they often do, it may cloud people's ability to evaluate the facts and other information they are hearing.

The second lesson I took away from the Harvard conference was that people are getting their news more and more frequently from social media like Facebook and Twitter where they tend to communicate with people like themselves—people they tend to know and trust. One panelist presented an analysis of over a million media references that people had posted on their Twitter and Facebook accounts. Early in the presidential campaign, those references tended to be from mainstream media sites like the *New York Times*, the *Wall Street Journal*, CNN, and network television news programs. In other words, postings of both center-left and center-right news sources were common. But as the campaign unfolded, these sources faded into the background while references to extreme right-wing sources with a proclivity for trafficking in fake news became more prominent. Topping the list of the most frequently mentioned sources were those from the Breitbart News Network and Fox News. There wasn't much comparable emerging on the left.

You may know that Rupert Murdoch, a very conservative and very wealthy Australian-born American media mogul, established Fox News. His empire also includes News Corp, 21st Century Fox, the large publishing house Harper Collins, and the *Wall Street Journal*. You probably know less about Breitbart, which Andrew Breitbart started in 2005 as Breitbart.com. Breitbart was a conservative who, ironically, had helped Arianna Huffington start the liberal *Huffington Post*. His idea was to create a website that would counter the so-called liberal media bias—occasionally, as it turned out, with vulgar anti-Semitic and Islamophobic views. He died suddenly of a heart attack at age forty-three, but his website lived on.[9] Libertarian hedge fund billionaire Robert Mercer gave $10 million to Steve Bannon, eventually Donald Trump's senior White House adviser, to help subsidize Breitbart. It is now the twenty-ninth most popular website in America, has two billion page visits a year, and is bigger than the *Huffington Post*, its inspiration, and PornHub. It is the biggest political site on both Facebook and Twitter.[10]

However, that's just the beginning. Mercer and his friends also seem to have their hands on other Internet sources of alternative facts and fake news. Before the 2016 election, a group of people bought several hundred Internet domain names at considerable cost to "weaponize" certain ideas. The plan was to repeatedly blast out certain messages in coordinated fashion so that people believed them. One ideational carpet-bombing network was set up during the election to saturate the public with pro-Trump information.[11] We also know, according to testimony before the Senate by James Clapper, former director of national intelligence, that the Russians engaged in these tactics too during the 2016 election using social media to spread fake news and pro-Trump messages.[12]

The point is that we need to be very careful these days when considering what's true and what's not. It's all too easy to find ourselves stuck in an echo chamber where we hear or read the same things repeatedly, and where we believe people we talk and listen to simply because what they say resonates with what we already think and makes us feel good regardless of the truth.

I have tried very hard *not* to write a book based on truthful hyperbole, alternative facts, or fake news. I have drawn my facts from many sources that most people would take as truthful. These include a variety of US government reports and databases; reputable news sources, including, for example, the *New York Times*, *The Economist*, and CNN; well-regarded public opinion polling organizations like Gallup and Pew Research; and several articles and books by respected scholars and professional journalists. In this way, I have tried to separate fiction from truth, and fake news from the real McCoy.

American Discontent

CHAPTER 1

How Did This Happen?

This is not just a story about Donald Trump's ascendance to the presidency of the United States. It's a story about America. It's a story about the decline of civil and sensible politics and their replacement with something much more divisive that may very well threaten US hegemony. It's a story about several long-developing economic, racial, ideological, and political trends in America that created the public discontent that Trump exploited to win the presidency of the United States.

Trump made billions of dollars building skyscrapers, high-end resorts, and golf courses, selling his brand and creating and starring in a popular reality television show. He had no political experience either running for or holding public office. His campaign was disorganized and poorly funded by conventional standards. His policy positions were ill-defined and vague and often boiled down to pithy sound bites like "We'll build a wall!"—which summed up a good deal of his views on how to handle the country's problems of immigration and job loss. During the campaign, he promised to renegotiate various free-trade agreements, pursue protectionist policies, and clamp down on immigration to the United States of Muslims and especially Syrian refugees, whom he considered to be the Trojan horse of radical Islamic terrorism. He also pledged to rethink America's commitment to the North Atlantic Treaty Organization (NATO) and make deals with Vladimir Putin, Russia's president, whose leadership he said he admired. His campaign was riddled with racist, misogynist, xenophobic, and nationalist hyperbole. Many of his views were transmitted instantly in 140 characters or less to his millions of Twitter followers. It was unorthodox, but it worked. Why? He was a pitchman extraordinaire in the right place at the right time with a knack for garnering publicity, distorting facts, and side-stepping scandal. In the extreme, some might say he used these skills to sucker people into supporting him. But there was much more to it than first meets the eye. Trump didn't suddenly come out of nowhere and win the White House just because he was a great pitchman.

My argument is that Donald Trump's rise to power was the culmination of a half century of change in America during which public discontent ebbed and flowed but reached unprecedented heights in the years prior to the election, creating a political tsunami that swept him into the White House. He, better than anyone else, managed to tap that discontent. It started during the 1970s with the decline of America's Golden Age of prosperity following World War II. Four distinct trends were involved and then a massive shock to the system. The first trend, and probably the most important, was the growing economic difficulties of many Americans. These stemmed initially from stagflation—the twin evils of economic stagnation and inflation—but then from globalization and increased international competition, all of which contributed to sluggish wage growth, rising inequality, and a disappearing American dream of upward mobility. The second trend was the emerging perception that many of these problems, as well as other social ills, were caused by people from racial and ethnic minorities, and most recently immigrants who were taking jobs away from Americans and who threatened the homeland and the American way of life. The third trend was a conservative shift in ideology where people came to believe that big government was a threat to America's future, that taxes had become too high, and that something had to be done about this to solve America's economic troubles. Many of the public's fears, anxieties, and beliefs about all of this were not borne out by the facts. Even though many Americans really were suffering economically from industrial decline, racial and ethnic minorities and immigrants had not caused these problems. Nor was smaller government a panacea for them. Nevertheless, Trump exploited each of these trends. But he also benefited from a fourth one to which each of the other three contributed—increasing political polarization, especially between the Republican and Democratic parties, the likes of which Americans hadn't seen in generations. A tipping point had been reached. And then suddenly the 2008 financial crisis hit, Barack Obama was elected the first African American president, and his administration moved quickly not only to resolve the crisis but also to overhaul the nation's health care system in bold fashion. Polarization in Washington turned into legislative gridlock, and public discontent soared. The tsunami had arrived. People were fed up with the status quo and saw Trump as their savior—the only one who, as his core campaign slogan promised, could "Make America Great Again!"

Professional football in America is played on Sunday afternoons. The next day fans gather around the water coolers, coffee machines, or lunch tables at work to discuss the games. The topic of conversation often ends up being why somebody's favorite team would have won if only they had passed or run the ball more often, kicked a field goal when they had the chance, or done something else differently. It's not unusual for fans to second-guess the team's quarterback, the guy who runs the offense, for calling the wrong play or making a bad decision at a crucial moment that cost their team the win. These fans are known as Monday morning quarterbacks. They exist elsewhere too.

My argument about Trump's rise to power differs from many on offer that focus on much more immediate factors with little appreciation for the deeper structural and historical trends that I address. Many of these arguments are the ruminations of Monday morning quarterbacks who very quickly tried to make sense of what had happened on Election Day in 2016. Many of their explanations for why Trump beat Hillary Clinton, his Democratic opponent, have been reported in the media. They are not wrong as far as they go. But they don't get to the more important factors underlying the election. They focus only on the tip of the iceberg.

To begin with, some people, like Trump confidante and political fixer Roger Stone, say that Trump won because of his media-savvy experience, showmanship, and celebrity—he knew how to pitch his message in effective ways.[1] "Make America Great Again," "Build a Wall," and "Drain the Swamp" were memorable phrases during the campaign that summarized his plans for improving the economy; keeping Mexican murderers, rapists, and gangsters out of the country and stopping others from taking jobs away from Americans; and cleaning up government. Observers have long recognized that Republicans generally have a way with words, framing their arguments in simple terms that resonate with people's basic feelings, values, and predispositions. George Lakoff's classic book, *Don't Think of an Elephant*, shows how for years Republicans have paid close attention to this, bringing memorable sound bites to public debates while their Democratic opponents bring facts and data that nobody remembers the next day.[2] It is no surprise, then, that Ronald Reagan, an actor by training, became the Republican governor of California and then president of the United States, or that Arnold Schwarzenegger, another Republican actor, eventually followed in his footsteps to the state house in Sacramento. Donald Trump was especially gifted in this regard, first honing his skills as a flamboyant pitchman for his far-flung business ventures and then starring in *The Apprentice*, the popular reality television show in which he searched for an able assistant to work for him in real life and dismissed inferior contestants every week with the simple yet again memorable phrase "You're fired!" As one observer put it, "If *The Apprentice* didn't get Trump elected, it is surely what made him electable."[3] Trump's appeal was based partly on the passion he could tap in his supporters. And he could do that because he told them with catchy phrases that what they already felt about race, class, immigration, government, and other things was right. It was okay, he said, to feel that way, and it was okay to ignore political correctness and the left-wing "PC police" that told them how they ought to feel.[4] A few people predicted more than a year before the election that his media skills could win Trump the nomination if not the White House too.[5]

Some say that Trump won because WikiLeaks publicized embarrassing emails from the Democratic National Committee and the Clinton campaign that were stolen by Russian computer hackers. Clinton herself has said this publicly.[6] Lending some credence to that charge, a subsequent investigation by the Office of the Director of National Intelligence concluded, "Russian President Vladimir Putin ordered an influence campaign in 2016 aimed at the U.S. presidential election. Russia's goals were to undermine public faith in the U.S. democratic process, denigrate Secretary Clinton, and harm her electability and potential presidency." The investigation went on to say that "Putin and the Russian Government developed a clear preference for President-elect Trump." The Federal Bureau of Investigation (FBI), the Central Intelligence Agency (CIA), and the National Security Agency supported these conclusions.[7] The report did not determine whether the leaks influenced the outcome of the election, but some people in addition to Clinton believed they did.

Some say that Trump won because eleven days before the election the FBI's director, James Comey, raised concerns anew about Clinton's mishandling of classified information on her private email server while she was secretary of state. An earlier FBI investigation had exonerated her. At that time Comey announced that the case was closed. However, in late October he informed Congress by letter that thousands of additional emails had been discovered on someone else's computer in a separate investigation that might implicate her again for the same thing. Suddenly, Clinton's trustworthiness, already a major issue in the campaign, was again being questioned. But then two days before the election Comey let her off the hook again, announcing that there was nothing new in this batch of emails after all. Nevertheless, Clinton has insisted that Comey's unprecedented announcement in October of an ongoing FBI investigation helped turn the tide in Trump's favor, especially among undecided voters in key battleground states. Addressing a group of donors soon after the election, she said, "There are lots of reasons why an election like this is not successful. . . . Our analysis is that Comey's letter raising doubts that were groundless, base-less . . . stopped our momentum."[8] The Office of the Inspector General launched an investigation into Comey's actions. Months later, Clinton reit-erated this accusation in her election memoir, *What Happened*, maintaining that "if not for the dramatic intervention of the FBI director in the final days, I believe that in spite of everything, we would have won the White House."[9] After all, she argued, the email story dominated headlines, crowd-ing out virtually everything else she and her campaign were saying or doing. She believed deeply that were it not for Comey, the press's obsession with her emails would have blown over.[10]

Some say that Trump won because the Clinton campaign never really got its act together. It was beset by feuding over strategy; relied too much on data analytics; failed to sense the national populist mood, particularly among poor, rural, white, working-class voters; and, as a result, neglected and lost Wisconsin, Michigan, and a few other key states with signifi-cant blue-collar constituencies.[11] For example, during the waning days of the campaign, the Service Employees International Union pleaded with Clinton's leadership team in Brooklyn to shift more resources to Michigan because local reconnaissance warned that she was losing her grip on that crucial state. The request was denied and Clinton lost Michigan. If things had been managed differently, maybe Clinton, not Trump, would have become president.[12] Perhaps this isn't surprising insofar as politicians are typically unresponsive to the interests of low-income citizens and some-times even the middle class. Arguably, one reason Mitt Romney lost to Obama in the 2012 presidential election was that Romney was caught on tape making disparaging remarks at a fundraiser about the less affluent 47 percent of the population that he said paid no income tax and were free-loading on government benefits of one kind or another.[13]

In contrast, some say that Trump won because he ran a brilliant campaign. According to Roger Stone, "Donald Trump is his own strategist, campaign manager, and tactician, and all credit for his incredible election belongs to him." In Stone's opinion, Trump's brilliance was on display throughout the campaign by his being able to dominate the media coverage with combative flair and outrageous language that appealed to working- and middle-class voters, by reading his crowds to gauge what resonated with them or not, and by speaking his mind in an era when people were fed up with political double-talk. Trump also shook up his leadership team several times during the campaign to bring in new ideas and fresh thinking when it was needed.[14] Notably, he brought in Steve Bannon, who afforded Trump access to an infrastructure of organizations, including Breitbart News, that helped gen-erate and spread many of the alternative facts and fake news that permeated the campaign to Trump's advantage.[15]

Some say that Trump won because he exploited a populist insurgency that was sickened with politics as usual in Washington. People wanted a president outside both the Republican and Democratic Party mainstream.[16] Moreover, even though his campaign statements were vague, misleading, or factually incorrect, enough of the electorate was so ill-informed that they still bought his populist line, and did so, ironically, despite his boasts of being filthy rich.[17] Research suggests that although much of the public is in the dark about most political issues, all else being equal, conservatives, Trump's bread and butter, tend to be less well informed than liberals.[18] According to PolitiFact, a nonpartisan fact-checking organization, nearly three-quarters of Trump's factual claims and statements on the campaign trail were either mostly or entirely false as compared to only about a quarter of Clinton's.[19] Trump, for example, said the following about Clinton's proposed immigration policy at a campaign rally in Albuquerque, New Mexico, on October 30, 2016: "She wants to let people just pour in. You could have 650 million people pour in, and we do nothing about it. Think of it. That's what could happen. You triple the size of our country in one week."[20] If he were right, it could mean that every person from South America, Central America, and Canada would move to the United States in that single week—roughly 3.9 million people per hour, nonstop, for 162 hours. Despite erroneous statements like this, many Trump supporters believed much of what he said. For instance, while Trump claimed that voter fraud was rampant in several states during the election—a claim that was proven to be patently false—60 percent of Trump voters surveyed a month after the election believed that millions of people had voted illegally for Clinton. Only 6 percent of Clinton voters believed this. Indicative of their unfailing faith in Trump's pronouncements, 86 percent of those who voted for him also believed that he was more credible than CNN, whereas 2 percent of Clinton voters believed the same.[21] Clinton was perceived as being far less trustworthy than Trump in many polls too.[22]

Some say that Trump won simply because so many people hated Clinton, believing that in addition to being dishonest she was also part of the Washington establishment, corrupt, incompetent, an abortion fanatic, and, of course, Bill Clinton's wife, not to mention a woman. People also blamed her for being too stiff and overly intellectual on the campaign trail, and lacking charisma.[23] Within days of the election, the conservative *National Review* posted an article with the following headline summing it up nicely: "Hillary Clinton lost because she's Hillary Clinton."[24]

Some say that Trump won because of the rise of social media.[25] Social media emerged during the campaign as an important source of information for many voters. Facebook and Twitter were particularly important, especially for younger people, who shifted their attention away from major news organizations. In February 2016, nearly half of Americans surveyed said they consumed news on Facebook—much of it neither filtered nor fact-checked, which opened the door for what came to be known as fake news and alternative facts. The rise of fake news was startling, such as the story that the pope had endorsed Donald Trump for president, which never happened but was still shared by over one million people on Facebook.[26] Lots of the fake news was pushed by the Breitbart News Network and Fox News during the campaign.[27]

Finally, by the same token, some say the mainstream media bears responsibility for Trump's victory because during much of the campaign it reported but failed to question the truthfulness of much of what was circulating on social media or said by the candidates, particularly Trump. When it did eventually raise questions, it picked on Trump more than Clinton, not surprisingly given his more cavalier handling of the facts. But this fed into Trump's repeated attacks on the media as being biased and dishonest. It may also have fueled many of his supporters' suspicions that the media was against him and therefore not to be trusted. Gallup reported in September 2016 that Americans' trust and confidence in the mass media had fallen to the lowest point since Gallup began polling on the subject—only 32 percent said that they had a great or fair amount of trust in mainstream television, radio, and newspaper news, down from 72 percent in 1976. Most of the decline was among Republicans—that is, Trump supporters.[28] Moreover, pursuit of the ratings cash cow meant that much of the mainstream media obsessed over sensationalistic stories like the Clinton email scandal or the possibility that she was running a secret pedophile ring in the basement of a Washington pizzeria rather than stories about the candidates' policy proposals.[29] The quest for ratings combined with Trump's flamboyant celebrity and media style, plus his provocative Tweets and other outrageous statements, meant that he garnered far more media coverage than anybody else in the campaign. When asked whether the media's ratings-driven pandering to sensationalism was good for the country's political discourse, a top executive from CBS television put it like this: "It may not be good for America, but it's damn good for CBS."[30]

WHAT'S MISSING?

There may be some truth to all this speculation about why Trump won. But this Monday morning quarterbacking ignores the underlying structural and historical factors that created an opening for him in the first place. Why was it, for example, that he could frame the immigration problem so effectively in terms of job loss and the threat of minorities streaming into the country intent on rape, murder, drug dealing, and terrorism? Perhaps because citizens had long-festering concerns about their jobs, their financial future, and the economy in the wake of the financial crisis, or because he was able to tap a growing undercurrent of racism that had been churning for many years in American society—sometimes cultivated deliberately by politicians. Perhaps racism also had something to do with the appeal of his call for countering terrorism by stopping Muslims from entering the country.

Why was it that Clinton was less trusted by many voters than Trump, even though Trump was significantly less truthful? Why did people hate her so much? Why was it that the WikiLeaks, Russian hacking, and Comey stories about Clinton's emails were taken as reasons to doubt her trustworthiness and competence? And why did people yearn for a populist outsider, very much unlike Clinton, for president? Perhaps it was because people no longer trusted their government—and people who had served in it like Clinton—because it was stuck in political gridlock. And perhaps the distrust in government and those associated with it was because political ideology had shifted so far to the right over the last few decades. Perhaps distrust was also due to political polarization in Washington.

Why did the Clinton campaign ignore key states, particularly in the old industrial heartland of the upper Midwest? Perhaps because it lost sight of the fact that the working and middle classes in the Rust Belt states that Democrats presumed she would win because they had been traditional Democratic strongholds had experienced so much economic hardship that they gave up hope that Democrats would ever really help them. Unfortunately for her, many of these people were deeply offended when at a campaign fundraiser she described half of all Trump supporters as a "basket of deplorables." This was a statement eerily reminiscent of Romney's crack about the 47 percent, and one that she regretted almost as soon as the words slipped past her lips and into the microphones of the press.

Why were voters increasingly inclined to believe fake news? Perhaps because as part of the general ideological polarization of politics, people had become less inclined to listen to all sides of an argument in the first place. And as the number of highly partisan news outlets, such as Fox News, MSNBC, Breitbart, and smash-mouth talk radio, proliferated, people simply tuned into news outlets that told them what they already believed. Conservatives tended to listen to conservative sources and liberals tended to listen to liberal ones.[31] Notably, a right-wing media ecosystem began to emerge following Reagan's election in 1980. Its growth accelerated after 2008 and especially during the 2016 election cycle. Judging from an analysis of millions of Twitter and Facebook communications, during the 2016 cycle that ecosystem garnered increasing attention among the public, shifted the mainstream media's attention to Trump's agenda, and through constant repetition gave fake news and alternative facts credibility. Nothing of this magnitude occurred on the left.[32] Nevertheless, these news outlets gave their audiences what they wanted to hear, creating an echo chamber where people insisted that anything that didn't square with their beliefs was rubbish.

What I am suggesting is that as plausible as these popular explanations are, they only scratch the surface. They certainly had some effect on the election, as contingencies always do. Hillary Clinton recognized many of these in her analysis of the election.[33] But Trump's ascendance to power was the manifestation of much deeper trends in society. Trump spoke to and capitalized on the discontent, angst, and anxiety among voters that was associated with these trends. Just as I was finishing this book, another book, *One Nation After Trump*, written by E. J. Dionne, Norman Ornstein and Thomas Mann, appeared. It suggested that understanding Trump's victory required "seeing that he represents an extreme acceleration of a process that was long under way." Their claim captures the essence of my argument.[34]

BUILDING BLOCKS

We don't have to start from scratch to understand what happened. There are already some possible explanations on offer about where the political polarization, gridlock, and public discontent came from. They provide some building blocks we can use to begin developing a more nuanced and complete analysis of Trump's rise to power.

One focuses on *ideas and ideology*, pointing, for example, to the rise of neoliberalism as it has spread into politics and mainstream public discourse. Neoliberalism, or market fundamentalism as it is sometimes known, is an extremely conservative policy playbook emphasizing the need for smaller government to solve many economic and social problems. This means cutting taxes, regulation, and government spending to the bone; balancing the government budget; and paying down the national debt.[35] Its proponents, such as former Speaker of the House Newt Gingrich, current Speaker of the House Paul Ryan, and the conservative wing of the Republican Party, especially in the House, have proven to be especially inflexible and divisive advocates of neoliberalism. Neoliberalism feeds into a winner-take-all mentality that is a recipe for polarization and gridlock, particularly during tough economic times.[36] The media echo chamber, discussed earlier, is also culpable in this regard insofar as certain newspapers, TV and radio programs, websites, and blogs on the right have engaged in increasingly partisan and inflammatory rhetoric pushing neoliberalism.[37] Not coincidentally, some blame this for a general dumbing down of political discourse in which people are more likely to believe fake news and alternative facts.[38]

Another helpful building block involves American *political institutions*.[39] Some people argue that the division of powers and system of checks and balances has always had the potential for stalemate whenever political and ideological divisions become more extreme.[40] Others have blamed the increased gerrymandering of congressional districts, which has created an increasing number of "safe seats" in the House, so called because they are virtually guaranteed to be controlled by the same party year after year. This encourages candidates from the party in control in safe districts to compete intensely among themselves for their party's nomination since the winner will likely win the general election too. This tends to bring out candidates with more extreme political and ideological views.[41] Another institutional explanation on offer involves campaign finance. Many argue that, thanks to changes in campaign finance laws, the demise of civility in American politics boils down to the increasingly vast sums of money flowing into politics from wealthy interests with extreme ideological axes to grind.[42] The fabulously wealthy libertarian brothers Charles and David Koch are often seen as poster boys for this trend.[43] A few observers have also said that the development of the modern primary system is to blame insofar as it created opportunities for activists to push their parties in more extreme directions when selecting candidates to run for president.[44]

Finally, many people attribute America's political problems to the *economy*, specifically economic stagnation, growing income inequality, the angst it has produced within the body politic, and the willingness of politicians to capitalize on it. Job loss, particularly in the industrial heartland, has politically energized working- and middle-class Americans who have faced increasing difficulties over the last few decades trying to make ends meet.[45] In turn, social movements have erupted on both sides of the political spectrum, pushing the Left and Right farther apart.[46] These included the Tea Party and Occupy Wall Street movements. This goes back to the notion that we are living in a winner-take-all society where the politics of austerity have pitted different groups against each other with nobody willing to compromise or cooperate with their opponents.[47]

Overall, then, we are facing a situation that resembles the fable of the three blind men and the elephant—each feeling a different part of the animal and offering wildly different descriptions of it and missing some parts altogether. Parsimony is a goal for most social scientists. However, life is complicated and sometimes it is difficult to boil things down to simple cause-and-effect relationships.[48] That's the case here. Several relatively distinct trends developed over a long period and eventually merged to produce the polarization, angst, and gridlock of today upon which Trump capitalized. Because it is a complicated story, a road map would be helpful to show what lies ahead.

THE ROAD MAP

Chapter 2 quickly outlines the overarching historical backdrop against which Trump staged his campaign—America's Golden Age. This was the time of greatness to which he referred constantly on the campaign trail and that was embodied in his campaign theme, "Make America Great Again!" This is important because he used it as a foil for showing how great America used to be and by implication what greatness would look like once he restored it as president.

However, the core of my argument is about four big historical trends. If a picture is worth a thousand words, then Figure 1.1 is helpful because it illustrates the basic flow of the argument and structure of the rest of the book with details in each box to be explained in subsequent chapters. The first trend is economic. Chapter 3 begins by showing how long-term trends in the economy beginning in the late 1960s and early 1970s, notably stagflation, automation, globalization, and increased international competition, caused working- and middle-class wage stagnation, rising inequality, and mounting levels of personal debt. These in turn caused many Americans to worry that the American Dream was slipping out of reach and that the chances for upward mobility were evaporating into thin air. They were right. This is a story of the decline of America's postwar Golden Age of prosperity. Trump took advantage of this by promising to be the best jobs-creating president God ever put on Earth and claiming that his economic program would boost economic growth beyond what most economists believed was possible.

Chapter 4 explains how this economic story and the angst it produced took on racial tones. This is the second trend. Again, Trump's promises played on public fears and concerns. For years minorities had been blamed for higher taxes, job loss, and depressed wages, as well as crime, terrorism, and a general assault on traditional American values. However, the facts were at odds with these perceptions. But that didn't matter to Trump—he disregarded the facts and capitalized on the public's misunderstandings, often in rather ugly ways. Racial scapegoating was not new to the United States. However, it took a more explicit tone in the Trump campaign, which emphasized recent immigration patterns—an influx of Hispanics from Mexico and Muslims from the Middle East that Trump said he would stop from entering the country by building a wall along the southern border, rounding up undocumented immigrants, deporting them, and tightening

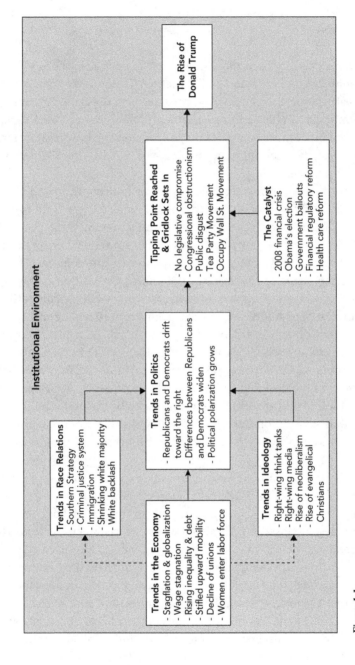

Figure 1.1:
The rise of Donald Trump.

up the immigration system overall. The point of this chapter is not so much to prove Trump or his supporters wrong, although that is an important part of the story, but to show how he was able to play upon the misguided beliefs of the electorate to help him win the election. The same is true of the next chapter.

Chapter 5 describes the third trend, how economic decline laid the foundation for a shift in ideology. By this point in the book it will be clear how clever Trump was at promising things during the campaign that resonated with the public's anxieties, ill-informed or not. This chapter digs deeper into how he did this, particularly insofar as his economic plan is concerned. Again, his views of problems and solutions were at odds with the facts. But what mattered in the end was how effectively he played upon people's perceptions and assumptions about the world. This is a story about the rise of neoliberalism as the cure for what ailed Americans and the American economy. Neoliberal ideology is a multidimensional phenomenon. It involves a taken-for-granted paradigm—a set of assumptions—about how the economy works, as well as specific policy recommendations derived from it. It also involves a variety of public sentiments—some might say values—deeply rooted in American culture about the appropriate role government ought to take in managing the economy and influencing people's lives. These sentiments and others provided raw materials with which Trump fabricated catchy rhetorical frames to garner public support for his policy ideas. Not everyone succumbed to the neoliberal mantra, but enough did to help Trump's cause.

Each of these three trends provided a certain amount of ammunition for Trump's campaign. But they also converged, delivering even more firepower by contributing to a fourth trend—growing political polarization. Chapter 6 explains how this happened. First, ideological trends—the rise of neoliberalism—pushed both Republicans and Democrats to the right. However, the Republicans moved farther than the Democrats in part because they also succumbed to pressure from conservative Evangelical Christians and in part because some of the more moderate Republicans defected to the Democratic Party in the wake of the Nixon Watergate scandal. Meanwhile, traditional New Deal Democrats helped anchor the Democratic Party to more liberal positions—even though that anchor was beginning to slip a bit thanks to the arrival of those post-Watergate Republican defectors. Second, economic trends were at work too. As stagflation and globalization unfolded, organized labor grew weaker and its support for the Democratic Party diminished, which was another reason the liberal Democratic anchor was slipping. An additional reason for that slippage was that big corporations' support for the Democratic Party eroded as it became harder for them to absorb the costs associated with the

Democrats' expensive government programs. But while economic issues were pushing both parties to the right, they also polarized them by driving wedges between generations and between men and women on important policy issues. Third, politics also became more polarized racially. White working-class voters switched from the Democratic to the Republican Party thanks to the so-called Southern Strategy, which insinuated that Democratic Party policies were threatening white privileges. This sparked a white backlash against Democratic policies. Topping it all off, immigration and then the 9/11 terrorist attacks racialized political divisions further.

By the time the 2008 financial crisis hit and Obama was elected president, polarization had reached a tipping point. Chapter 7 explains that the financial crisis and Obama's presidency provided the catalyst that pushed things over the edge into extreme political gridlock in Washington, something with which Americans became thoroughly disgusted. The financial crisis exacerbated America's economic woes and made people angry. The fact that Obama was America's first African American president made things worse. So did his moves to handle the financial crisis and Great Recession, as well as to reform the national health care system. Trump tapped the public's anger and disgust, turning it to his electoral advantage. He claimed that as a billionaire, he didn't need anybody's money to win office. Nor was he an insider to Washington politics. He promised that because he wasn't beholden to anyone, he would unify the country and cut through the gridlock by "draining the swamp" in Washington—ridding it of backroom deals that favored special interests rather than the public. And if Congress didn't cooperate, he said that he would move unilaterally by issuing executive orders that would get the job done. Among other things he promised to immediately scrap Obama's two signature programs—financial regulation and health care reform—that had helped transform polarization into gridlock in the first place.

Overall, then, Trump just happened to be in the right place at the right time. He rose to power thanks to slowly developing economic, racial, ideological, and political trends and then a massive catalyst that suddenly triggered a partisan explosion. Chapter 8 wraps things up by providing evidence from exit polls that the issues I have described and that Trump tapped did in fact resonate with voters enough to sweep him into office. However, this last chapter also argues that Trump's success helped transform American politics in ways that are reminiscent of what has happened in several European countries in the sense that politics is no longer just about traditional liberal and conservative issues like taxes, spending, and regulation but also about issues of globalization. In other words, American politics has taken a new form, which is polarized in new ways. This threatens the hegemony the United States has enjoyed since World War II.

None of this took place in a vacuum. It unfolded in an institutional environment that tended to channel economic, racial, ideological, and political forces in certain directions. The shaded background in Figure 1.1 represents this institutional environment. I've already mentioned some of these institutions: the system of checks and balances, gerrymandering, campaign finance laws, and the presidential primary system. But there are more. For example, America's two-party system based on winner-take-all elections increased the possibility of polarization and gridlock. In European countries with electoral systems based on proportional representation, if a party wins more than a certain percentage of the vote, say, 5 percent, then it gets a roughly comparable number of seats in parliament. As a result, there are often several parties represented in the legislature, which means that to get anything done, including often forming a government to begin with, compromises are required, deals must be cut, and, as a result, politics gravitate toward the middle of the political spectrum, not the polarized extremes. Nevertheless, polarization is not inevitable in a two-party winner-take-all system. If it were, it would have occurred long ago in America. Another important institution was the American criminal justice system, which generated animosities and conflicts among racial groups that contributed to polarization. So did passing voter identification laws requiring voters to prove their residency to receive a ballot—an institutional change intended to undermine the electoral power of minority groups, among others. And underneath it all was America's federalist system, which afforded state governments lots of leeway in writing their own rules in the first place.

Additionally, Americans embraced several institutionalized values that came into play during the 2016 presidential campaign and were particularly important for Trump's rise to power. One is a long-standing distrust of intellectuals stretching back to the seventeenth century. Americans have always placed high value on common sense and pragmatism while frequently questioning the legitimacy and relevance of lofty intellectuals. Anti-intellectualism gradually pervaded religious doctrine; the realm of business, particularly with the advent of business schools and the economics profession; and, perhaps ironically, the educational system where teachers were supposed to instill in their students practical knowledge necessary for later life.[49] These values even appeared occasionally among intellectuals, such as in sociologist C. Wright Mill's classic, *The Sociological Imagination,* in which he slammed "grand theory" in the social sciences and those who propagated it for being excessively verbose and out of touch with the real world.[50]

Another important set of values are those associated with populism. Populism was occasionally related to the sort of anti-intellectualism I just described. But more often it took two different forms. One involved left-wing sentiments against moneyed interests, such as in the nineteenth century when midwestern farmers raged against bankers, railroads, monopolies, and financial speculators who exploited the working class or didn't appear to contribute anything of real value to society. Another involved right-wing sentiments held by people who believed that religious, racial, ethnic, or immigrant groups other than their own threatened their status and position in society. This brand of populism often went hand in hand with nationalism.[51]

Two more sets of values are important for my argument. One was the belief in laissez-faire. Americans have long valued individual initiative in free markets as the key to economic success, upward mobility, and the American Dream.[52] The other was American beliefs in the sanctity of the traditional nuclear family. All of these institutional factors and a few others contributed to Donald Trump's victory and are discussed along the way in various chapters.

Of course, there is one more important institution. One question people have asked me is how Hillary Clinton could have won nearly three million more votes than Donald Trump in the general election but still lost the White House. The answer is that Trump won seventy-four more votes than she did in the Electoral College. The Electoral College is the mechanism established by the US Constitution for the indirect election of the president where citizens in each state vote in a general election to pick "electors" who ultimately choose the winner. The Electoral College votes in almost every state are distributed on a winner-take-all basis.[53] If they had been distributed proportionally, then Hillary Clinton would have won.* However, a second and more interesting question is, why Clinton didn't bury Trump in a massive landslide of popular votes in the first place and effectively take the Electoral College out of play? In other words, why was the election as close as it was? She had far more experience than Trump in the executive branch when as First Lady she spearheaded a major health care initiative in her husband's administration, and then served as secretary of state under Obama. She also had more experience in Congress, where she served for eight years as the junior senator from New York. She even had experience in the judicial branch as a lawyer. Trump had no experience in government at all. Yet her margin of victory in the popular vote was only a smidgeon over 2 percent. The answer to this second question lies at the heart of this book.

* The fact that some states (Maine and Nebraska) have recently replaced winner-take-all systems for allocating Electoral College votes with proportional systems suggests that some people recognize the problem.

Some of my colleagues talk about the "red thread" running through an argument—that is, the central story line that ties all the details and complexities together. It's not unlike the little girl in the red coat who appeared for a moment every now and then in Steven Spielberg's otherwise black-and-white movie, *Schindler's List*, and whose presence was a reminder of how obvious the horrors of Nazi Germany should have been to the world, especially insofar as they brutalized children. Perhaps I shouldn't have been surprised, then, when people asked me to pick the one thing above all others that best explains Trump's rise to power. I hate the question given the complexities involved. But if forced to answer, and at the risk of being accused of reducing everything to economics, I would say that the backbone of my argument—the red thread—is the story of economic change. Much of Trump's campaigning, beginning with his central "Make America Great Again!" slogan, zeroed in on the economy. When he announced his candidacy in Trump Tower, nearly all he talked about were economic issues—jobs, wages, and trade. In fact, he opened his remarks by blasting China, Japan, and Mexico for beating America in trade. He said very little about national defense and nothing about social issues.[54] And why not? The national hangover left by the worst financial catastrophe in nearly a century still throbbed in the American psyche. Trump clearly understood Bill Clinton's most famous electioneering principle: "It's the economy, stupid!" Unlike other recent Republican nominees for president, Trump downplayed social issues and zeroed in almost entirely on the economy.[55]

But Trump was a master at wrapping economic issues in nationalist, xenophobic, racist, and in some cases sexist rhetoric. And therein lies the complexity of my argument. Consider race and ethnicity for a minute. For years lots of politicians had been blaming African Americans, Mexican immigrants, and the Chinese for the economic trials and tribulations of the white working and middle classes. Trump did too. Yet racism in America can't be simply reduced to economic issues. Certainly, the anti-Muslim sentiment that Trump tapped during the campaign had nothing to do with economics—it was all about perceived terrorist and cultural threats to America. The same was true of ideology. The nation's economic malaise created an opportunity for neoliberalism to become the guiding light for many policymakers, but anti–big government sentiments, not to mention traditional family and religious values, had been around since the Revolution and they also mattered in Trump's rise to power. My point is that economic factors facilitated many—but by no means all—of the racial, ideological, and political changes that helped pave the way for his victory. We can't boil it all down to the economy even if the economy is the most important part of the story—the red thread. This is why there are dotted rather than solid causal arrows in Figure 1.1 running from economic trends to racial and ideological trends—they represent these less deterministic effects.

These complexities are why Trump's rise to power tends to defy lots of conventional wisdom on presidential electoral politics. Thomas Frank's bestseller, *What's the Matter with Kansas?*, for example, argues that most people vote against their economic interests because they are suckered by a bait-and-switch strategy honed over the years mainly by conservative Republicans. During elections, politicians promise to protect traditional middle-American cultural values but then once in office act in the economic interests of corporations and the wealthy. In Frank's words, "values may matter most to voters, but they always take a backseat to the needs of money once the elections are won."[56] But in Trump's case, as I have noted, economic, not social, issues were at the heart of the campaign even though he often cloaked them in cultural trappings, such as immigration.

In contrast, and in response to Frank's argument, political scientist Larry Bartels believes that economics outweighs values and social issues when it comes to deciding presidential elections. He argues that Republicans win the presidency when incomes among the affluent are rising in the year before the election, and when campaign contributions favor the Republican candidate.[57] Consistent with his view, incomes of the wealthy were rising during the 2016 election cycle. But other economic issues were involved too, such as jobs and trade. Moreover, Trump was outspent nearly two to one by Clinton ($795 million to $408 million), especially when it came to outside money, where Clinton enjoyed a three-to-one advantage ($231 million to $75 million).[58]

The point is that we need a more nuanced analysis to explain Trump's rise to power. As Katherine Cramer found in her study of Wisconsin gubernatorial politics, people's conservative inclinations nowadays are a combination of economic and cultural concerns that form what she calls a politics of resentment, where people who need help from the government but don't get it are offended when they see their government helping people who they believe don't need it.[59]

CONCLUSION

Before digging into the trends that brought Trump to power, we need to pause for a minute and consider the core message of his campaign—the notion that America had fallen from greatness and that he would restore that greatness if elected president. He referred frequently during the campaign to a bygone era when the United States was king of the hill, prosperity was widespread, people were happy, and life was wonderful. He blamed the demise of American greatness on mainstream politicians, wasteful and corrupt government, foreigners, bad trade deals, and, of course, Barack Obama. The next chapter takes a closer look at his nostalgic view.

CHAPTER 2

Make America Great Again

One day during the campaign a reporter asked Trump to explain what he meant by "Make America Great Again!" He wanted to know what historical moment Trump had in mind when he thought that America was still great. It was a reasonable question. After all, this was Trump's core campaign slogan. It was stitched in white letters on the red baseball cap he wore to rallies. It was plastered across the front of the podiums he spoke from. Sometimes it was hung behind him at the venues where he appeared. It was displayed by supporters on millions of yard signs and bumper stickers from coast to coast. And it promised that even though America wasn't great anymore, Trump would restore that greatness if he was elected president. The question was also worth asking because knowing when America had been great would give voters a glimpse of what greatness might look like on Trump's watch. However, Trump's answer was a little vague. American greatness could have been either the early twentieth century or the mid-twentieth century. According to Trump, these were times when "we were not pushed around, we were respected by everybody, we had just won a war, we were pretty much doing what we had to do."[1]

If Trump was referring to the early twentieth century, it must have been the interwar period because America had won World War I and was fast becoming an economic powerhouse. Coincidentally, whether he realized it or not, that era also had the America First Movement, much like Trump's "Make America Great Again" crusade. The America First Movement had its own high-profile celebrity too—Charles Lindbergh, the first pilot to have flown alone nonstop across the Atlantic Ocean. We can push the comparison even further. As the Nazis ramped up for World War II, Lindbergh visited Germany and was impressed with its military and industrial might.

The Germans were equally impressed with him. In 1938, Hermann Göring presented Lindbergh with the Commander Cross of the Order of the German Eagle, a prestigious award from Adolph Hitler. You see, Lindbergh was also known for his anti-Semitism, nationalism, and isolationist foreign policy views, which appealed to Hitler and which were eloquently portrayed in Philip Roth's novel *The Plot Against America*, in which Lindbergh becomes president. Others have drawn parallels between the America First Movement and certain aspects of Trump's campaign, including his degrading remarks about religious and other minorities, his nationalism, and his public admiration for an authoritarian leader—Russian president Vladimir Putin.[2]

However, Trump also seemed to refer to the 1950s and 1960s—America's postwar Golden Age. This was probably the time most Trump supporters assumed he had in mind when he talked about making America great again. It was also a time with which they were familiar, having grown up in it, like me, or having heard about it from their parents or grandparents. This era would have had the most resonance for voters. But what did the Golden Age look like? How golden was it?

THE GOLDEN AGE

World War II devastated much of Europe and Japan, but it was a boon to the United States because America emerged from the war as the capitalist world's hegemonic power. It was a time when the United States had become the most powerful nation-state on earth in terms of its economic, military, political, and ideological resources and influence. Not even the Soviet Union, America's archenemy during the Cold War, could match US power on all four dimensions. Today many people view the early postwar decades as America's Golden Age—a time of unprecedented prosperity at home and strength abroad.

The United States had the richest and most productive *economy* in the world immediately after the war and was considerably less dependent on foreign trade than most other countries. The sheer size of the US economy in 1950, roughly $1.5 trillion in gross domestic product (GDP), was larger than all the West European economies combined and about three times larger than the Soviet Union's. American GDP per capita (in 1990 dollars) was $9,561, more than twice what it was for Western Europe. And labor productivity in America that year was $12.65 per hour, while in the twelve large Western European economies it averaged only $5.54 per hour.[3] Moreover, in what we now refer to as the capital–labor accord, many big businesses and unions agreed to peg wage increases to productivity increases and provide union workers with a variety of health care, pension, and other benefits. The rising economic tide would lift all boats. A moment of relatively peaceful labor–management relations ensued from the late 1940s through the early 1970s.[4] Because America's market was so large and important to world trade, its ability to restrict access to that market afforded it considerable leverage over other countries. Moreover, US corporations were the most technologically advanced and competitive and had the largest cash reserves in the world.[5]

This translated into prosperity for many Americans. Unemployment was low, averaging about 4.8 percent between 1948 and 1973, some years as low as 3 percent.[6] During those years average wages grew by over 91 percent.[7] And between 1940 and 1970, the percentage of households owning their own homes jumped from 44 percent to 63 percent.[8]

Government had a hand in all of this. For example, the Eisenhower administration signed legislation to spend $25 billion between 1957 and 1969 to build an interstate highway system, which created thousands of well-paying jobs and dramatically improved the ability of businesses to transport goods.[9] The space program was launched, pumping billions more into the development of new technologies.[10] And Congress passed the Servicemen's Readjustment Act of 1944, commonly known as the GI Bill, which established hospitals, vocational training programs, and unemployment benefits for veterans. It also provided veterans with low-cost mortgage loans and stipends for tuition and living expenses for college. Between 1944 and 1956, 7.8 million veterans benefited from this educational and training assistance. In its peak year, 49 percent of all college admissions were veterans. Not only did this improve the nation's human capital but it also helped keep unemployment rates low by preventing a flood of military veterans returning from the war from suddenly swamping the labor market. Furthermore, by 1952, the program had extended 2.4 million home loans to World War II veterans. All of this helped stimulate the economy by boosting the demand for goods and services.[11] So did various pieces of federal housing legislation in the late 1940s and 1950s, which provided incentives for financing, building, and buying affordable housing. In particular, the Housing Act of 1948 provided liberal mortgage insurance through the Federal Housing Administration for low-cost housing. Real estate developers jumped at the opportunity, triggering a massive boom in housing construction and suburbanization. Levittown, Long Island, was perhaps the most famous of many housing developments built thanks to the GI Bill and these other federal programs. When it was finished in 1951, Levittown sported over 17,000 homes.[12] The American Dream of steady well-paid work and home ownership was becoming a reality for millions of people who constituted a growing and vibrant middle class.

American prosperity helped finance government programs at home that further improved standards of living. Notably, in 1965, President Lyndon Johnson signed legislation establishing the Medicare and Medicaid health insurance programs. Medicare was a universal program that provided health insurance to everyone over the age of sixty-five years. Medicaid was a means-tested program that covered poor people and their children. Furthermore, other programs for the poor were expanded in the 1960s. Eligibility for the Aid to Families with Dependent Children (AFDC) program, which was originally designed as part of the 1935 Social Security Act to provide cash assistance to white single mothers who did not work, was expanded to include families and African Americans. Expenditures for a number of other social programs were also expanded.[13]

US hegemony also stemmed from American *military* prowess. Consider 1968, the height of the Cold War and Vietnam War. The United States alone accounted for 42 percent of all military spending worldwide. The comparable figure for the Soviet Union, the nearest competitor, was 28 percent. Put differently, the Americans spent $401 per capita for defense, while the Soviets spent $231 per capita. Moreover, the United States was the dominant force in the North Atlantic Treaty Organization (NATO), the postwar Western European military bulwark against Soviet aggression, which by 1970 accounted for half of all military spending worldwide, a third more than the Warsaw Pact.[14] Since World War II, roughly three-quarters of NATO's budget had come from the United States.[15] Not surprisingly, NATO's Supreme Allied Commanders have always been from the US military, although its secretary general, the top civilian post, has not. US military reach elsewhere was also impressive. At the end of World War II the United States had over 2,000 military sites around the world—the first truly global network of bases, dwarfing even that of the British Empire during its heyday. Although the number declined somewhat since then, there were still about 1,600 US bases abroad in the late 1980s.[16]

Due to its economic and military might, the United States projected *political* power around the world in the decades immediately following the war. The US-financed Marshall Plan, for example, helped not only rebuild the war-torn world so as to prevent another world war but also created markets abroad for American companies. This was only the beginning. The United States constructed a liberal-capitalist international political order based on multilateral principles and rules largely devised and approved by Washington. European anxiety that the Americans might defect from NATO created incentives for Europeans, particularly the German government, to conform to American wishes. International security issues were not typically invoked by the United States to induce cooperation among its allies, but they were in the background and everybody knew it. Cooperation was based as well on other institutions crafted in the interests of the United States but with clear benefits to its allies. The United Nations is perhaps the most obvious example—one where the United States held a permanent position on the Security Council, affording it the ability to veto any policy proposals it did not like.

Robert Keohane, the astute international relations scholar, has argued that institution building supported US political hegemony by delivering three key benefits to the capitalist world. First was a stable international monetary system, based on the Bretton Woods agreements of 1944, that established the International Monetary Fund (IMF) and the International Bank for Reconstruction and Development (IBRD), later known as the World Bank, and set up the dollar as the world's reserve currency—the international medium of exchange. Second was the provision of open markets for goods, based in part on the General Agreement on Tariffs and Trade (GATT) but also on the US government's ability to convince other countries to reduce tariffs and other barriers to free trade. Third was providing countries with access to oil at stable prices. This was less a matter of building formal than informal institutions, such as fostering friendly political relations with oil-producing countries like Saudi Arabia, which then helped US oil companies operating overseas to supply oil to Europe and Japan.[17]

Certainly US political hegemony fed back into its economic hegemony. Because the Bretton Woods agreement established the dollar as the world's reserve currency, the United States enjoyed privileges of seigniorage, which meant, among other things, that it could borrow with ease compared to other countries because people wanted to have dollars, especially when international markets were unsettled and dollars offered a safe haven. And thanks to the tidal wave of petrodollars that flowed into the international financial system after the price of oil skyrocketed in the 1970s, there was plenty of money available to borrow. Money also became available as savings accumulated in other countries. The upshot of all this was that the United States was able to subsidize prosperity through borrowing. This is why, for example, by 2008, the United States had outstanding debt to the Chinese of $1.3 trillion. One downside, of course, was that the US government continued to run up fiscal deficits and debt year after year, but nobody seemed to worry too much about that.[18]

Finally, American hegemony had an *ideological* dimension—the very notion of liberal capitalism in the first place. To a considerable extent this was spearheaded by the diffusion of US economic thought, heavily influenced by Keynesianism during this period, through much of the capitalist world. The American perspective privileged neoclassical thinking over more heterodox approaches like institutional or development economics.[19] One vehicle for this dissemination was the set of international organizations noted earlier like the IMF and IBRD, which used these ideas during the first few postwar decades to guide how they advised and otherwise helped countries with their fiscal and monetary problems. Another vehicle was the development of the economics profession itself, heavily influenced by American economists and their economic theories, which commanded great respect in the international economics community. Because economists came to occupy key positions in national governments and were often trained in economics departments at US universities, the American economics profession had considerable influence abroad.[20] Of course, the Cold War also meant that US hegemony entailed a relentless attack on totalitarian communist ideology proselytizing instead for freedom, individual choice, capitalism, democracy, and human rights. As a result, having crushed fascism during the war and then thwarting the advance of communism beyond the Iron Curtain in Europe, if not in China, the American ideology of liberalism in politics and economics dominated most of the advanced capitalist world. It was also hegemonic in many less developed countries, at least in rhetoric if not always in practice.[21]

Remember as well the cultural façade against which American ideological hegemony was displayed. Core beliefs in individualism, hard work, freedom, and economic opportunity—the American Dream—have long been part of American culture. Horace Greeley's famous 1865 dictum "Go west, young man," advised people to take advantage of their freedom and head to the frontier to improve their lives. American history books and literature are filled with stories about the struggles of pioneers heading westward to find a homestead, work the land, and stake claims for themselves and their families—through good times and bad. During the nineteenth century Horatio Alger's rags-to-riches novels portrayed the vast rewards individual initiative could bring to downtrodden Americans, while in the twentieth century John Steinbeck's magnificent novel *The Grapes of Wrath* showcased the moral virtues and honor of hard work and self-sacrifice displayed by dispossessed farmers from the country's heartland. American music has also long glorified hard-working men and women. Woody Guthrie, Pete Seeger, Dolly Parton, Sam Cooke, Bruce Springsteen, and many other artists have celebrated this in their music. So has much American art, notably Frederick Remington's classic paintings and sculptures of cowboys taming the Wild West. And let's not forget the traditional nuclear family, another aspect of Golden Age ideology, where men were supposed to be the breadwinners and women were supposed to take care of the home and kids.

This snapshot of postwar America is intended to provide a glimpse of the America that Trump seemed to recall when he promised that he would "Make America Great Again." It's a snapshot of prosperity at home and strength and influence abroad. It was an image of the past often signified in the media during the 1960s. For example, TV sitcoms like *Leave It to Beaver* and *Father Knows Best* portrayed prosperous, white, middle-class, nuclear families living happily in America's suburban homes where it was literally the father who was in charge and really did know best. Westerns like *Bonanza* and *Gunsmoke* displayed the virtues of individualism and freedom that presumably had made America great in the first place. Movies like *The Longest Day*, portraying the Allied invasion of Europe on D-Day, and *Sands of Iwo Jima*, starring the quintessential American hero John Wayne, showed how US military strength had defeated fascism and made the world a better and safer place.

But this was an incomplete picture of America's Golden Age. Just like there is a dark side to the moon, there was also a dark side to the immediate postwar era that is often forgotten, which leads to an overly nostalgic view of those years. This is important for two reasons. First, the fact that Trump never acknowledged this part of the history during the campaign was indicative of his willingness to massage, distort, or ignore the facts to suit his purposes—a habit that we will see repeatedly in subsequent chapters. Second, even during the Golden Age, signs were developing that America might be headed toward political polarization. And these signs foreshadowed trends that helped lay the foundation for Trump's rise to the presidency. Let's take a closer look at what the nostalgic view of the Golden Age leaves out.

ANOTHER LOOK

Economic prosperity did not reach all corners of American society. The rising tide, as it turned out, did not lift all boats. Inequality and poverty were significant problems, especially for minorities.[22] In fact, 22.4 percent of all Americans lived in poverty in 1959—something that did not go unnoticed by the media, which occasionally drew attention to it in dramatic fashion.[23] Edward R. Murrow, a long-time correspondent for CBS News, aired a documentary on Thanksgiving Day, 1960, entitled *Harvest of Shame* that chronicled the harsh conditions of migrant agricultural workers in the United States. In 1962, Michael Harrington published *The Other America*, a book that received national recognition for documenting widespread poverty in America and that caught the eye of President John Kennedy, who started thinking about what would eventually become known as the War on Poverty under his successor, Lyndon Johnson. But despite this attention, some worried that as long as suburban middle-class America was growing, most Americans would not pay much heed to these things or for that matter much of anything political. The sociologist C. Wright Mills warned in his 1951 classic, *White Collar*, that the middle class was becoming alienated and politically apathetic.[24]

Although the capital–labor accord had certainly made things better for the average American worker, trouble was brewing beneath the surface there too. First, unionization rates peaked in the late 1950s at about 37 percent of the labor force and declined steadily thereafter—even though public support for unions remained well above 60 percent through the 1960s.[25] This mattered because it was partly the strength of organized labor that had led to the accord in the first place. Second, declining unionization meant a decline in the bargaining power of organized labor, which would eventually hurt labor's ability to win wage and benefit increases on par with what they had been achieving previously. The advantages of unionization in this regard were clear. Union workers earned considerably more than nonunion workers in comparable jobs.[26] Third, the declining strength of labor unions meant that organized labor was losing influence over policymaking in Washington for things like stronger labor legislation and expanded social programs. For example, Congress passed the Landrum-Griffin Act in 1959, tightening prohibitions on secondary boycotts and limiting picketing for union recognition. But even before then and despite the capital–labor accord, organized labor's political clout was always somewhat tenuous. A case in point was the Taft-Hartley Act passed in 1947, which limited the power and activities of labor unions and led to a reduction in the number of labor victories at the National Labor Relations Board. Moreover, some state legislatures like Indiana and Ohio began passing antilabor legislation in the 1950s.[27]

During the Golden Age, US military strength certainly helped ensure the security interests of the Western world and defend American interests abroad. But there was frequently a nasty side to this insofar as the United States supported a variety of right-wing dictators around the world between 1945 and 1970. These included, for example, tyrants in Thailand, Greece, Indonesia, Iran, the Philippines, Paraguay, Panama, Haiti, Honduras, Guatemala, and Venezuela. One of the most infamous cases was in 1973 when the CIA helped orchestrate a coup d'état that toppled the democratically elected socialist government of Salvador Allende in Chile and brought General Augusto Pinochet to power.[28] Decades later Pinochet would be convicted of murder, torture, and other human rights violations committed by his regime. American military intervention in Southeast Asia took all this to another level. US military advisers first went to South Vietnam in 1950 to help prevent the spread of communism in the region—an adventure that escalated through the 1960s and early 1970s, costing more than 58,000 American lives and perhaps as many as 1.4 million lives overall on both sides, including civilian casualties. The war, of course, triggered major protests, unrest, and civil disobedience across the United States.

Fervent anticommunist ideology informed much American foreign policy immediately after World War II and throughout the Cold War years. But it also had domestic ramifications because it helped lay the foundation for extreme right-wing political activity. In 1950, Wisconsin Senator Joseph McCarthy launched his crusade to root out communists in the military, government, and other walks of life—an ideological witch hunt that culminated in his 1954 Senate hearings where he grilled witnesses to determine whether they were members of the Communist Party or would name people who were. Despite widespread anticommunist ideology in Congress and elsewhere, McCarthy eventually went too far and was censured by his Senate colleagues and crucified in the media by Murrow, the CBS commentator, whose scathing rebuttal of McCarthy's criticism of a CBS report about his anticommunist crusade was devastating to the senator's reputation and public standing. It was a particularly dark time in America insofar as many liberals and conservatives in government "were themselves acting to exclude, persecute, fire and even imprison Communists."[29] McCarthy's demise, however, did not extinguish right-wing extremism. The John Birch Society, for instance, was founded in 1958 to advocate a fiercely anticommunist and pro–small government ideology. It never wavered from these goals and is still in existence today.[30]

Ideological extremism also took a racist form and spilled over into politics during the Golden Age. Although the number of lynchings of African Americans declined after World War II, it was compensated for by an increase in the use of court-imposed capital punishment often by accelerated trial, which disproportionately targeted blacks, especially in the South.[31] Beyond that, Jim Crow was a fixture in the South for decades after the war ended—a system of rules and laws treating blacks and whites differently based on assumptions of white supremacy. These included, for example, poll taxes and other means of preventing African Americans from voting, and rules mandating segregated schools, restaurants, hotels, and public transportation. Much of this was finally put to rest when Lyndon Johnson signed the Civil Rights Act of 1964 and the Voting Rights Act of 1965. The civil rights movement had brought enormous pressure for these reforms, but international pressure also contributed insofar as the continued mistreatment of African Americans created serious problems for America's advocacy of democracy, freedom, and human rights abroad during the Cold War.[32] Nevertheless, some forms of racism persisted, including the white supremacist Ku Klux Klan.

Finally, signs were beginning to emerge in the 1950s and early 1960s that the conventional ideal of a nuclear family—breadwinning dad, homemaking mom, and the kids—was beginning to change. The percentage of single-parent households, rather low at that time, was beginning to increase, as was the percentage of children born out of wedlock. Mothers were also moving into the labor market as breadwinners both in single-parent and married families. These were trends that were just beginning and were evident among all racial groups, although whites remained more closely in sync with the nuclear family ideal than others.[33]

CONCLUSION

Overall, then, despite the prosperity America was experiencing thanks to its hegemonic position during the Golden Age, there were troubling undercurrents stirring that Trump conveniently ignored in his promises about how he was going to "Make America Great Again." Hints that these undercurrents might lead to trouble were seen from time to time. The nonviolent civil rights movement was one such hint during the 1950s and early 1960s. It seemed to subside after the Civil Rights and Voting Rights Acts were passed, at least until riots exploded in Newark, Detroit, Chicago, Washington, and other cities in the second half of the 1960s amid complaints of persistent racial injustice, police brutality, inequality, and poverty in black neighborhoods. The Black Power Movement, highly critical of the civil rights movement and epitomized by the Black Panther Party, which was more open to the use of violence, persisted into the 1970s. Violence was triggered as well by the assassinations of civil rights leaders Malcolm X in 1965 and Dr. Martin Luther King Jr. three years later. Things calmed down around the country after Washington beefed up social programs like AFDC to appease residents, mostly black, who lived in the affected neighborhoods.[34] But these undercurrents were even felt occasionally in the bucolic suburbs, including mine, about twelve miles from Newark, New Jersey, where racial tensions got hot enough in the late 1960s to close my high school more than once while I was a student. The day after Dr. King was killed, a friend and I, two middle-class white kids, were jumped in an otherwise deserted school hallway by a bunch of black kids we had never seen before.

The antiwar movement was another hint that America was not the picture of peace and tranquility seen on TV sitcoms. The movement disappeared once President Richard Nixon pulled troops out of Vietnam and then Saigon fell to the Viet Cong in 1975. But this was not before violence broke out in the streets at the Chicago Democratic National Convention in the summer of 1968, pitting police against students and other antiwar demonstrators. It was not before National Guard troops killed four students at an antiwar demonstration in 1970 at Kent State University in Ohio. And it was not before four other antiwar protestors blew up the Army Mathematics Research Center at the University of Wisconsin-Madison that same year, accidentally killing one person and injuring three others. Of course, the fact that the United States was defeated in Vietnam was an indication that its military power might be slipping.

The counterculture, the summer of love, hippies, Woodstock, an emergent drug culture, rock 'n roll, the popularization of communal living, and the advent of the birth control pill suggested that social norms were changing in America too. The watchwords of the day were "Question Authority!" On the radio Bob Dylan was singing about how times were changing and Marvin Gaye wanted to know what's going on. College students were reading James Baldwin, Herbert Marcuse, Ralph Ellison, Franz Fanon, Tom Wolfe, Ken Kesey, and various other critical, antiestablishment, and New Left authors. So while McCarthy and the John Birch Society, among others, were pushing some people's thinking to the right, the counterculture was pushing others to the left—an early indication that political and ideological polarization was beginning to percolate through society.

There was certainly much good happening during the postwar Golden Age, but it was by no means good for everyone. In hindsight, it now seems that what was not so good presaged the growth of several economic, racial, ideological, and political trends that would eventually polarize America in ways that were then impossible to foresee but that would wreak havoc in national policymaking and lay the foundation for Trump's rise to power. The rest of the book examines this claim in detail, starting with changes in the economy.

CHAPTER 3

Economy and Class

What goes up must come down. This was as true of the postwar American economy as it was in Newtonian physics. Beginning in the 1970s, the economy began to run into trouble as US firms became less competitive internationally. During America's Golden Age, Europe and Japan were rebuilding their economies from World War II's devastation—and doing so with the latest cutting-edge technologies and organizational practices. As a result, foreign manufacturers of automobiles, steel, machine tools, consumer electronics, and many other products began to encroach on markets both in the United States and abroad that had been dominated by American companies. Because foreign manufacturers often produced goods with higher quality and lower prices, American firms started having a hard time keeping up. US economic hegemony began to slip. The effects on the working and middle classes were profound. Jobs were lost, wages stagnated more or less for the bottom three-quarters of the population, family debt increased, economic inequality got worse, and the possibility of upward mobility deteriorated, all fostering an environment in which people's angst and anxiety about the economy blossomed. This chapter explains how this happened. This is the beginning of the red thread mentioned in chapter 1 that connects many of the details in the chapters that lie ahead.

Eventually, Donald Trump would capitalize on the situation, promising to turn things around. At rally after rally and in repeated interviews during the campaign he assured the public, "We're going to have job growth like you've never seen. . . . In fact, I will be the greatest president for jobs that God ever created!"[1] The irony, of course, was that as the election drew near, there were clear indications that things had already started to get better on Obama's watch. But neither Trump nor his supporters seemed to notice.

The signs were hard to miss in the 1970s that the competitiveness of US firms in international and domestic markets was eroding. The automobile industry illustrates the story particularly well because throughout the Golden Age and even before, it was the quintessential source of well-paying jobs for millions of Americans. US automobile manufacturers were world leaders during the Golden Age. In 1961, the Big Three—General Motors, Ford, and Chrysler—enjoyed nearly 86 percent of the US automobile market. Toyota and Honda had not yet arrived.[2] Volkswagen was still a bit player despite having introduced the Beetle to the American market in 1949.

The Big Three relied on a Fordist production model, so called because it was pioneered by Henry Ford in the early twentieth century. It involved large vertically integrated firms and production facilities, like Ford's gargantuan River Rouge Plant in Dearborn, Michigan. The plant's footprint exceeded one square mile and included docks along the Rouge River, an internal railroad line to move material, an electricity-generating plant, a steel mill, and over one hundred thousand employees that manufactured virtually all the components needed to make Ford cars. Fordism also involved managerial hierarchies, rigid work rules, and bureaucratic agreements with unions to handle labor–management relations and set wages and benefits.[3] It was a wonderful way to mass-produce cars and all sorts of other goods on a large scale at relatively low cost thanks to its economies of scale, which is why many industries in the United States adopted the Fordist model and prospered from it during the Golden Age.

But things were changing. By 1980, the Big Three's hold on the American market had slipped to about 74 percent—a slide that would continue for the next thirty years. By 2014, they held only 45 percent of the domestic market, by which time Toyota and Honda had grabbed nearly a quarter of it, initially by selling small, inexpensive but higher-quality and more fuel-efficient cars, later branching out into trucks, SUVs, and more upscale models. Volkswagen had become another major competitor.[4] Fuel efficiency became a concern after the price of oil on world markets quadrupled in 1973 following an embargo by the Organization of Arab Petroleum Exporting Countries (OPEC) in reaction to American support for Israel in the Yom Kippur war. In the twenty years since 1967, the United States went from having a trade surplus in cars, exporting more than it imported, to having a $60 billion deficit. This was the single largest contribution to the country's trade deficit of any industry. And profit margins were being squeezed too.[5]

The Big Three tried to keep pace with their foreign competitors but fell short, sometimes in almost laughable ways, particularly when it came to quality. People who bought cars made in the United States by the Big Three in the mid-1980s reported twice as many defects within the first three months of their purchase than those who bought Japanese cars.[6] My small 1975 Ford Pinto serves as exhibit A. It was only about three years old when the cheap plastic steering wheel cracked right down the middle on one very cold New Hampshire winter night. The door handle pulled off a few days later. The muffler fell off on the way home from Boston the next month. The car eventually died completely, which was probably a good thing because it was discovered later that Pinto gas tanks might rupture and explode when rear-ended by another car—a danger that Ford hid from the public for many years.[7] As for General Motors, during the 1970s, it produced its own subcompact response to the foreign competition—the lightweight Chevy Vega, a car with an aluminum alloy cylinder block that was prone to intense vibration, noise, and overheating at high speed, sometimes completely ruining the engine. The Vega was manufactured in a state-of-the-art plant in Lordstown, Ohio, that rolled cars off the assembly line faster than one every minute—a breakneck pace unheard of in the industry. But this contributed to shoddy assembly and lousy paint jobs that caused the body to rust badly and required frequent visits to the repair shop. The speed of the assembly line was so fast and unrelenting that in 1972 it triggered a month-long wild-cat strike by workers suffering from what became known as the "blue collar blues"![8]

The Big Three soon realized that at the rate they were going, they were no match for German precision engineering and well-trained workers, who were able to spot and correct manufacturing errors quickly and efficiently, or Japanese producers, who relied on flexible production methods and just-in-time supply chains that cut costs and enabled manufacturers to offer consumers a much wider choice of vehicle styles and options than the American companies. Japanese flexibility was impressive. For example, they could switch dies in an automobile manufacturing plant in five minutes, while it took up to a day in an American plant. The Japanese product cycle was shorter too—7.5 years from initial conception of a car to the day the last one rolled off the assembly line. In the United States the product cycle was 13 to 15 years. This meant that the Japanese were more innovative, more in sync with the latest automotive and production technologies, and more in tune with changing consumer tastes. Eventually American manufacturers caught on and began emulating these techniques.[9]

The Big Three took three particularly important steps to try to catch up. First, taking a page out of the Japanese playbook, they began to upgrade their production technologies, often replacing workers with machines, and decentralizing their operations—shifting to what is now known as the post-Fordist production model. This involved downsizing through layoffs and outsourcing more work to an increasingly dense network of independent suppliers organized in just-in-time delivery systems where suppliers delivered their products just in time for assemblers to use them.[10] This reduced inventory costs, allowed for more flexibility in managing production, and enabled the auto companies to play one supplier off of another to reduce the costs of the components they needed.[11]

Second, they began moving assembly and supply operations out of the Midwest to other parts of the country, particularly those with weaker unions and cheaper labor costs. Eventually, they went even farther afield, shifting some operations to Mexico where labor was even cheaper and to Canada where, for instance, the costs of providing health insurance to workers was greatly reduced. By 1987, General Motors had twenty-three plants operating south of the Rio Grande. The North American Free Trade Agreement (NAFTA) accelerated these trends, but outsourcing stretched far beyond the NAFTA region to countries all over the world. NAFTA and globalization also meant that Japanese, German, and eventually South Korean automobile manufacturers set up production facilities inside the United States to avoid tariffs on vehicles they would have had to import otherwise.[12]

Third, the Big Three revisited long-standing principles in labor contracts. In 1950, Walter Reuther, president of the United Automobile Workers (UAW), negotiated the "Treaty of Detroit" with General Motors. This was a five-year contract that included cost-of-living wage adjustments, a sound pension plan, a no-strike pledge, and, finally, agreements to let management run the company and link wages to productivity, something known as the annual improvement factor (AIF). Ford and Chrysler followed suit. This became a model for many other US industries—the capital–labor accord mentioned in chapter 1. But in 1979, when the Shah of Iran was overthrown and Iranian oil shipments to the United States were reduced, the price of gasoline skyrocketed for the second time that decade, sending the economy into recession and dealing a crippling blow to US automobile manufacturers who still had not fully grasped the importance of fuel efficiency. Manufacturers demanded and won an end to the AIF. Wages began to lag productivity growth. In the years that followed, workers ended up making additional concessions in wages, benefits, hiring, and the collective bargaining process itself.[13]

Similar stories were unfolding in other manufacturing industries across the United States, including steel, textiles, machine tools, consumer electronics, semiconductors, computers, copiers, and more.[14] Figure 3.1 shows how traditional manufacturing industries—the backbone of the economy during the Golden Age—were losing market share both domestically and internationally during the 1960s and 1970s. As a result, as Figure 3.2 shows, manufacturing was giving way to services as the primary source of economic

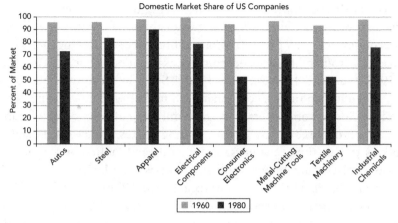

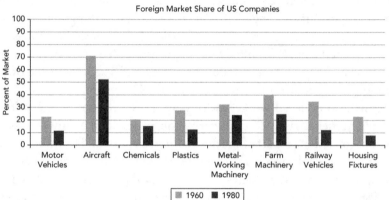

Figure 3.1:
Shrinking markets for US products, 1960–1980.
Source: Business Week Team 1982, p. 14.

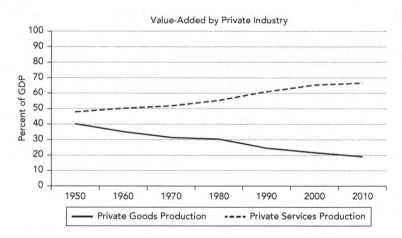

Figure 3.2:
The decline of manufacturing in the United States, 1950–2010.
Source: US Bureau of Economic Analysis 2016.

growth in the economy. Furthermore, during these years manufacturing jobs disappeared steadily—declining from about 24 percent of all jobs in the economy to only 9 percent.[15] Corporations were also seeing their profits squeezed. Profitability dropped from a peak profit rate of nearly 10 percent in 1965 to around 4.5 percent by 1980.[16] So, as in the automobile industry, in an effort to reduce costs, many US firms began downsizing, which involved closing some operations and combining others, selling off superfluous parts of the company, imposing hiring freezes, firing workers, shifting workers to part-time schedules, and offering early retirement packages.[17] It also involved outsourcing to other countries like Mexico, Singapore, Sri Lanka, and Brazil where wages were much lower. Recent data from the US Commerce Department show that during the early 2000s, American-based multinationals added 2.4 million jobs overseas while cutting 2.9 million jobs at home. Outsourcing often involved assembling things like television screens, radio circuit boards, engine blocks, and automobile chassis with parts exported from the United States. The assembled product would then be imported back to America. Between 1969 and 1983, the value of such reimports jumped from $1.8 billion to nearly $22 billion.[18]

Firms also replaced workers with new, more productive technologies. The phenomenal rise of computerization meant that many less skilled workers got laid off as part of the downsizing movement. However, this also meant that new jobs were created for more skilled workers at higher wages as long as the new technologies they used raised their productivity enough to offset the wage increase.[19] Given that the Trump campaign persistently blamed trade and outsourcing for the loss of manufacturing jobs, it is worth noting that conservative and liberal economists alike disagree vehemently with his claim. A report from the conservative Heritage Foundation, for example, based on data from the US Bureau of Labor Statistics, found that trade with China or elsewhere was not to blame but that "U.S. manufacturing employment has fallen primarily because U.S. businesses have changed how they manufacture goods. Advances in computers and robotics enable machines to perform many rote tasks that once required human labor. Manufacturers have replaced human labor with these machines in their production processes."[20] Some estimate that as much as 85 percent of the job losses in manufacturing from 2000 to 2010 were from technology and productivity improvements, not from trade or outsourcing, which only accounted for 13 percent.[21] Many liberals, including Paul Krugman, winner of the Nobel Prize in Economics and an expert on trade, agreed that trade was not the culprit.[22]

Another strategy firms used to improve the bottom line was to shift some of their resources from manufacturing to various financial investment opportunities. General Motors, for instance, expanded GMAC, a bank holding company that initially offered automobile financing, into all sorts of financial services. Doing this enabled firms to detach earnings from production and exclude the general workforce from revenue generation. In turn, this reduced workers' share of the firm's income, increased top executives' share, and, as a result, contributed to increased income inequality.[23] More on that later.

Employers also cut back on benefits packages. Sixty-three percent of the civilian workforce during the early 1990s was covered by employer-provided health plans, but by 2010 only 54 percent were covered. Put differently, the number of Americans without health insurance increased from about 34 million to 51 million during that period. It was worse for young workers. Since 2000, the share of recent college graduates with health insurance provided by their employer dropped by 22 percent. Recent high school graduates suffered a 14 percent decline. And for those people who were lucky enough to be covered by an employer plan, more and more of them had to chip in to cover the premiums at a time when the cost of health insurance was shooting up beyond the rate of inflation. That meant that costs were being shifted from the employers to the employees.[24]

By the same token, fewer employers offered their workers traditional pension plans that guaranteed retirees a monthly benefit. Between 1980 and 2008, the proportion of private sector workers participating in these defined benefit pension plans dropped from 38 percent to 20 percent. Instead, many firms switched to 401(k) plans where the employee and sometimes the employer contributed to an investment account with no clearly defined benefit. Employee contributions were voluntary, so the benefit depended partly on how much they contributed. But it also depended on how well their investment portfolio did, so, for instance, if the stock market crashed and decimated the portfolio, as occurred to many people during the 2008 financial crisis, the retiree would suffer the consequences. Saving for retirement became more voluntary and much riskier. According to the US Social Security Administration, the likelihood that the baby boom generation, born between 1946 and 1964, will not have enough retirement income to sustain them for the rest of their lives has increased accordingly.[25]

The impetus for reforming US corporations and reducing costs by automation, cutting wages and benefits, and outsourcing good manufacturing jobs did not come entirely from inside corporate boardrooms where executives worried about shrinking market share and profit margins. Pressure also came from the outside world. For example, thanks partly to deregulation since the 1970s, buyer–supplier relationships changed. To an increasing extent suppliers had to deal with larger buyers like Walmart or Target who pressed them to cut costs, including wages.[26] Another example comes from the world of high-stakes finance. The 1980s was a time of hostile corporate takeovers, where corporate raiders like Kohlberg Kravis Roberts & Co. (KKR), a huge private equity firm, and T. Boone Pickens, chairman of BP Capital Management, a large hedge fund, would spot what they believed to be underperforming but potentially lucrative firms and tender an offer to the firm's stockholders to buy them out and seize control of the company. If they succeeded, they often reorganized the firm, firing top management, selling off subsidiaries unrelated to the firm's core mission, and often outsourcing many remaining operations.[27] The idea was to make firms leaner, more efficient, and more profitable.[28] One of the most notorious cases was KKR's leveraged buyout of RJR Nabisco, maker of Oreo cookies and other food products, in 1988 for $25 billion. Once the deal was done, 40 percent of the workforce was laid off, including the CEO; Nabisco's food and cigarette businesses were separated; and operations in Britain and famous food brands like Del Monte and Chun King were sold.[29] Firms increasingly took preemptive action to guard against hostile takeovers like this. According to Steve Pearlstein, a Pulitzer Prize–winning professor of public and international affairs, beginning in the 1980s, "Corporate executives came to fear that if they did not run their businesses with the aim of maximizing short-term profits and share prices, their companies would become takeover targets and they would be out of a job. Overnight, outsourcing became a manhood test for corporate executives."[30]

The impact of all this for workers was clear—good jobs were lost. As workers were forced to find new jobs, they often suffered "job skidding" where, for example, a well-paid middle manager at Nabisco would be laid off and then get a new job with lower pay and worse benefits as an assistant manager at the local McDonald's. If those who lost these jobs in manufacturing were well educated or managed to get retrained with new skills, there might have been opportunities for good jobs in the service sector, particularly as computerization came into its own and the technology sector flourished. But for those without those credentials and training, service sector jobs were less attractive.[31] Put differently, in the new "knowledge economy," those with the right knowledge prospered, and those without did not.

Job loss in manufacturing was important precisely because manufacturing jobs tend on average to pay more than jobs in other sectors of the economy. In other words, there is a significant "wage premium" for manufacturing jobs. The average wage premium in 2012–2013 for US manufacturing workers without a college degree was $1.78 per hour (10.9 percent more than comparable nonmanufacturing workers earned). In some states the wage premium was much higher, particularly in places that produced high-tech or capital-intensive goods, such as aircraft, autos, and refined petroleum products. The wage premium for non-college-educated workers in Michigan is still among the highest, despite what happened to the automobile industry, at \$3.35 per hour (21.9 percent). Other high-end examples include Louisiana (\$3.06 per hour, 19.6 percent), with its large fossil fuel industry, and Washington (\$3.13 per hour, 17.6 percent), with its aerospace and computer industries.[32] High-paying manufacturing jobs had provided a solid economic foundation for working- and middle-class families during the Golden Age. As those jobs were lost, that foundation began to crumble, with dire consequences for people's pocketbooks. This provided fodder for Donald Trump's promise to workers that he would be God's greatest job creator, bringing back good manufacturing jobs to the United States.

One reason the manufacturing sector has a wage premium is because of its comparatively high rate of unionization compared to the service sector.[33] Another reason these good manufacturing jobs were being lost was, as I explained in chapter 1, that the percentage of workers belonging to unions dropped steadily from its peak of about a third in the late 1950s to about 11 percent in 2015.* Had organized labor been stronger it might have been able to defend against much of this job loss, not to mention cuts in wages and benefits. For example, in countries like Sweden and Denmark, where unions represent well over 60 percent of workers, organized labor has been able to prevent some plants from being closed and some jobs from being lost. Unions are also strong enough to negotiate with employers to figure out ways to reorganize production, shift production to new products, and retrain workers for new jobs, something that happens frequently in countries like Germany that have extensive apprenticeship and job reskilling programs.[34] For all these reasons, understanding the demise of organized labor requires a closer look.[35]

THE DEMISE OF ORGANIZED LABOR

Although it has declined since the early 1950s, public support for unions has never slipped below 50 percent over the last ninety years.[36] So there must be some other reason for the decline of organized labor and unionization rates. In fact, there are several, but it is important to keep in mind that most of the decline has occurred in the private sector, not the public sector, where roughly 28 to 42 percent of federal, state, and local government workers are union members, compared to about 7 percent in the private sector. But unionization rates have slipped for everyone.[37] Why?

---

* Today only a small fraction of unionized workers are in the private sector. The number of workers belonging to public sector unions outnumbers those belonging to private sector unions more than five to one (Hirsch and Macpherson 2016).

First is the shift from a manufacturing to a service-based economy. Some service workers are highly educated professionals, such as doctors, lawyers, nurses, and professors. As professionals, they expect to be allowed to think for themselves and act with autonomy on the job. Doctors, for instance, bridle at the thought that somebody else should tell them how much time they can spend with a patient, what diagnostic tests they can order, and what medications they can prescribe. Such independence does not lend itself to joining a union that negotiates contracts that might limit doctors' autonomy. This may explain why few doctors belong to unions or organize strikes.[38] The same can be said for many other professions in the United States. But other service workers are much less well educated and lack this kind of professional socialization. Some clean hospitals, office buildings, and hotels; some work in restaurants and bars; some pick vegetables and fruit in the fields. And often these are part-time workers, women, and sometimes recent immigrants to the United States. They too have been hard to organize, in part because traditional unions like the UAW, the Teamsters, or the United Steel Workers only have experience organizing America's smokestack industries.[39]

Second, the business community has become especially skilled and more aggressive at opposing unionization drives and decertifying unions that are already in place. Even during the Golden Age, organizations like the National Association of Manufacturers offered seminars to teach employers how to do this, as did an expanding number of specialized consultant firms. This caught many labor leaders napping, but they eventually fought back. Since 1960, the number of unfair labor practices filed with the National Labor Relations Board (NLRB) rose steadily. During the 1970s, there was a 216 percent increase in the number of workers reinstated in their jobs by the NLRB after having been fired for union activity, and a 128 percent increase in the number of workers awarded back pay by the NLRB.[40] But despite winning these legal battles, the labor movement lost the larger war. According to Jake Rosenfeld, an expert on organized labor, "This period corresponded first with a decline in union [certification] win rates, and subsequently with a dramatic decrease in union election drives."[41]

Third, as noted in chapter 1, the federal government contributed to the decline of unions by passing legislation like the Taft-Hartley and Landrum-Griffin Acts that made unionization more difficult. Moreover, in the 1960s and 1970s, a rift between the liberal wing of the Democratic Party and organized labor developed over the Vietnam War. George Meany, president of the American Federation of Labor and Congress of Industrial Organizations (AFL-CIO) and a fervent anticommunist, came to believe that liberal extremists had taken over the party, culminating in its nomination of Senator George McGovern, a liberal antiwar candidate from South

Dakota, to run against Richard Nixon for the White House in 1972. This undermined the Democratic coalition that had supported progressive social policy and labor interests in Congress since World War II. It made it especially difficult for labor to toughen the National Labor Relations Act in ways that would have countered the aggressive antiunion tactics of employers. Rosenfeld summarized the dismal political situation for labor during this time: "Congress did not pass and therefore the president did not sign any major piece of legislation altering the basic framework governing collective bargaining. . . . It left labor largely powerless to combat employers' legal and illegal tactics during organizing campaigns and decertification drives."[42]

Sometimes the government took much stronger steps against organized labor. The most famous was Ronald Reagan's move as president in 1981 to fire striking air traffic control workers and replace them with military personnel—a decisive move that destroyed the 14,500-member Professional Air Traffic Controllers union and triggered a resurgence of strike breaking and tougher negotiating positions by corporations in several industries.[43] Large companies were so emboldened that they abandoned pattern bargaining in the 1980s. Pattern bargaining was a system where a union and a major employer would negotiate a contract and then the other firms in the industry would agree to similar contracts to avoid a confrontation with the union. This is what happened in the Treaty of Detroit in 1950 when General Motors and the UAW agreed to terms and then Ford and Chrysler followed suit. The shift away from pattern bargaining made for much more variability in union agreements, which increasingly included reductions in benefits, wage freezes or concessions, and the introduction of two-tiered employment schemes where the pay scales and benefits of workers who had been with the company for a while were grandfathered in under terms of the old contract but more recent workers were brought in with much less attractive compensation packages.[44]

Finally, the assault on unions also played out at the state level thanks to American federalism, where lots of policymaking was left up to the discretion of the states. Some state governments tried to eviscerate public sector unions in various ways to help balance state budgets. Wisconsin Governor Scott Walker, for instance, made a national reputation for himself trying to do this.[45] Furthermore, nineteen states passed right-to-work legislation between 1944 and 1963, after which there was a lull for more than a decade. But in 1976, the trend began anew. By 2017, another eight states had passed such laws either by statute or by constitutional amendment.[46] The Republican-controlled government in my state, New Hampshire, nearly passed a right-to-work proposal in early 2017. In right-to-work states, workers are not required to join a union if they work in a union-organized shop.

Nor are they required to pay union dues. In states without right-to-work laws, they are. So when I worked in an aluminum die-casting factory in New Jersey one summer during college running punch presses, drill presses, and grinders, I had to join the International Brotherhood of Teamsters and have dues deducted automatically from my weekly paycheck. The same was true another summer when I worked in the machine shop of a factory making metal screening and other types of wire cloth and had to join the United Steel Workers union. Had these plants been in Mississippi, Alabama, Louisiana, or some other right-to-work state, I would have had no such obligation even if it had been a union shop.[†] Right-to-work laws, of course, tend to diminish union memberships and the finances upon which unions depend.

Federalism and the lack of centralization in the United States is one reason unionization rates have always been lower than in many Western European countries and one reason they have declined more precipitously in America than across the Atlantic. In many European countries labor law is determined at the national not the local level, and labor agreements are negotiated between unions and employer associations representing all workers and firms in an industry or economic sector. The agreement applies to everyone, so wages and benefits are standardized for all firms regardless of whether they are unionized. As a result, in contrast to the United States, there is little incentive for an employer to oppose unionization in a plant—it won't have any effect on the company's labor costs because they have to pay the same either way. Moreover, national law in some European countries stipulates that certain welfare benefits, notably unemployment insurance, are organized through the unions so that only members are eligible for benefits, a system that also encourages union membership.[47]

But what does any of this have to do with Donald Trump? A lot, because it went a long way in laying the groundwork for his economic pitch to voters. How? By generating lots of economic stress and anxiety for many American families—problems he promised to solve.

TOUGH TIMES FOR AMERICAN FAMILIES

Reminiscent of the Lordstown automobile plant, there is a famous scene in Charlie Chaplin's 1936 movie *Modern Times* where he is working on an assembly line screwing nuts onto pieces of machinery. As the line continues

---

† Variation in labor law across states also helps explain the variation in the union wage premiums across states.

to speed up, he has to work faster and faster just to keep pace. Eventually, he can't and has a nervous breakdown. The symbolism is hard to miss—as times change, people have to work harder and harder in order not to fall behind, and the chances that they might actually get ahead diminish. This is exactly what happened to millions of Americans as the Golden Age of prosperity slipped away.

Rising international competition, falling market shares, profit squeezes, outsourcing, the loss of manufacturing jobs, the rise of the service sector, technological innovation, automation, and the weakening of unions had profound and disturbing effects for working- and middle-class Americans. Less skilled workers have been hurt the most, but some college-educated workers have been hurt too. The story begins with wage stagnation and growing income inequality. Between 1973 and 2000, the median wage remained flat, inched up about fifty cents an hour during the next few years, but then stalled again. This was a tough problem for middle- and working-class families during the latter half of the 1970s and early 1980s when, thanks to the rising costs of food, raw materials, and oil, inflation hit double digits, only to be brought under control by a severe tightening of monetary policy that threw the economy into a deep recession. The go-go 1990s provided only a brief respite driven by the dot-com bubble, low interest rates, and a flood of cash from abroad.[48] The upshot of all this, as Figure 3.3 shows, was that average incomes for the bottom three-fifths of the income distribution improved only slightly after the mid-1960s.

At the same time, things were much better for people at the top. While wages were stagnating at the bottom, economic productivity continued to

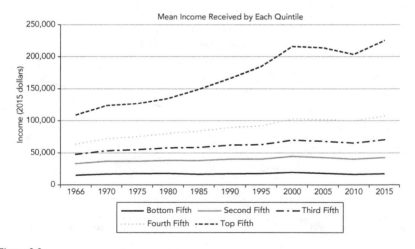

Figure 3.3:
Changing income over time, 1966–2015.
Source: US Census Bureau 2017c, Table F-3.

rise steadily as it had since the 1940s. This meant that the financial gains from increased productivity were no longer being shared by everybody but were going to people at the top of the income distribution.[49] Among other things, this reflected the demise of the AIF discussed earlier. Figure 3.3 also shows that income for the top two-fifths of the income distribution and especially the highest fifth increased appreciably. This was also due to the fact that these people owned most of the wealth in the country—stocks, bonds, bank accounts, real estate, and other income-generating assets. Since the early 1960s, the top fifth of the population has owned over 80 percent of the nation's wealth, and by 2010, that figure was just shy of 90 percent.[50] Wealth generates income, especially during boom times when the stock and bond markets create big profits as they did during the 1990s and again after 2010, or when real estate prices are rising as they were in the early 2000s.

In short, the rich got much richer than everybody else. Figure 3.4 shows that from 1970 through 2015, income inequality, measured by the Gini coefficient, grew steadily. The Gini coefficient is a standard measure of income inequality ranging from 0 to 1. A coefficient of 0 represents perfect equality where everyone in society gets the same income. A coefficient of 1 represents perfect inequality where one person gets it all. Income inequality in the United States in 2015 was on par with that of Turkey and Estonia, and was roughly twice as high as the average for the Organisation for Economic Cooperation and Development (OECD), the group of the thirty-five mostly high-income democratic market economies in Europe, North America, and East Asia. Taxes and government transfer programs reduced income inequality in America by about 18 percent, but this was again well below the OECD average—nearly half of the OECD countries

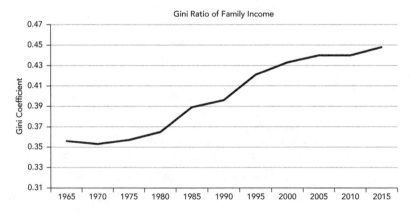

Figure 3.4:
Growing income inequality, 1960–2015.
Source: US Census Bureau 2017c, Table F-4.

reduced inequality in this way by 30 percent or more.[51] Declining union membership accounted for 20 percent of the increase in earnings inequality in the United States since the 1970s.[52]

To make ends meet, the average American family had several options. One was to work more hours, with women entering the labor force in increasing numbers as second breadwinners. For instance, from 1970 to 1997, the average time married couples spent working for pay jumped from about fifty-two to sixty-two hours per week. And thanks in part to more women entering the labor force, traditional families where the adult male was the only breadwinner, as represented in those 1960s TV sitcoms mentioned in chapter 1, dropped from about 24 percent to 7 percent of all families between 1970 and 2000.[53] One side effect was that parents had less time to spend with their kids, such as helping them with their homework, a trend which sociologists have shown tends to put kids at a disadvantage in terms of how well they do in school and, as a result, how well they do later in life.[54]

The second option was to save less money—or spend money already saved. The amount of money the average American saved rose from about 7.5 percent of their earnings in 1960 to a little over 12 percent by 1975 but then began dropping. By 2005, the personal savings rate dipped below zero, which meant that on average people were not saving anything but instead were beginning to tap whatever money they had managed to save up to that point, including saving accounts and those personal retirement accounts I mentioned earlier. The ramifications are especially scary when we consider retirement savings. Nowadays the median retirement account balance is $3,000 for all working-age households and $12,000 for those households near retirement. Put differently, 92 percent of working households do not meet conservative retirement savings targets for their age and income. If we consider not just their savings but the rest of their net worth, including their house if they own one, it still looks like 65 percent will fall short of having enough money to sustain themselves through retirement.[55] This short-term strategy for making ends meet will have disastrous long-term consequences, as many senior citizens are beginning to discover.

Borrowing was the third option families used to meet their financial needs. According to the US Federal Reserve, "Since 1960, the growth rate of real [inflation adjusted] household debt in the United States has far outpaced the growth rates of real disposable income and real household wealth. . . . Beginning in 2000, however, the pace of debt accumulation accelerated dramatically." Much of the run-up in debt during the twenty-first century was mortgage related. Rising mortgage debt became the big story in the early 2000s not just because people were trying to make ends meet but also because a combination of other factors, including low interest rates, weak lending standards, the spread of deceptive and exotic mortgages, and the growth of a global market for securitized loans, promoted increased borrowing.[56] I will have more to say about this in chapter 7. But what matters now is that from 1973 to 2011, average household debt mushroomed from 67 percent to 119 percent of disposable personal income.[57] And shouldering this debt proved to be increasingly difficult. Figure 3.5 tells the story. The share of households incurring especially high debt burdens and having trouble paying their bills on time increased during the 1990s and early 2000s. The middle fifth of households was particularly hard hit in terms of the percentage increase of households with debt problems. Borrowing was necessary for the baby boom generation to maintain the same standard of living as their parents' generation. It's even harder for today's young adults—the millennial generation, born between 1981 and 1997. For instance, since the 2008 financial crisis, while most types of household debt started to decline, student debt continued to grow—and at an accelerating pace—more than doubling between 2001 and 2013.[58] Why

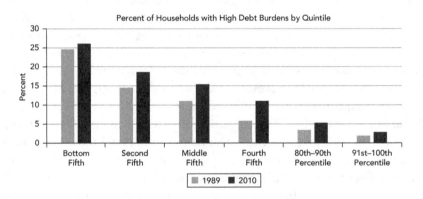

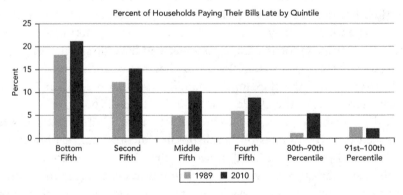

Figure 3.5:
Rising debt and financial difficulty, 1989–2010.

Source: Mishel et al. 2012, pp. 408–409.

Note: High debt burden is a ratio of debt service payments to income greater than 40 percent. Late payment for bills is any bill due 60 days or more.

American families with increasingly tenuous earnings and savings profiles, and therefore worse credit ratings, were able to borrow so much money is clear—banks and other lending institutions faced a looser regulatory environment and found profitable ways to lend to riskier customers. How they did it is again a subject best left for chapter 7.[59]

Government policies also contributed to growing inequality in the first place. Consider tax policy first. Beginning with the Carter administration, the United States pursued several regressive tax reforms, so called because they benefited higher-income groups the most and in some cases actually hurt the middle and working classes.[60] When Reagan came into office in 1981, he quickly signed what at the time was the largest tax cut in US history, with benefits disproportionately going to the higher-income groups. From 1977 to 1988, people in the bottom half of the income distribution saw their federal taxes *rise* by as much as 1.5 percent, while those in the top half saw their taxes *fall*, often by much more than that. Taxes for the top 5 percent of the income distribution dropped by 2.5 percent, while taxes for the richest 1 percent dropped by 6 percent.[61] The George H. W. Bush and Clinton administrations raised taxes a bit and expanded the Earned Income Tax Credit (EITC), which helped raise incomes a little for those at the bottom.[62] But then George W. Bush pursued regressive tax cuts with a vengeance during the early 2000s. Figure 3.6 shows that by 2010, the benefits of his first three tax cuts were disproportionately skewed in favor of wealthier people. We'll see why in chapter 5. Those at the very top of the income distribution—the richest 1 percent like Bill Gates, Warren Buffett, and Donald Trump—received the most generous cuts (roughly a 25 percent reduction), while those in the middle like police officers and school teachers got the least generous cuts (less than a 10 percent reduction).

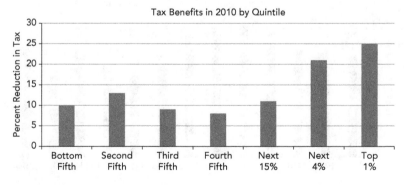

Figure 3.6:
Distribution of benefits from the first three George W. Bush tax cuts.
Source: Adapted from Leicht and Fitzgerald 2007, p. 195.

Social policies also exacerbated inequality. To begin with, the value of the federal minimum wage peaked in 1968 at $10.34 (in 2012 dollars).[63] As Figure 3.7 shows, taking into account the effect of inflation, it declined steadily thereafter, rebounding slightly in the early 2000s but never returning to anywhere near its high point. Furthermore, in 1964, President Lyndon Johnson launched his War on Poverty, which expanded some old social programs, such as AFDC, and established new ones, notably Medicare and Medicaid, two health insurance programs for the elderly and poor. But when Reagan took office, his administration reduced program budgets for AFDC, job training, unemployment insurance, and more. Perhaps most important, in 1996, the Clinton administration, which came into office promising to "end welfare as we know it," passed the Temporary Assistance to Needy Families (TANF) program—a major reform that limited to five years the amount of federal income assistance people could receive over the course of their lifetimes. It also imposed activation and workfare policies. That is, states administering welfare benefits could demand that recipients enroll in job training programs and find work according to rules set at the state level. The idea was to create incentives for people to get off welfare and into the labor force. The problem was that TANF was needed most when people were out of work and job opportunities were scarce—during recessions. This was a Catch 22 dilemma. Lane Kenworthy, an expert on welfare policy, concluded that during the 2008–2009 recession and its aftermath, "the five-year lifetime limit instituted in the mid-1990s has proved too strict, causing needless hardship and suffering."[64] The recession was also a time when Congress made it increasingly difficult, if not impossible, for welfare benefits, including the extension of unemployment compensation, to keep pace with need. The point is that since the 1970s, most

Figure 3.7:
The federal minimum wage, 1950–2010.
Source: US Department of Labor 2017.

of these programs have remained in place but have expanded at a much slower pace than before. The major exception was AFDC, where inflation-adjusted benefit levels decreased and then TANF set limits on how long you could receive benefits.[65]

In sum, in addition to the changes in the economy noted earlier, both regressive tax reforms and rolling back social programs contributed to growing economic stress and inequality in the United States. A recent report from Stanford University's Center on Poverty and Inequality concludes that the United States is an inequality-producing machine on steroids—even compared to relatively stingy welfare regimes in other Anglo-Saxon countries—thanks to its "distinctively anemic safety net and a distinctively unequal distribution of wealth."[66] As a result, like Charlie Chaplin's dilemma on the assembly line, many people have had to run faster and faster just to stay in the same place economically, let alone get ahead. Some have failed to do so, which is why the middle class has been shrinking and inequality has been growing. Between 1971 and 2015, the share of adults living in middle-class households dropped steadily from 61 to 50 percent.[67] Nowadays, American middle-class prosperity has become more of an illusion than a reality because it is based increasingly on overwork and debt.[68]

This translated into three things of political importance: growing concerns about inequality, the economy, and upward mobility. Consider inequality first. According to Gallup Polling over the last thirty years, roughly 60 percent of Americans believed that income and wealth were distributed unfairly, which is why Obama, as well as Hillary Clinton and Bernie Sanders, made the issue a core part of their presidential campaigns. People with lower incomes were more likely to believe that inequality was unfair than were people with higher incomes. Although less than half of Republicans held this view, enough did so that some Republicans in the 2016 campaign addressed the issue, assuming that independents, Hispanics, and other voter groups felt it was important. As we shall see, Trump was not among them, even though roughly a third of his supporters felt that the issue was important. There were also partisan differences in how to deal with inequality. Democrats wanted to reduce wealth at the top of the socioeconomic scale by, for example, taxing the rich, while Republicans wanted to create opportunities for people at the bottom to climb the economic ladder by their own initiative. Nevertheless, the percentage of Americans believing that government should do more to redistribute wealth by taxing the rich heavily rose since the 1970s, and especially between 2000 and 2015, during which time the percentage of Americans favoring heavy taxes on the rich rose from 45 to 52 percent.[69]

Second, what about economic angst? People's views on the economy, whether it is doing well or not, and their economic confidence rises and falls more or less as does the state of the economy.[70] Although that confidence hit a major low point during the first few years of the Great Recession, it recovered to a degree by the time the election approached in 2016.[71] Nevertheless, a Marketplace-Edison Research Poll found that by October 2016, over a third of Americans polled said that they lost sleep worrying about their finances—up eleven points from the previous year. Nearly a third worried of not being able to pay their mortgages—up ten points from the previous year. Nearly a third were afraid that they might lose their job in the next six months—up ten points from the previous year. And two-thirds said they felt financially insecure at least occasionally.[72] According to Gallup Polling, in the run-up to the 2016 election, the economy remained the leading issue in Americans' minds when they were asked what they thought the biggest problem facing the country was—about 40 percent of Americans believed this, with Republicans being much more concerned than Democrats by a two-to-one margin.[73] Moreover, by 2015, more than two-thirds of Americans believed that the economic system unfairly favored powerful interests, with only 31 percent reporting that it was generally fair to most Americans.[74]

Much of this stemmed from underlying trends in the economy described earlier, notably the gradual disappearance of good jobs. Figure 3.8 shows that since the turn of the century, a majority of Americans believe that it has been a bad time to find a quality job, with the percentage skyrocketing, of course, when the financial crisis and Great Recession hit, but staying above 50 percent throughout the period. Furthermore, Americans had become more pessimistic about job security. Nearly two-thirds of those surveyed in 2016 felt that there was less job security now than in the past, and half

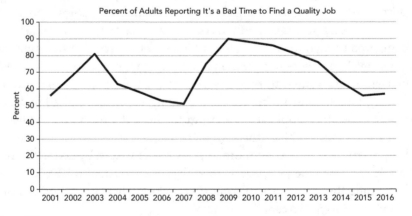

Figure 3.8:
Persistent economic angst and anxiety, 2001–2016.
Source: Gallup Polling 2017f.

believed it would get worse in the future. Importantly, given Trump's claims about the evils of outsourcing, 80 percent said that the greatest danger to American jobs was outsourcing work to foreign countries.[75] All of this made sense because since 2000, the civilian employment rate for prime-age men older than sixteen years of age dropped from about 72 percent to roughly 66 percent.[76] The decline in health care and pension benefits, described earlier, surely contributed to economic angst too.

Finally, the third politically important concern involved changes in economic mobility, of which there are two basic types.[77] *Generational* mobility refers to the odds that people will do significantly better or worse economically during their lifetimes. *Intergenerational* mobility refers to the odds that their kids will do better or worse as adults than their parents did. There is considerable generational mobility in the United States, but most of it—roughly two-thirds—occurs over short distances within the national income distribution.[78] It's as if we were sitting next to each other in a restaurant and switched chairs at the same modestly set table—the middle-class table—rather than you moving to a more opulent table, a higher economic class, or a more spartan table, a lower economic class. But here's the thing. As income inequality increases, as it has in America, children from more affluent families start farther ahead of those from poorer families. In other words, the tables in the restaurant are moved farther apart, maybe into different rooms, which according to some researchers tends to make both types of mobility less likely. There was considerable mobility from 1950 to 1980, but then both individual and intergenerational mobility stalled.[79] According to economist Lawrence Mishel and his team, "today's middle-income families may not be doing as well as those of previous generations, and children may not achieve the economic success of their parents."[80] As it turned out, concern about the deterioration of upward mobility was an especially important reason people supported Trump.[81]

The problems of economic hardship that I have been describing have long affected social solidarity in America. Lillian Rubin, a sociologist, psychotherapist, and internationally renowned author, interviewed nearly four hundred working-class people and found that the deteriorating economic conditions in the late 1980s and early 1990s caused people to be angry about taxes, welfare programs, immigrants, and racial minorities. They also tended to lose hope for their future, and worry that their kids would not have a better future than their own had been. These concerns were worse for men than women because the men were often the ones being laid off or suffering from intermittent employment. In turn, people tended to lash out at other groups within the working class, blaming them for their troubles. Why? She found that people needed scapegoats or they would blame themselves. So, whites blamed people of color for coming into the country and competing with them for jobs. Hispanics were resentful of African Americans because they believed that the blacks had been more vocal and therefore rewarded with affirmative action assistance, whereas Hispanics had been neglected because they had been quiet. African Americans were resentful due to their history of racial oppression and slavery at the hands of whites. Rubin also discovered a resurgence of white ethnic pride, seen, for example, in the formation of white ethnic clubs and associations, because as the number of immigrants of color coming to America increased, their sheer visibility compared to the white immigrants who preceded them caused whites to think more about their own ethnic and racial heritage. Rage and racism were the result, although curiously, when the people she interviewed could set aside the issue of race and ethnicity, they often found lots of common ground in their shared working-class experiences.[82]

More than two decades later another sociologist, Arlie Russell Hochschild, interviewing working-class whites in poor Louisiana communities found much the same thing—deep bitterness, particularly among members of the Tea Party Movement, that minorities had in effect cut in line ahead of them to receive special consideration and a leg up in the competition for jobs and education. They perceived that the chances for upward mobility, both for themselves and their kids, were disappearing.[83] More generally, what is involved here is a politics of resentment, which in fact can take many forms. For instance, residents of rural areas may resent people living in urban areas; less well-educated people may have disdain for intellectual elites; and those without government benefits may begrudge those that have them.[84] We will return to the issue of race and racial resentment in chapter 4. But first, how did Trump capitalize on the economic concerns of working- and middle-class Americans that I have described?

TRUMP TAPS THE DISCONTENT

Trump drew political strength from the economic discontent that had developed around the decline of the Golden Age. In addition to promising to bring jobs back as God's best presidential job creator, he pledged to bring traditional American manufacturing back to its former glory. This included, notably, reviving industries like steel production and coal mining that had long been in decline. For example, Trump repeatedly said that he would bring coal mining jobs back to West Virginia, Pennsylvania, and other former coal mining hubs. At a campaign rally in Pennsylvania, he proudly held up a sign proclaiming in big bold letters that "Trump Digs Coal." And despite a mountain of evidence that reviving the coal industry was impossible because demand for coal over the last decades had dropped and that restoring coal mining jobs would also be difficult due to automation, his supporters believed him.[85] Driving home from work one day shortly after the election, I listened to a coal miner from West Virginia being interviewed on the radio. He explained that he had lost his job back home and moved his family to Wyoming, where he was now working in the biggest coal mine in the country. He said he voted for Trump because he had promised to resurrect mining jobs back east. He also said that if Trump didn't deliver on his promise within eighteen months, he would vote Democratic in the 2018 midterm elections. He was not the only one enamored with Trump's promise. As one West Virginia delegate to the 2016 Republican National Convention told the crowd, "Tens of thousands of coal miners have lost their jobs over the last seven-and-a-half years under this [Obama] administration—it's time we change course with a man named Donald J. Trump."[86]

In another pledge to bring jobs back, Trump said that he would throttle unfair foreign competition by ripping up the NAFTA agreement and renegotiating the trade deal with Mexico. Time and time again he promised that he would "entirely renegotiate NAFTA" or "terminate it" because it "has destroyed our country." He also took aim at China because "they're not playing fairly." He set this theme when he announced his candidacy for president and started talking about unemployed Americans: "They can't get jobs, because there are no jobs, because China has our jobs and Mexico has our jobs."[87] He even lambasted some American companies for taking advantage of trade agreements like NAFTA, claiming at one point that Ford planned to "fire all its employees in the United States" after the automobile giant announced it was planning to move its small car production to Mexico over the next two years.[88] Never mind that his pledge to slap hefty import tariffs on Chinese, American, and other companies like these would lead to higher prices for Americans who wanted to buy their products—his supporters still lapped it up.

Trump promised working- and middle-class workers that their wages would go up too if he was elected president, the implication being that this would restore the chances for upward mobility, among other things. He hammered on this theme in a flurry of tweets in December 2015. In one tweet he complained, "The middle-class has worked so hard, are not getting the kind of jobs that they have long dreamed of—and no effective raise in years. BAD." In another tweet he said, "Wages in our country are too low, good jobs are too few, and people have lost faith in our leaders. We need smart and strong leadership now!" His plan for fixing wages and restoring upward mobility was to take a tougher stance on trade by imposing tariffs at the border, lower the corporate tax rate to stop firms from outsourcing jobs, boost economic growth, and tighten the borders so that immigrants wouldn't get in and steal jobs from American workers—a topic that is at the heart of the next chapter.[89]

The one issue discussed previously that Trump did not seem keen on addressing was inequality. This shouldn't be surprising. He was, after all, a billionaire. He talked often about lowering taxes on corporations and the wealthy and sometimes the middle class, but he never said much publicly about inequality. This put him very much at odds with Hillary Clinton and especially Vermont Senator Bernie Sanders, who built most of his run for the Democratic presidential nomination on America's vast and growing inequality. However, Trump's silence on income inequality didn't matter. Why? An analyst from the Brookings Institution explained:

> As a general rule, Americans are not as troubled by the gap between the rich and the rest as the citizens of other nations, so long as they feel that wealth is earned fairly. The health of the American dream is not captured by narrow measures of income inequality. Rather, it is about equality in both the sense and the substance of real opportunity, of individual possibility.[90]

The issue wasn't inequality per se but rather perceptions of the prospects for upward mobility—making a better life for you and your kids. Others have agreed.[91] Francesco Duina found exactly this in *Broke and Patriotic*, his study of why poor Americans are so patriotic—despite their misfortunes they believe that America is still the land of milk and honey, and that anybody can make it if they work hard enough and catch a few breaks.[92] This made sense insofar as Trump's support tended to be strongest in areas of the country where prospects for the future and upward mobility had dimmed the most.[93] According to Pew Research, there isn't any group in America more pessimistic about their chances for economic improvement than the white working class, who, as it happens, also tend to blame government for their problems.[94] And many of these folks were Trump supporters.

CONCLUSION

Serious political consequences followed from all of this. As jobs were lost, economic stress mounted, income inequality grew, and mobility diminished, the middle class grew smaller.[95] Throughout the Golden Age the middle class helped anchor American politics in a relatively centrist position. We will see later that once that anchor began to slip, Democrats and Republicans tended to drift farther apart. At the same time, it gave Donald Trump an issue that would help propel him to the White House—his promise to bring jobs back to America.

Trump exploited the job issue, other economic problems described earlier, and the angst they produced for many Americans. His solutions, however, were at odds with what most experts said had caused these problems and what they believed would actually solve them. In particular, Trump persistently blamed international trade for job loss and wage stagnation, but the real culprits were often automation, computerization, and corporate moves to streamline their operations to compete more effectively in an increasingly competitive economic world.

But Trump's economic pitch also had a racial angle to it. As Lillian Rubin's research foreshadowed, and Arlie Hochschild's confirmed, racial and ethnic fault lines within the working and middle classes expanded as America's Golden Age receded into memory. MIT economist Michael Piore has argued that identity politics like this became the norm in America, fragmenting the electorate and further undermining trust and solidarity.[96] This gave Trump's campaign an additional issue to work with—the scapegoating that Rubin warned about. Indeed, his campaign speeches were peppered with all sorts of disparaging remarks about Hispanics who were ostensibly flooding across the border taking jobs away from Americans; Muslims who threatened the homeland's security; and African Americans who he intimated were causing all sorts of crime and mayhem in American cities. Issues of race and ethnicity played a big role in Trump's rise to power, as the next chapter explains.

CHAPTER 4
Race and Ethnicity

Dog whistles are curiosities. They emit a sound so high pitched that people can't hear it but dogs can. Owners use them to train their dogs to sit, come, fetch, and do other things. Dog whistles provide a wonderful metaphor for describing how racially coded appeals have been used politically in America with significant effect. Conservatives as far back as the 1960s like Arizona Senator and one-time Republican presidential nominee Barry Goldwater used racial innuendo to attract white voters by hinting—but not saying out loud—that African Americans were creating all sorts of problems for whites. The use of "dog whistle politics" has been all too ubiquitous in America.[1]

Donald Trump's campaign threw dog whistle politics aside in favor of clearly audible and racially charged promises to voters as part of his "Make America Great Again" campaign. One promise was that he would build a wall along the southern border to keep out Mexicans and other Hispanic immigrants who he claimed not only were taking jobs away from hard-working Americans but also were criminals, rapists, and drug dealers—"bad hombres" in his terms.[2] He also said that he would deport all undocumented immigrants, estimated to be about eleven million people. He softened that statement a bit during an interview with *60 Minutes*, a popular television news program, after he was elected, but not by much:

> What we are going to do is get the people that are criminal and have criminal records—gang members, drug dealers, we have a lot of these people, probably two million, it could be even three million. We are getting them out of our country or we are going to incarcerate. . . . But we're getting them out of our country, they're here illegally.[3]

Another promise was that he would crack down on migration from Muslim countries, particularly Syria, because those were the places spawning what he called radical Islamic terrorists, who wanted to come to America and destroy it. At one point his campaign issued a press release stating that if elected, he would have "a total and complete shutdown of Muslims entering the United States."[4] Finally, he assured voters that he would solve the problems of crime, decay, and devastation in America's cities, which he implied were largely the doing of African Americans. He put it this way at a rally in Toledo, Ohio: "The violence. The death. The lack of education. No jobs. We're going to work with the African American community and we're going to solve the problem of the inner city."[5]

Much of this sounded like the racial and ethnic scapegoating that Lillian Rubin and Arlie Hochschild found among demoralized working-class families mentioned briefly in the previous chapter. It resonated with Trump's supporters and helped him win in the primaries and the general election. The clear majority of them favored deporting undocumented immigrants and building the wall.[6] Trump's supporters were also far more inclined to view African Americans as criminal and violent, not to mention unintelligent and lazy, than many of his opponents' supporters in the primaries and general election.[7] But why? Were Hispanic and other immigrants really flooding the country and causing all sorts of economic and social problems like he said? Were Muslims the overwhelming terrorist threat he assumed? Was the African American community in such terrible shape as he implied? The answer to all these questions is no. There was plenty of evidence casting doubt on the truthfulness of Trump's claims about these groups of people, yet he continued to make these claims and promises—even in his inaugural address.[8] In the end, however, the truth didn't matter because his pronouncements resonated with voters' fears that the United States was under siege from a growing number of racial and ethnic threats. These fears had been brewing for a long time, due in part to the trends of wage stagnation and job loss I described in chapter 3. But other trends were involved too, including a growing white backlash against African Americans, Hispanics, and Muslims; the country's changing racial and ethnic demography; and various trends in the criminal justice system. The increased threat of terrorism, triggered by the attacks on the United States on September 11, 2001, helped ramp things up too. Politicians had been stirring up these fears, often for decades, for their own strategic purposes and often by using those political dog whistles.

The previous chapter showed that Trump's claims and promises capitalized on real trends—wage stagnation, industrial decline, job loss, mounting debt, and stifled mobility—which everybody recognized. His description of these trends was frequently right, but his explanations for them were often wrong. But when it came to issues of race and ethnicity, the facts pointed one way while people's perceptions pointed the other way—and Trump exploited that. In this case, as we shall see, it was often the perception rather than the reality that mattered.

THE POLITICS OF RACE AND ETHNICITY

It goes without saying that problems of racism have long run deep in American politics. There are plenty of examples. It began with the persecution of Native Americans and slavery in the 1600s. There was the vicious and bloody Civil War in the nineteenth century, followed by Jim Crow during the Reconstruction era, with its history of political intimidation, oppression, and lynching of African Americans. There was the internment of Japanese Americans during World War II. Racism reared its ugly head again in the 1960s in places like Montgomery, Birmingham, and Selma, Alabama, where police used dogs, nightsticks, and water cannons to try to silence African American civil rights protesters. But beginning in the 1960s, racism gradually assumed a more modern guise that is particularly relevant to my argument about Trump—dog whistle politics.

Barry Goldwater, Richard Nixon, and other Republicans pioneered the so-called Southern Strategy in the 1960s and 1970s. The Southern Strategy was a plan to get white working-class voters from the South to desert the Democratic Party and vote Republican, often by hinting but not saying explicitly that the Democrats were doing things that benefited African Americans at the expense of whites. Ever since the Civil War, southern segregationists had hated the Republican Party—the despised party of Abraham Lincoln that had launched the "War of Northern Aggression" and dismantled slavery in the South. But as the Democratic Party began to warm slowly to civil rights issues, beginning with Franklin Roosevelt and running up through the Kennedy and Johnson administrations, it gradually alienated many southern Democrats, the so-called Dixiecrats. Goldwater and Nixon saw an opening for the Republican Party to make inroads south of the Mason-Dixon Line by developing the Southern Strategy, which appealed to whites whose power was threatened by the civil rights movement and the expansion of the franchise.[9] But credit must be given as well to George Wallace, four-term Democratic governor of Alabama and a rabid segregationist who ran surprisingly strong campaigns for the Democratic Party's presidential nomination in 1964, and then for the presidency itself as an independent in 1968. Wallace showed Republicans that there was political gold to be mined by pandering to the racist sentiments of some white Americans. He won about 13 percent of the popular vote in 1968 and carried five southern states, which certainly showed others that the Southern Strategy had legs.

In part, the Southern Strategy blamed the tax burden being shouldered by white working- and middle-class families on the government's need to pay for social programs that benefited "other" people. The implication was that the other people were people of color, notably poor African Americans. During the 1970s, many people's taxes were rising—but more because inflation pushed them into higher tax brackets than because of the fiscal requirements of the welfare state. Besides, the number of poor whites in America far exceeded the number of poor blacks, so whites benefited more than blacks from these programs. Nevertheless, many Republicans and some conservative Democrats embraced the Southern Strategy and continued to use it well into the 1990s, mixing issues of race and class into a toxic political brew.[10] To be sure, some white working- and middle-class folks were simply fed up with *anyone*, regardless of race, who in their view was lazy and sponged off the welfare state.[11] But the point is that the Southern Strategy worked. Many white voters grew skeptical of Democratic Party social programs that had been first established by Roosevelt's New Deal in the 1930s and beefed up since then, especially by Johnson's Great Society initiatives in the 1960s. They began turning against the welfare state, taxes, the Democratic Party, and what they perceived to be big government.[12]

Several scholars have shown that thanks to the Southern Strategy, a significant and mostly white part of the American working and middle classes began shifting politically to the right. This helped foster two things. One was the rise of increasingly conservative Republican and occasionally Democratic politicians, particularly but not exclusively in the southern Bible belt, a subject we will set aside until chapter 6.[13] The other was a white backlash against minorities and the policies allegedly designed to help them.[14] As sociologists Doug McAdam and Karina Kloos explain, it began in the South in the 1960s as opposition to the civil rights movement but then spread northward, "inspiring a more general 'backlash' by racial conservatives all over the country."[15]

In Cicero, Illinois, for instance, demonstrators advocating racially open housing were attacked in 1966 by white opponents wielding bricks and bottles. Opposition to school busing was another indication that the white backlash had spread to the North. When I was growing up in New Jersey in the 1960s, my town began busing kids from black neighborhoods to middle schools in white neighborhoods and vice versa. The idea was to ensure equal educational opportunities for everyone. I remember some of my friends' parents being furious about it. As late as the mid-1970s, communities like South Boston were still deeply divided over court-ordered school busing to the point where there were antibusing demonstrations that occasionally turned violent.

There were also lots of legal challenges where whites took aim at affirmative action laws. One very high-profile case was Allan Bakke's 1974 lawsuit against the Regents of the University of California, in which he alleged that he had been denied admission to medical school because he was a white man and because minorities were given special consideration in the admissions process. He eventually won his case in the US Supreme Court, which affirmed in a deeply divided decision the university's right to consider race among other things as an admissions criterion if this didn't involve racial quotas.

The white backlash continued to ebb and flow over the years, reaching a crescendo with Barack Obama's election as president and the rise of the Tea Party Movement.[16] But public opinion polls reflected white backlash too. About a third of white adults in 2015 believed that the country had made all the changes necessary to give blacks equal rights with whites. In other words, well over fifty-three million people felt that we did not need to do anything more to make amends for the historically racist treatment of African Americans. Enough was enough. Only about a tenth of African Americans agreed.[17]

A final example of the growing white backlash, although one targeting more than just African Americans, is the recent attack on voting rights—an institutional change tied to demographic trends. Thanks to higher birth rates and immigration, the Hispanic population grew significantly during the 1990s and 2000s. A *Time Magazine* cover story in 1990 was entitled "America's Changing Colors: What Will the U.S. Be Like When Whites Are No Longer the Majority?"[18] By the time Trump launched his bid for the presidency, Hispanics constituted a larger percentage of the population than African Americans (17.6 percent vs. 13.3 percent). The US Census Bureau predicted that by 2044, non-Hispanic whites would be a minority in the country.[19] This scared Republican leaders, who began worrying that the country's electoral base was tilting more and more in favor of the Democrats. Most Hispanic immigrants and their children were relatively poor and uneducated—precisely the sort of people that tended historically to vote for Democrats. Indeed, Obama won the presidency twice garnering a large majority of the minority vote, including Hispanics and African Americans. But even before Obama's election, conservative whites worried increasingly that they were losing control of their country. As a result, in several states in the early 2000s, Republicans passed laws designed ostensibly to reduce voter fraud, which in fact had been virtually nonexistent for decades, but that made it more difficult for poor minorities to vote. For example, several states passed laws requiring voters to show government-issued identification, such as a driver license, birth certificate, or state identification card, at polling places to get a ballot. People without such proof of residency because, for instance, they did not own a car or could not afford the fee for an ID card were disenfranchised.* In some states, the impact if not the discriminatory intent was so obvious that the courts struck down the laws. A federal court ruled that North Carolina's 2013 voter ID law "targeted African Americans with almost surgical precision."[20] But Republicans didn't stop there. In Texas, they filed lawsuits that succeeded in overturning certain provisions of the 1965 Voting Rights Act that protected minorities from being disenfranchised. Texas convinced the courts that it was no longer necessary for the US Department of Justice to oversee voter registration and voting there. The Justice Department had done so previously because Texas, among other southern states, had engaged in all sorts of egregious violations of the voting rights of minorities.[21]

Trump made the most of this, defending tighter voter restrictions because in his view voter fraud was rampant, particularly among undocumented immigrants, which was another reason he believed that immigration should be restricted. In a statement to reporters at Trump Tower in October 2016, he said that the Obama administration was conspiring against him to rig the election. When asked how, he explained, "They're letting people pour into the country so they can go vote before the election."[22] Polling less than a month before the election found that 41 percent of Americans (73 percent of Republicans vs. 17 percent of Democrats) believed that the election was probably rigged, which suggested that voters may have been swayed by Trump's repeated warnings about widespread voter fraud.[23] Among Republicans, 60 percent believed that undocumented immigrants would be voting illegally in the election.[24] Even after he won the presidency, Trump told congressional leaders at a White House reception that he would have won the popular vote had three million to five million undocumented immigrants not voted illegally for Hillary Clinton.[25] This was an astounding claim. There was no proof behind the numbers. And even if the numbers were true, it would mean that these people had all voted miraculously for the same candidate![26] This was conspiracy theory gone wild.

But the more important point is that, having been nurtured for decades by the Southern Strategy, by the time Trump decided to run for office, many white Americans, particularly Republicans, were not inclined to defend programs that supported or protected the rights and interests of minority

---

* Some university students going to school outside their home states were also targeted in this way. Students tend to be more liberal and vote Democrat more than the average American (Waldman 2016, chap. 12).

groups.[27] As noted earlier, far fewer whites than blacks said the country still had work to do for blacks to achieve equal rights with whites. There were, however, significant partisan differences depending on people's political affiliation. In May 2016, nearly 60 percent of white Republicans said that too much attention is paid nowadays to race and racial issues, while only 20 percent of white Democrats agreed. Similarly, only 36 percent of white Republicans felt that more changes were needed to give blacks equal rights with whites, while 78 percent of white Democrats believed that.[28] Not surprisingly, then, Republicans were much less inclined than Democrats to support affirmative action, voting rights, and social programs that would improve the economic situation of African Americans or other minorities, or the taxes that paid for these things.[†]

Trump's position on voter fraud is important for two more general reasons. First, it shows how he abandoned subtle dog whistle politics and did not hesitate to openly accuse minorities of all sorts of things, some more sinister than others.[‡] Second, it exemplified his misunderstanding of the facts and his willingness to either twist or ignore them entirely to woo voters. Nowhere was this more evident than when it came to issues of race and inequality.

RACE AND INEQUALITY

African Americans and Hispanics have fared worse historically than whites in terms of their socioeconomic position. Figure 4.1 shows that in 1975, the median family income for African Americans and Hispanics was about the same, roughly $37,000, adjusted for inflation. It increased by about 24 percent by 2015. Meanwhile, median family income for whites in 1975 was nearly twice as high—just shy of $60,000—and rose 38 percent by 2015. In other words, the income gap between whites, on the one hand, and blacks and Hispanics, on the other hand, was large and became even larger, with whites on top. Furthermore, as Figure 4.2 illustrates, the poverty rates for African Americans and Hispanics were substantially higher than they

† Americans do not tend to support government programs that help the less fortunate despite rising inequality and poverty. This may be because Americans hold optimistic views of mobility, which curb their enthusiasm for redistributive policies (Manza and Brooks 2016). Ironically, however, the United States has less mobility than many other advanced countries (Corak 2016).

‡ Trump was not the first presidential candidate to abandon dog whistle politics. Still smarting from his defeat by Obama in the 2012 presidential election, Mitt Romney blamed his loss on Obama's habit of bestowing policy gifts on "dependent segments" of the population. He named them openly—African Americans and Hispanics (McAdam and Kloos 2014, p. 275).

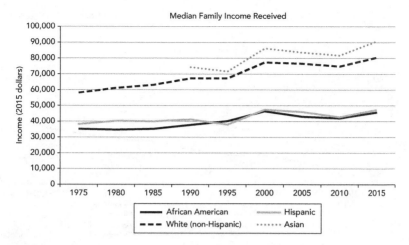

Figure 4.1:
Income inequality by race, 1975–2015.
Source: US Census Bureau 2017c, Table F-5.

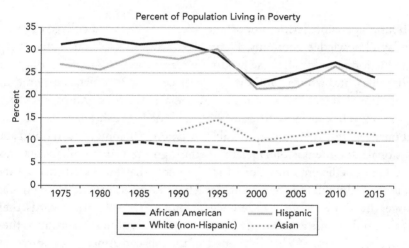

Figure 4.2:
Poverty rate by race, 1975–2015.
Source: US Census Bureau 2017b, Table 2.

were for whites. This was due partly to the fact that working-class African Americans had depended to a considerable extent on well-paid blue-collar manufacturing jobs in the smokestack industries that had been vanishing slowly since the 1970s. As those jobs disappeared, their economic situations deteriorated.[29] But educational differences mattered too.

High school and college graduation rates rose for these groups between 1975 and 2015. However, while high school graduation rates for African Americans and whites improved to a point where the gap between them nearly vanished, reaching about 88 percent in 2015, Hispanics lagged at

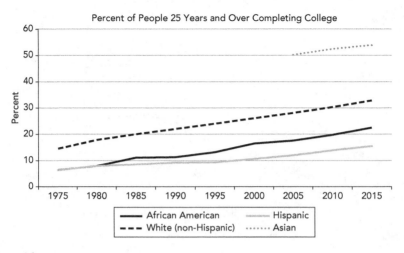

Figure 4.3:
Educational attainment by race, 1975–2015.
Source: US Census Bureau 2017d, Table A-2.

about 67 percent.[30] More important given the need for a college degree in today's knowledge economy, Figure 4.3 shows that although the college graduation rates for all these groups increased after 1975, blacks outpaced Hispanics, and whites continued to outpace both. In short, economic and educational inequality persisted across racial and ethnic groups.

We must be careful not to paint with too broad a brush. I have been talking about averages. There is considerable variation in income, poverty, and educational attainment *within* racial and ethnic groups too. Recall, for instance, the Gini coefficients mentioned in chapter 3 that measured income inequality. Although the coefficients for African Americans and Hispanics are larger than for whites, the differences are not extreme. In other words, there is almost the same amount of income inequality within each group as there is between them.[31] What happened in the African American community helps illustrate why. Simply put, a separation occurred historically in the black community along class lines. A black middle class emerged receiving a big boost from the 1960s civil rights legislation, which opened up job opportunities, especially in the public sector where it was easier to monitor and enforce the law. To be sure, just as black working-class households began to slip economically since the 1970s, so did many black middle-class households, whose wealth and neighborhood resources didn't stack up compared to their white counterparts.[32] More important, however, for my argument and for reasons discussed later, a distinct black underclass also developed, characterized by extreme poverty, high rates of female-headed households, out-of-wedlock births, joblessness, crime, drug abuse, and other social problems.[33]

Different sides of African American life were on display on television in the late 1970s and 1980s. On one side, *The Jeffersons*, with its catchy theme song "Movin' on Up," was a sitcom developed by Normal Lear about an upwardly mobile middle-class African American family in New York City that had moved from Queens to Manhattan thanks to George Jefferson's successful dry-cleaning business. On the other side, although not as destitute as the underclass, *Sanford and Sons*, another sitcom by Lear and starring Redd Foxx, a comedian famous for his raunchy comedy records, portrayed Fred Sanford and his son Lamont as two African Americans living in the Watts section of Los Angeles and struggling to make ends meet running Fred's languishing junk yard—an enterprise that never seemed to generate enough cash to pay off their debts, causing Fred to concoct all manner of get-rich-quick schemes.

Two points are important here, both about misperceptions. First, understanding the economic situations of different racial and ethnic groups requires some nuance—it's not cut and dried. Trump either did not understand this or refused to acknowledge it when, for instance, he addressed a crowd in Michigan during the campaign and described African American communities like this: "You live in your poverty, your schools are no good, you have no jobs, 58 percent of your youth is unemployed." What he neglected to note among other things was that about 50 percent of white youth was unemployed too because these figures included high school students not in the labor market, and that three-quarters of the black community was *not* living in poverty (see Figure 4.2 again).[34] Furthermore, according to the US Census Bureau, in 2015 there were nearly three times as many whites living in poverty as blacks simply because there were so many more white people living in America to begin with.[35]

The second important point is that many Americans misunderstood the situation too. Even though African Americans on average have substantially lower incomes, less education, and more poverty than whites, a Pew Research Center poll in 2016 found that less than half of the whites and Hispanics surveyed knew that blacks tended to fare worse than whites. Blacks were more aware of the situation. Nevertheless, only 60 percent of the African Americans polled knew this about their situation.[36]

Many Americans believe that inequality boils down to the attitudes and behaviors of people in different groups. Public opinion polls since the late 1960s show that Americans feel strongly that individuals are largely responsible for their own economic situations. This reflects the country's long-standing cultural values, discussed in chapter 1, that hold hard work and self-reliance in high regard. For example, in 2007, two-thirds of all Americans believed that personal factors rather than racial discrimination explained why many African Americans had trouble getting ahead in life.

This view, however, was not held equally across racial and ethnic groups. Seventy-one percent of whites and most Hispanics believed that it was black people's own fault that they had not gotten ahead. This stands in sharp contrast to other countries where a substantial majority of citizens think that poverty and joblessness are caused by structural factors like low wages or meager job opportunities, not laziness, lack of ambition, or other personal attributes. It turns out that African Americans put far more weight on structural factors too.[37] As recently as 2016, blacks were much more likely than whites to say that lower-quality schools (75 percent vs. 53 percent) and lack of jobs (66 percent vs. 45 percent) are major factors holding black people back. And 70 percent of blacks believed that racial discrimination was still an important factor, as compared to only 36 percent of whites. In short, whites tend to blame the victims of financial distress for their own troubles, whereas blacks tend to blame society's opportunity structure.[38] Some have argued that this is because whites tend to suffer from "color blind racism" where they rationalize black people's lower socioeconomic status as the product of market dynamics and imputed cultural limitations.[39] Blaming the victim like this has long been a feature of racial politics in America.[40] But which perceptions are right?

The bottom line, according to the best social science research, is that it isn't individual attributes, laziness, or lack of ambition but deeper structural factors that matter most. Let's return to the example of the black underclass. William Julius Wilson, one of America's foremost experts on the subject, interviewed people living in some of the poorest African American urban neighborhoods in the United States. Contrary to public perceptions (and conservative rhetoric) that the persistence of the underclass was due to black people's poor work habits, moral decay, and other cultural deficiencies, Wilson found that the problem was a lack of economic opportunity, migration of relatively better-off members of the African American community to more affluent neighborhoods elsewhere, and, as a result, the deterioration of critical community institutions for those left behind, including a diminishing tax base, failing schools, and civic disengagement. Crime, drugs, out-of-wedlock births, and female-headed single-parent families became prevalent even though most people living in these communities still subscribed to conventional middle-class values, including a desire for legitimate jobs and traditional family life. However, they recognized that their chances of achieving these dreams were extremely slim given the scarcity of economic opportunities available to them. Without legitimate work, people turned to dealing drugs, prostitution, and other forms of crime to make ends meet—it was their survival strategy. And without a sufficient pool of "marriageable" men, due to high rates of male unemployment and incarceration, discussed later, women often chose to raise their kids alone rather than marrying the fathers and having to worry about them too. In other words, what might look like dysfunctional underclass culture turned out to be a necessary adaptation to economic circumstances largely beyond people's control.[41]

This is not to say that culture (or racial prejudice) doesn't matter or that it doesn't contribute to the ongoing plight of poor African Americans.[§] It feeds back in a vicious cycle, further hobbling people's chances of upward mobility. But Wilson's point was that its origins were structural and historical. When I explain this to my students, many are often surprised. In fact, many people do not realize this, which helps explain why, on the one hand, Trump's message resonated with white voters who believed overwhelmingly that blacks were to blame for their own misfortunes while, on the other hand, it offended black voters who did not believe this. Capturing the sentiment of many African Americans, Alexis Scott, former publisher of the *Atlanta Daily World*, a black-owned newspaper, had this to say about Trump: "He is giving voice to every stereotype he's ever heard" about black people.[42] Here again is the red thread in my argument. Trump made inner-city social problems a racial and cultural issue when it was more a long-standing economic issue—and it worked like a charm given people's misunderstandings of the causes, consequences, trends, and racial characteristics of inequality in America. Misperceptions also helped him appeal to voters on the issue of race and crime.

RACE AND CRIME

How many times have we seen drug dealers and gang members played by African Americans or Hispanics in the movies and on television? A lot. This was another stereotype that Trump used. He equated violent crime with African Americans and Hispanics, particularly immigrants from Mexico. Here again he played to public misperceptions and fears about the threats posed to America by different racial and ethnic groups. Just like the issue of race and inequality, misperceptions about race and crime have a long history in America insofar as dreadfully racist criminal justice practices are concerned. Racial profiling is one example, highlighted, for instance, in 2014 when a white police officer in Ferguson, Missouri, shot to death Michael Brown, an unarmed black teenager—an incident that sparked days

§ Many studies report that implicit racial discrimination still plays a role in who gets interviewed and hired for jobs (O'Flaherty 2015, chap. 5).

of rioting in that community. Opposition to profiling was also at the heart of the Black Lives Matter Movement. But the point is that, as was true for the issue of race and inequality, Trump was not the first politician to twist the issue of race and crime to his political advantage.

Politicians have used the issue of crime in the United States to mobilize voters—particularly white voters—for decades as part of their strategies for winning elections. Indeed, years ago campaigning on a law-and-order platform became an integral part of many Democratic and Republican campaigns.[43] For instance, electoral politics helped motivate Governor Nelson Rockefeller of New York in 1973 to pass the so-called Rockefeller Drug Laws in that state that established harsh mandatory prison sentences for the illegal possession or sale of drugs. It was a political move that garnered much national attention and eventually helped propel Rockefeller to the vice presidency of the United States. And it significantly increased the New York State prison population. At the national level Nixon launched the War on Drugs in 1971. Forty years later it had cost $1 trillion and triggered a sharp rise in incarceration. During the Golden Age, the number of people serving time in state and federal prison hovered around 200,000. But beginning in 1974, it rose steadily, hitting nearly 1.5 million by 2015.** Poor communities of color were hit hardest.[44] Nixon's motivation was entirely political. Many years later one of his closest aides, John Ehrlichman, explained that the Nixon campaign in 1968, and the Nixon White House after that, had two enemies: the anti–Vietnam War Left and black people. The idea was that

> by getting the public to associate the hippies with marijuana and blacks with heroin, and then criminalizing both heavily, we could disrupt those communities. We could arrest their leaders, raid their homes, break up their meetings, and vilify them night after night on the evening news. Did we know we were lying about the drugs? Of course we did.[45]

Since then every president has found it useful for one reason or another to mobilize voters around drug-related and other kinds of crime. This included Bill Clinton, who signed legislation in 1994 providing funds for tens of thousands of new police officers and imposing the famous "three strikes" mandate whereby people convicted three times of certain crimes,

---

** Thanks in large part to increasingly tough drug laws, incarceration rates in the United States during the 1980s and 1990s were ten times higher than in Europe (Western and Beckett 1999). Between 2005 and 2007, about 24 percent of all inmates of federal and state prisons were serving time for drug-related offenses. Over half of all federal inmates were doing so (Sabol and West 2008, pp. 21–22). Perhaps as many as 20 percent of these people had been convicted of offenses related to the possession and sale of marijuana—not hard drugs like heroin or cocaine (US Department of Justice 2003, p. 444).

including drug crimes, were automatically sentenced to life in prison. In turn, rates of incarceration in state and federal prisons soared, especially among people of color.[46]

Trump took advantage of the long political tradition of racial scapegoating bolstered by public misperceptions about the relationship between race and crime. We have already seen that he blamed African Americans and Hispanics for crime in America, particularly violent crime like rape and murder. This resonated with the public's perceptions too. Americans—and whites in particular—consistently associate these two groups with criminal activity. One national survey found in 2010 that whites overestimated the percentage of burglaries, illegal drug sales, and juvenile crime committed by African Americans by 20 to 30 percent. Other studies report similar results. Furthermore, according to the General Social Survey, most Americans believe that blacks are more prone to violence than Hispanics, and even more so than whites.[47]

But these perceptions do not fit the data very well. Consider men serving time in state and federal prisons for violent crime. According to the US Department of Justice's 2015 statistics, 57 percent of the African American prisoners and 59 percent of the Hispanic prisoners were locked up for violent crimes, including murder, manslaughter, rape, or sexual assault, but only 48 percent of the white prisoners were in for that reason.[48] This is consistent with the perception that African Americans and Hispanics are more violent and criminally inclined than whites. However, these numbers overlook one crucial fact—those who end up doing jail time are not necessarily the ones who commit crime. The Justice Department also reports that from 2008 to 2012, the rate of violent crime among whites (56.4 incidents per 1,000) was slightly *higher* than it was for blacks (51.3 per 1,000), and *much higher* than it was for Hispanics (27.8 per 1,000).[49]

This evidence raises two important points. First, Trump's insistence that Hispanic criminals are flowing across the border in droves is misleading. In fact, immigrants overall have lower crime rates than native-born citizens.[50] According to the Cato Institute, a conservative think tank, "By race and ethnicity, every group of legal and illegal immigrants has a lower incarceration rate than their native peers. Even the incarceration rate for illegal immigrants is lower than the incarceration rate for native white Americans."[51] This includes Hispanic immigrants. This conclusion is reinforced by the fact that if we consider the *entire* US prison population, not just violent offenders, the proportion of Hispanic immigrants in prison is low compared to other groups, presumably because they try very hard to abide by the law to avoid deportation.[52]

Second, to a significant degree incarceration is often a matter of race, whereas the commission of crime is often a matter of class. Insofar as economics and race intersect, here is the red thread in my argument again. Sociologists Robert Sampson and Janet Lauritsen, for example, note that differences in crime rates among racial and ethnic groups stem in part from social forces that "concentrate race with poverty."[53] This conclusion is bolstered by Figure 4.4, which shows how frequently households in different income groups are likely to be victimized by crime. Victimization is clearly associated with class. The higher the income group, the less likely the household is to be victimized regardless of its race.

Why might there be such a discrepancy between those who commit crime and those who serve time for it? First, behind these numbers were racist police practices, especially racial profiling and the increased likelihood that cops would bust people who were more visible to them like blacks dealing crack cocaine on the streets in open-air markets in poor neighborhoods than whites dealing powdered coke in the privacy of their homes and apartments in more affluent areas.[54] In fact, even though African Americans are less likely than whites to use illegal drugs, they are three to four times more likely to be arrested on drug charges, and are six to seven times more likely to be in prison for drug offenses.[55] More specifically, when it comes to marijuana, whites and blacks use it at about the same rate, but blacks are three times more likely to be busted, charged, and convicted than whites.[56] Second, in experiments, when subjects were tested for their implicit racial biases—that is, the propensity to assume the worst of people of color without realizing it—researchers found whites to be biased even when they explicitly disavowed being prejudiced. Implicit bias against African Americans and Hispanics has also been found among criminal justice officials, including police, prosecutors, defense lawyers, jurors, and judges. Some studies have found that implicit bias leads to higher bail and

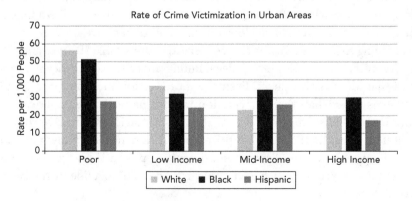

Figure 4.4:
Violent urban crime by race and ethnicity, 2008–2012.
Source: Harrell et al. 2014, appendix 8.

harsher sentences for people of color than for whites, especially among juvenile offenders.[57] The effect of implicit bias is especially strong when it comes to drugs.[58] Given the War on Drugs, it's no wonder that the number of African Americans and Hispanics in prison has grown over the years.

The point is that Trump catered to the misperceptions of Americans who believed that minorities were the ones responsible for crime in America. In fact, had he been better informed or less inclined to misconstrue the facts, he might have argued that crime was an artifact of the tough times he correctly blamed on wage stagnation, rising debt, stifled mobility, and the other economic trends discussed in chapter 3. But again, what mattered was how well he tapped voters' perceptions of the truth, not the truth itself. And Trump was a master at that. Many Americans shared his misperceptions, which is why Trump's scapegoating of minorities on these issues resonated among his supporters. But he scapegoated minorities for other things too—some economic, some not.

IMMIGRATION AND JOBS

Immigration was one of the most important issues in Trump's campaign. At least since the 1980s, a threat narrative had emerged in American politics that linked immigration to a host of economic and social problems. It was an issue with two dimensions—Hispanic and Muslim. On the Hispanic side, he expressed deep concern especially about those "bad hombres" from Mexico streaming across the border not only creating criminal mayhem, which we now know to have been blown way out of proportion, but also taking jobs away from American workers. Insofar as crime was concerned, Hispanic immigrants have long been portrayed by politicians as a threat to the nation. Because many came illegally, they were framed automatically as dangerous criminals. Furthermore, during the Nicaraguan Contra War in the 1980s, they were pictured as communists; during the War on Terror, they were labeled as terrorists; and during the 2014 international Ebola epidemic, they were portrayed as a danger to public health. These claims were far from the truth.[59] But insofar as jobs were concerned, during a campaign speech in Phoenix, Arizona, Trump called for a crackdown on undocumented immigration because "most illegal immigrants in our country are lower-skilled workers with less education who compete directly against vulnerable American workers. . . . These illegal workers draw much more out from the system than they will ever pay in."[60] He also insisted that they drive down wages. Once again, the red thread of economic trends got tangled up with racial issues.

Trump's pitch about Hispanic immigrants was well placed. An increasing percentage of the white population believed that immigrants, especially

Hispanic immigrants, were a burden on the nation, adding to problems of crime, competing with other Americans for jobs, benefiting from social programs, and more. As politicians pandered to these beliefs, more whites defected from the Democratic Party into the arms of the Republicans, especially if they lived in areas where immigration was just beginning to increase and as the mainstream media began to report negative images of immigrants. Support for more conservative policies, such as lower taxes and less spending on welfare programs and education, grew accordingly. In short, a white backlash developed against immigrants in general but Hispanic immigrants in particular.[61] Trump tapped into that backlash.

Many of Trump's supporters said they believed his claims about immigration, jobs, and wages. A Pew Research Center poll a few months before the election found that two-thirds of registered voters who said they supported Trump reported that they thought immigration was a "very big problem" for the United States—even bigger than terrorism, crime, race relations, or the availability of good jobs.[62] But that's only half the story, because although Trump's account of the immigration issue fit their perceptions, it did not fit the facts.

First, it is true that Mexicans constituted slightly more than half of all undocumented immigrants in the United States in 2014.[63] And since 1980, there was an increase in undocumented migration to the United States from Mexico. However, the number of undocumented Mexicans peaked at about 7 million in 2008 and then fell back to about 6.6 million by 2010. Moreover, migration was a two-way street. Beefing up security along the southern border actually reduced the *outflow* of undocumented migrants, which was a major reason the net rate of undocumented migration grew during the 1990s—not just because people were coming into the United States but also because they couldn't leave. Nevertheless, and despite Trump's claims to the contrary, between 2009 and 2014, more Mexicans *left* the United States than arrived, mostly to return to their families and because job opportunities since the Great Recession had diminished. In other words, to the extent that there was a flood of immigration at all, it was flowing more to the south than to the north. Most people did not realize this.[64]

Second, a report from the National Academies of Science, written by an eminent team of demographers, economists, and sociologists, found that Mexican immigrants were not taking jobs from Americans or depressing wages. Tomatoes illustrate the point. When the federal government banned the use of Mexican farm workers in 1964, rather than hiring Americans, California tomato growers replaced them with tomato-picking machines. In fact, most economists agree that immigrants—including poorly educated Mexicans—don't undermine employment opportunities for Americans.

They also find that immigration enhances economic growth, as well as the lives of immigrants and people already living here. The US Chamber of Commerce agreed too, reporting that immigrants in general tend to have skill levels at either the very high or very low levels and thus do not tend to compete with Americans for jobs. Insofar as most Hispanic immigrants are concerned, they work in low-wage jobs where, according to most economists, they don't disadvantage American workers. But the point is that immigrants do jobs that most Americans either don't want or don't have the skills to do—they complement rather than steal jobs from native-born Americans. Incidentally, immigrants will also help replace workers in jobs performed by the baby boom generation as it moves into retirement. This was something else that most people did not know.[65]

Third, immigrants do not sap welfare and other services in America to the extent often assumed. This misunderstanding has long been a political flashpoint. To begin with, the law forbids immigrants—both legal and undocumented—from using many services until they have established permanent residency and been in the United States for five years. The two big exceptions are elementary public education and emergency health care. In fact, evidence shows that Hispanics who are in the United States legally and who are entitled to various federal benefits are often reluctant to apply for them simply for fear of deportation.[66] The conservative Heritage Foundation estimates that the average undocumented immigrant household costs taxpayers $14,387 per year. However, the Chamber of Commerce argues that even if we accept this estimate, most economists see these costs as an investment in America's future because the children receiving these benefits will eventually become workers and taxpayers.[67] Moreover, even undocumented immigrants pay many of the same taxes as US citizens. They pay sales, property, and excise taxes; automobile registration fees; and even federal income tax and Social Security and Medicare taxes insofar as they must provide their employers with counterfeit documents.[68] The best evidence suggests that at least half of undocumented immigrant households currently file income tax returns using Individual Tax Identification Numbers, and many who do not file income tax returns still have taxes deducted from their paychecks. Collectively, undocumented immigrants in the United States pay an estimated total of $11.6 billion annually just in state and local taxes.[69] In addition, the Social Security Administration estimated that in 2010, undocumented workers paid about $12 billion into the administration's trust fund.[70] So to claim, as Trump did during the campaign, that undocumented immigrants will take more out of the system than they will ever put in is questionable. Again, most Americans did not know this, which is why Trump's message resonated with them.[71]

Overall, then, it is far from clear how much of a burden immigrants from Mexico and other countries really are. They do not take jobs from Americans or push down their wages. They pay billions of dollars each year in taxes. And they do not pose nearly as serious a criminal threat to society as Trump claimed and his supporters assumed. Yet it was in places throughout the United States where the growth of Hispanic and other nonwhite populations had been growing the fastest since 2000 that Trump was most likely to attract white supporters who had previously voted Democrat. This included, for example, rural counties in the Midwest that were crucial for his victory in the general election.[72] This suggests that whites were perceiving demographic change as a real threat insofar as they saw themselves gradually being outnumbered by immigrants who might eventually knock them off their perch in the racial pecking order. As noted earlier, this sort of concern had long been a source of racism and anti-immigrant sentiment in the United States.[73]

It is worth noting that mainstream Republicans had moved away from anti-immigrant rhetoric before this. As president, for example, George W. Bush proclaimed on more than one occasion that we are a nation of immigrants. And although he called for tougher border security, he also advocated a middle-ground approach between an automatic path to citizenship and mass deportation. His brother, Jeb, occasionally addressed crowds in Spanish when he was governor of Florida, which has a large Spanish-speaking immigrant contingent, and when he ran for the Republican presidential nomination. And Marco Rubio, another one of Trump's opponents in the primary, was also much less critical of immigrants than Trump was. The point is that Trump came down hard on an issue that clicked with his constituents but that others in his own party had treated more gingerly. Whether his fierce anti-immigration views stemmed from an insightful reading of the Tea Party Movement, listening to his inner circle of advisers like Steve Bannon, or something else is unclear. But it worked.

IMMIGRATION AND TERRORISM

What about Muslims, the other side of the anti-immigrant coin in the Trump campaign? Trump constantly raised concerns about the dangers of radical Islamist terrorists. His concern was that our borders were so porous that terrorists could easily sneak into the country and kill innocent Americans. A week after taking office, Trump signed an executive order titled "Protection of the Nation from Foreign Terrorist Entry into the United States" to solve the problem. The background for this was that the United States had experienced terrorist attacks at the hands of Muslims associated with or proclaiming allegiance to various terrorist organizations in the Middle East, notably Al Qaeda and the Islamic State in Iraq and Syria (ISIS). On September 11, 2001, Al Qaeda operatives hijacked four commercial airliners and used them to demolish the twin towers in New York City and hit the Pentagon. The fourth plane crashed in Pennsylvania. Furthermore, a married couple—one born in America and the other in Pakistan—inspired by radical jihad killed fourteen people in a 2015 shooting spree in San Bernardino, California. And a lone gunman praising ISIS opened fire the next year in an Orlando, Florida, nightclub, killing forty-nine partygoers. There were other incidents as well. To some people Trump's concern seemed to be justified insofar as there were three million Muslims living in the United States. Maybe there were more radical Islamist terrorists hiding among them! Indeed, nearly as many Trump supporters believed that terrorism was a serious problem as believed that immigration was.[74] The facts, however, pointed in a very different direction.

Since the 9/11 attacks until 2017, there were only 123 fatalities in the United States at the hands of Muslim extremists. Only a quarter of the terrorists involved in these killings were Muslim-born immigrants. To put this in broader perspective, during that same fifteen-year period, there were over 240,000 murders in the United States, including mass shootings like the one at Sandy Hook Elementary School in Connecticut that left twenty-six people dead, most of them young children. This meant that attacks by Muslims accounted for only a miniscule 0.0005 percent of all murders in America.[75]

Without diminishing the obvious importance of keeping terrorism at bay, it seemed like the situation was well under control. Trump's campaign promise to shut down Muslim immigration was akin to killing a fly with an M1 Abrams tank—a sixty-one-ton weapon with enough firepower in its 105-mm cannon to take out enemy forces over a mile away. Nevertheless, Trump supporters in general and in the right-wing media, including Fox News and the Breitbart News Network, insisted that radical Islamist terrorism was a major threat in America, even though the FBI didn't even mention it in its 2014 report, "National Threat Assessment for Domestic Extremism." The FBI was far more concerned about other groups, such as white supremacists, black nationalists, Puerto Rican nationalists, animal rights groups, and radical antiabortion crusaders.[76] But the important point, again, is not so much that Trump's rhetoric did not mesh with the facts but that it did mesh with his supporters' perceptions. Furthermore, targeting Muslims as the source of terrorism on US soil added an additional layer to Trump's explicit racial and ethnic scapegoating, which meant that it resonated with many Americans' general perceptions about racial and ethnic minorities.

But there was a second way in which Trump scapegoated Muslims that had little to do with terrorism. Many of those worried about Muslim immigration believed that Muslims wanted to destroy American values and replace them with Islamic Shari 'a law. In fact, many people believing this did not understand what Shari 'a law is and assumed that it is simply a recipe for extreme brutality and oppression for those, particularly women, who violated strict Islamic moral codes. For example, Newt Gingrich, former Speaker of the House and a close adviser to Trump during the campaign, charged that every Muslim in America who believes in Shari 'a "should be deported." Why? Because according to Gingrich, Shari 'a "is a moral threat to the survival of freedom in the United States and in the world as we know it."[77] Yet as is true of the Bible's teachings, there are many interpretations of Shari 'a, only some of which can be construed as the sort of radical Islamic fundamentalism about which Gingrich and other Trump supporters were so worried. Nevertheless, ten years after 9/11, nearly one in three Americans believed that Muslim Americans wanted to establish Shari 'a as the law of the land in the United States. And almost 60 percent of white evangelical Protestants believed that the values of Islam were at odds with American values. How Shari 'a law could come to dominate American society given that Muslims were barely 1 percent of the population is anyone's guess.[78] What matters, however, is that many Americans believed it and so were sympathetic to Trump's appeals for clamping down on Muslims.

In fact, anti-Muslim sentiment in America had been growing prior to the 2016 presidential campaign. For instance, between 1996 and 2015, the years for which the FBI posts hate crime statistics on its website, the number of hate crimes against Muslims increased tenfold. Furthermore, the FBI reported a 65 percent increase in anti-Muslim hate crimes just between 2014 and 2015. Some observers have argued that by playing on the public's Islamophobia, Trump's inflammatory anti-Muslim campaign rhetoric exacerbated the situation. The number of anti-Muslim attacks in 2015 was the highest since 2001.[79] Whether Trump's rhetoric is responsible or not, the broader lesson is that there has been a persistent and in some cases growing undercurrent of racial and ethnic animosity in America that Trump exploited for political advantage.

CONCLUSION

To summarize, Trump's willingness to disparage racial and ethnic minorities and immigrants resonated with voters, but not because this was something new and exciting to them in American politics. His appeals resonated with the public for three basic reasons. First, by linking issues of race to the problems of job loss, inequality, and poverty, he mixed the issues of race and class in ways that helped people rationalize their economic situations. Scapegoating minorities for their troubles was the key. Second, people were misinformed about much of what he was talking about. So was he, unless he simply twisted and distorted the facts to fit his pitch. As I explained in chapter 1, the media was culpable here insofar as it did not do more to challenge Trump's facts and claims or confront the so-called alternative facts and fake news being circulated on the Internet and elsewhere about these issues. Third, the public had been primed for Trump's talking points for decades thanks to the Southern Strategy, dog whistle politics, and various other trends in society. He capitalized on this by conjuring up fears and anxieties about African American crime in inner cities, Hispanic immigrants taking jobs away from Americans, and radical Islamic terrorists coming to kill innocent citizens and destroy American values. Some of these concerns had been cultivated over the years by politicians, some were rooted in shifting demographics, and some were associated with 9/11 and a few subsequent killings. Trump turned it all to his advantage and threw dog whistle politics out the window. He didn't start from scratch; he had plenty of material to work with.

When it came to immigration, once in office Trump moved quickly to deliver the goods as promised. During his first week as president, he signed an executive order directing the secretary of homeland security to begin planning, designing, and building the wall along the border with Mexico; to build detention facilities nearby to deal with asylum claims; to hire five thousand Border Patrol agents; and to empower state and local law enforcement to act as immigration officers. The same week he signed a second executive order instructing the secretary to prioritize certain undocumented immigrants for removal—both convicted criminals and people merely charged with a crime but not yet tried in court. The order also prohibited federal funding for sanctuary cities where local officials declined to help enforce federal immigration laws.[80] Finally, as mentioned earlier, a third executive order temporarily banned anyone from entering the United States from seven predominantly Muslim countries in the Middle East and Africa. Scapegoating had become administration policy.

In 2004, Barack Obama addressed the Democratic National Convention and uttered what are now these famous words: "There's not a black America and white America and Latino America; there's the United States of America." Four years later he became America's first African American president, and many people thought this was the beginning of a new era in US history—a postracial era—reversing, at long last, trends that had been in motion for a very long time. The fact that Donald Trump won office eight years after that by scapegoating racial and ethnic minorities proved that a postracial America was a dream not yet realized. In fact, Obama's presidency heightened rather than diminished racial divisions within American politics, tilling the soil even deeper for the growth of Trump's supporters. But before we get to that, we need to examine a third trend underpinning Trump's popular appeal—the rise of neoliberalism, a conservative ideology that had become increasingly important in US politics at least since the days of Ronald Reagan because it promised to rejuvenate the economy, put people back to work, grow their incomes, and restore the American Dream.

CHAPTER 5
Ideas and Ideology

In the huge television hit *Mad Men*, a saga about the world of corporate advertising in the 1960s, Jon Hamm plays the character of Don Draper, a heavy-drinking, womanizing, Madison Avenue marketing guru. In one episode Draper is pitching an ad campaign to a prospective client, the manufacturer of Lucky Strike cigarettes, at a time when national concerns over the dangerous health effects of smoking are on the rise. His pitch is short and sweet: "Everybody else's tobacco is poisonous. Lucky Strikes' . . . is *toasted*." In other words, forget that they might kill you—they taste good. What Draper knows is that one word or phrase can make or break a product.

Donald Trump knew this too. His promise to "Make America Great Again" was a wonderful catchphrase. After all, what red-blooded American wouldn't want to make his or her country great? Who wouldn't want more jobs, better wages, and a stronger economy? But the slogan's strength was also its Achilles heel—it immediately required clarification and specifics. How exactly would America be made great? What policies would be required? And why would they work? It seemed like Trump was at a disadvantage here because compared to Hillary Clinton, he was short on details. Her campaign website posted forty-one policy position papers with supporting details and documentation.[1] Trump's website had a measly fifteen with far fewer specifics.[2] One might have thought that this gave Clinton a clear advantage—she had details and facts, while he didn't. But in the end it didn't matter. He won the election anyway.

One reason was that Trump's rhetoric, claims, and promises resonated with a number of ideas and ideological beliefs held deeply by many Americans. He didn't need facts because ideas and ideology sufficed. Facts often got in his way. Indeed, the vagueness and superficiality of Trump's policy proposals left him plenty of room to play on people's ideological predispositions. This chapter examines the most important of these—people's conservative beliefs about the economy and government—which were central to Trump's campaign because they helped him draw the road map that he promised would lead to a greater America. Indeed, economic issues were at the forefront of his campaign; he downplayed most other traditional Republican talking points, such as abortion and family values.[3] I'll have a few things to say at the end about how he used ideology to handle certain women's issues because they became a flashpoint later in the campaign. But the main argument of this chapter is that Trump capitalized on an important ideological trend that had been developing since the 1970s—the rise of neoliberalism. However, before digging into this, I need to introduce a few terms that will come in handy along the way.

WHAT'S IN AN IDEA?

When people talk about ideas or ideology, what they mean is often pretty fuzzy, so let me clarify. In this chapter four types of ideas come into play.[4] One type is what we can call a policy program or *plan*. This is basically a prescription for solving a policy problem. Policy plans explain how changing things like the law or a regulation, spending more money, or fiddling with the tax code will fix a problem. So, for instance, we might lower interest rates to increase home sales. Politicians are constantly coming up with and arguing over plans to do things like reduce unemployment, boost economic growth, improve the health care system, or clean up the environment.

Another type of idea is a policy *paradigm*, like Keynesianism or neoliberalism, discussed later. Paradigms also stipulate causal relationships just like policy plans do. But unlike plans, paradigms are ideas that are often taken for granted and sit in the background of policymaking deliberations, often quite invisibly insofar as everybody just assumes them to be true. That's why people rarely argue over them. Like blinders on a race horse, paradigms limit what people can see and what plans they can imagine in the first place.

A third type of idea is what social scientists call a *frame*, which is typically a memorable metaphor or catchy phrase designed to make a policy plan sound appealing. Framing is what Don Draper was so good at. Trump, for instance, talked about "draining the swamp" in Washington when he referred to his plan for cleaning up government waste and corruption.

Finally, there are *public sentiments*. These are the values and normative beliefs people have about the way things ought to be. Like frames, they don't involve much causal logic, but unlike frames, which are very much in the foreground of political discourse, public sentiments tend to be taken for granted and reside in the background. Examples would be people's beliefs about whether socialism is good or bad, or whether we should aspire to the traditional nuclear family ideal where dad is the breadwinner, mom is the homemaker, and together they raise a couple of kids.

To keep things simple, let's just say that these ideas, and particularly paradigms and public sentiments, taken as a whole constitute what we might call ideology.* How does all this help us understand Trump's phenomenal success during the campaign? Let's begin with the rise of the neoliberal paradigm—one of the most important ideological trends in recent American history.

THE RISE OF THE NEOLIBERAL PARADIGM

The Golden Age in America was a time when Keynesianism was the policy paradigm that virtually all politicians used to help them manage the economy. President Richard Nixon confirmed this in 1971 when he declared famously that "We're all Keynesians now!" The basic idea, developed by the British economist John Maynard Keynes, was that government would regulate spending to counteract a market economy's inherent instability. How? By priming the pump that fueled economic growth. During economic recessions, the government would lower interest rates and taxes and increase public investment to stimulate aggregate demand—even if this meant borrowing money and incurring budget deficits in the short term. Furthermore, government would reduce income inequality, thereby increasing the propensity for more people to buy things, which would stimulate demand even more. However, during economic booms, government would do the opposite to avoid inflation by preventing aggregate demand from exceeding supply and therefore pushing up prices. Policymakers would stop pumping up demand and instead rein it in by raising taxes and interest rates and reducing government spending. Overall, then, government would strive to modulate aggregate demand in ways that would keep the economy on an even keel by stimulating growth and keeping unemployment low but without creating excessive inflation.[5] The crucial underlying assumption is that there is an inverse relationship between unemployment and inflation: like a playground seesaw, as one side goes up the other goes down, and vice versa. The trick is to keep it balanced.

Policymakers embraced Keynesianism not only in the United States but also in many advanced capitalist countries during the 1940s and 1950s

---

* This is consistent with what most people think ideologies are. Merriam-Webster's dictionary defines ideology as "a systematic body of concepts especially about human life or culture . . . the integrated assertions, theories and aims that constitute a sociopolitical program."

as a way of avoiding a relapse into a second Great Depression.[6] But things began to change in the late 1960s and early 1970s. Thanks to bad harvests around the world and deals to sell American grain to the Russians, prices for food and raw materials began to escalate in the United States. Making matters worse, the price of oil skyrocketed suddenly in the wake of the 1973 Organization of the Petroleum Exporting Countries (OPEC) oil crisis. The tradeoff between unemployment and inflation that Keynesians had assumed broke down. The seesaw was busted. The crisis ushered in a period of stagflation where both unemployment and economic stagnation on one side and inflation on the other side rose in lock step. Keynesianism was thrown into question and a war of ideas erupted as economists and policymakers searched for answers to the stagflation riddle. Neoliberalism won—a victory marked by Ronald Reagan's election as president in 1980.[7]

At the core, and contrary to Keynesianism, neoliberalism assumes that markets tend to be self-correcting and that governments would do well to leave them alone for the most part even when they run into trouble. Otherwise, policymakers will probably make things worse.[8] For instance, some economists argue that people are adept at anticipating government policy interventions based on what they learn from past experience. As a result, people's rational expectations undermine the intended effects of those interventions.[9] Consider fiscal policy. If the government decided on a tax cut financed by higher borrowing to stimulate aggregate demand, rational consumers would save the tax cut rather than spending it in antic-ipation of having to pay for tax increases later to pay off the debt incurred earlier from all that borrowing. The tax cut would have no effect. Others worry about the time it takes for policy to begin working because there is often a time lag. So, for example, if policymakers decide to increase spend-ing to stimulate the economy during a downturn, by the time that spending reaches the economy, the economy may already have recovered so the stim-ulus might trigger inflation, thereby doing more harm than good.[10] Making matters worse, some believe that policymakers are often less interested in serving the public interest than feathering their own nests or kowtowing to various lobbies and constituents, which means that government policy is often inappropriate and ineffectual in solving society's problems in the first place.[11] The policy implications of all this are clear: government's role in managing the economy should be minimal, which means that government spending, taxing, and regulation should be pared to the bone to let markets operate freely and as efficiently as possible.

Neoliberal ideas had been around since the 1930s.[12] But it took a while before they took center stage, replacing the old Keynesian paradigm. Several things helped that happen. First, beginning in the mid-1970s, a very con-servative group of think tanks including the Heritage Foundation, the Cato

Institute, and the National Center for Policy Analysis came on the scene in Washington. In contrast to the older and typically more moderate think tanks like the Brookings Institution, these new ones were ideologically motivated, touted neoliberalism, and pushed it in very aggressive ways into the political mainstream. Heritage, for instance, wrote *Mandate for Leadership*, a hefty volume of policy briefs that laid out a blueprint for reforming all aspects of public policy for the incoming Reagan administration—a document that reputedly guided the Reagan White House's initial budget-, tax-, and regulation-cutting efforts.[13] Much of this was funded, often quietly, by very conservative philanthropic organizations like the Olin Foundation and wealthy people like Joseph Coors, the beer tycoon, and Richard Mellon Scaife, principal heir to the Mellon banking and oil fortune, who were pivotal in founding Heritage, and later David and Charles Koch, who were key benefactors of Cato, the most libertarian outfit of them all.[14] The comparative financial advantage of these think tanks compared to many others was clear to me when a colleague and I visited them to collect data for another research project. Both Heritage and Cato had opulent office spaces. Heritage's lobby, for instance, was a pristine, wood-paneled affair leading to suites of spacious conference rooms with lots of amenities. Their counterparts on the left had nothing even close, where on one occasion we sat on folding chairs in a conference room with somebody's half-eaten lunch on an empty Ikea book case in the corner.

Second, conservatives not only poured big money into Washington think tanks but also gave millions of dollars to entice several of the nation's law schools to teach a conservative brand of judicial theory—the law and economics approach—based on neoliberalism in a deliberate effort to push the judicial system to the right.[15] Similar moves were made later on university campuses including Brown, Cornell, Dartmouth, the University of Virginia, the University of Texas, and the University of Colorado, where conservative money helped establish programs to teach undergraduates the virtues of free market capitalism as espoused by Adam Smith, Friedrich Hayek, Ayn Rand, Milton Friedman, and others, and supported scholars who were doing research and developing theories that supported conservative views. This was a strategy conservatives developed to counteract what they perceived to have been a liberal takeover of higher education in America, and to legitimize their political agenda.[16]

Third, corporations began lobbying for neoliberalism. Beginning in the early 1970s, to compensate for inflation, unions demanded higher wages, which cut into corporate profits. In some industries, such as construction, cost-of-living clauses in union contracts automatically pushed up wages faster than productivity, which meant that employers were getting less value from their workers for every dollar they paid in wages. Corporations desperately wanted to stop this, partly because they believed that wage demands rather than exogenous shocks from rising food and energy prices were causing inflation. As a result, large firms started lobbying in a much more systematic and organized fashion, urging the government to forget about balancing inflation against employment and focus instead on jacking up interest rates. There were two reasons for this. One was to bring inflation under control. The other was because they believed that higher interest rates would lead to significantly higher unemployment, which would reduce wage demands and labor costs and, as a result, increase their profits.[17] Toward these ends, a community of leading CEOs formed the Business Roundtable in 1972 after which corporate lobbying, previously not very effective, came into its own, wielding tremendous influence in Congress. Nowadays corporations spend about $2.6 billion a year lobbying and the biggest firms often have a hundred or more lobbyists working for them. They outspend the lobbying of labor unions and public interest groups combined by a thirty-four-to-one margin.[18]

Fourth, more and more private money flowed into politics thanks to changes in campaign finance laws. However, Republicans outspent Democrats in thirteen of the sixteen presidential elections prior to 2016.[19] It began with the proliferation of political action committees in the 1970s and 1980s, accelerated after that, but really took off thanks to a landmark Supreme Court decision in 2010. For decades, most campaign contributions came from wealthy people, most of whom tended to be Republicans and therefore conservative. But in the *Citizens United v. Federal Election Commission* decision, the court allowed corporations and unions to spend unlimited amounts of money on direct advocacy for or against political candidates. The result was a sudden flood of outside money into political campaigns, nearly quadrupling between the 2010 and 2012 election cycles. Most of the increase was from conservative sources, which outspent liberals two to one. Much of this so-called dark money was donated to nonprofit organizations that used it to back the candidates of their choice and without having to report where the money came from. The agenda being pushed was often neoliberalism.[20]

Fifth, certain quarters of the media began pushing the neoliberal agenda with a vengeance. Neoliberalism was extolled, for example, by editorialists like Jude Wanniski writing frequently in the *Wall Street Journal*. Authors like George Gilder whose 1981 best seller, *Wealth and Poverty*, was subsidized by the conservative Manhattan Institute and adopted as a book-of-the-month club selection received lots of media coverage.[21] Charles Murray's *Losing Ground*, a conservative critique of social policy, was another big hit.[22] Both were heavily criticized by the left. The emergence of flamboyant talk radio stars helped the cause too. For instance, Rush Limbaugh's show debuted in 1984 and eventually captivated an estimated weekly audience of 14.5 million listeners.[23] By 2016, the top ten most popular radio talk shows in America featured conservatives typically lambasting the Obama administration. These shows were hosted by Limbaugh (number one), Sean Hannity (number two), Mark Levin (number four), Glenn Beck (number five), Michael Savage (number seven), and Mike Gallagher (number ten), all with millions of listeners every day. Only two left-wing political shows made the list, not counting Howard Stern (number six), who specialized in outrageous and sometimes indecent political incorrectness, and Dave Ramsey (number three), who hosted a show about financial matters.[24] And, of course, Fox News, America's iconic conservative cable news channel, contributed too. Founded in 1996, Fox was run by former Republican Party media expert Roger Ailes. It became a media giant pushing the neoliberal agenda, particularly with on-air hosts like Bill O'Reilly, Tucker Carlson, Sean Hannity, and Glenn Beck.[25] In 2016, Fox News viewership topped all cable news channels, and for years *The O'Reilly Factor* was the top news program in the country until O'Reilly was fired unceremoniously in 2017 for sexually harassing a number of women at the station.[26]

A final reason behind the rise of neoliberalism was the fall of the Berlin Wall in 1989 and subsequently the collapse of the Soviet Union. Once the Cold War had been won, it was easy for advocates of neoliberalism to declare victory for their world view. In other words, the market economy had triumphed over state socialist planning. This opened the door for much cheerleading for market fundamentalism all around the world. This was especially evident in those postcommunist countries of Eastern and Central Europe and then Russia in the early 1990s that engaged in shock therapy where leaders moved as quickly as possible to privatize state-owned enterprises and create markets for everything. These were initiatives often supported, if not pushed aggressively, by the United States, various Western European governments, the International Monetary Fund (IMF), and other international organizations, often embracing neoliberalism.

Neoliberalism really hit its policymaking stride during the Reagan administration. As he was discussing stagflation during his 1981 inaugural address, Reagan remarked famously that "In this present crisis, government is not the solution to our problem; government *is* the problem!" Once the shift from Keynesianism to neoliberalism was underway, policymakers became increasingly enamored with cutting three things: taxes, spending, and regulations. To begin with, their desire to cut taxes focused particularly on the wealthy and corporations, not so much to stimulate aggregate demand, as Keynesians would have wanted, but to spur investment. Neoliberals argued that cutting taxes on the wealthy and corporations would give them more money to invest in ways that would spark economic growth and job creation without boosting aggregate demand and exacerbating inflation. This was referred to as supply-side economics because it was intended to increase the supply of investment capital to the economy. It was an integral piece of the neoliberal package. Furthermore, it was believed that the revenue lost today through lower tax rates would be more than made up for tomorrow by revenue generated later from the economic growth the lower rates would stimulate.[27]

Cutting government spending was next. There were several reasons for this. One was to reduce government borrowing, which was believed to be crowding out private actors from the capital markets, thereby stifling investment and growth. Another reason was to diminish budget deficits, which became an obsession of both political parties. And a third was to reduce incentives for people to act in ways contrary to the country's best economic interests. The logic was that because the social safety net had presumably become increasingly generous since the 1960s, people had fewer incentives either to seek gainful employment or, if they had a job, to work hard at it. Why? Because government programs had reduced the fear of unemployment—the government's social safety net would take care of you if you didn't have a job. Hence, not only had public policy unintentionally fueled higher unemployment but also it had undermined hard work and productivity and, therefore, the nation's economic competitiveness. In short, the allegation was that government spending on social programs had unintentionally made people lazy.[28] And, as I explained in chapter 4, it was often implied that these were people of color. As researchers at the Urban Institute concluded about Reagan's first term in office, "In characterizing the federal government as more of a problem than a solution, the president clearly struck a popular chord with the country."[29] And he did it with flare, even before becoming president. In 1976, he described what he called a "welfare queen," who turned out later to be fictional but not before the term had entered the American lexicon, where it is still used widely today. Here's how he depicted this fake freeloader: "She used 80 names, 30 addresses, 15 telephone numbers to collect food stamps, Social Security, veterans' benefits for four nonexistent deceased veteran husbands, as well as welfare. Her tax-free income alone has been running $150,000 a year."[30] The imagery stuck in people's minds like glue.

Finally, policymakers began to cut regulations, which were reputedly expensive for firms to comply with and, therefore, another reason investment capital was in short supply. Besides, they believed that one way to reduce the size of big government and unleash the power of the market was to reduce government regulation. As a result, although the federal budget increased steadily from $1.7 trillion to $3.8 trillion from 1980 to 2015 (in 2016 constant dollars), one cabinet-level department took a particularly big hit. The Department of Labor suffered a 47 percent budget cut during this period despite a huge but temporary spike in 2010 associated with the Great Recession. Furthermore, regulatory agencies that conservatives felt were particularly onerous to business had their budgets cut too, including the Environmental Protection Agency and the Securities and Exchange Commission.[31]

Successive presidents after Reagan didn't veer too far from the neoliberal script. George H. W. Bush, for instance, who had exclaimed during his presidential campaign that people should "Read my lips. No new taxes!," eventually did raise taxes—but to reduce a budget deficit that neoliberals hated. Clinton raised taxes too for the same reason. Recall that he also signed major legislation overhauling the federal welfare system by limiting lifetime eligibility to certain benefits and linking eligibility to the recipient's efforts to find a job—a move designed to get people off welfare and put those welfare queens out of business. And he passed legislation that kept federal regulators off the back of the banking and financial services industries in ways that also helped foment the 2008 financial crisis. Finally, as we saw in chapter 3, George W. Bush pursued neoliberal supply-side tax cuts during his presidency.

Overall, then, a series of changes and challenges to the economy—the red thread in my argument—opened the door to a fundamental ideological shift in how policymakers dealt with the county's economic problems. The trend was toward neoliberalism as the new operating paradigm. But how did Trump's economic plan compare to it?

TRUMP'S ECONOMIC PLAN

Trump's plan was pretty simple and straightforward. He promised during the campaign that he would lower taxes by $4.4 trillion over a decade and simplify the tax code. In particular, he said that no business would pay more than 15 percent of its income in taxes—a dramatic reduction from the 35 percent marginal corporate tax rate in place at the time. He also promised to reduce government spending by $1 trillion over the next decade and slash "excessive regulations" that he claimed cost Americans almost $2 trillion a year. Finally, he said he would scrap trade agreements like the North American Free Trade Agreement (NAFTA) and the more recent Trans-Pacific Partnership, and roll back restrictions on offshore oil and gas drilling. Doing all of this, he claimed, would create twenty-five million new jobs over the next decade and boost economic growth to at least 3.5 percent annually.[32] America would be great again. Most of his plan was straight out of the neoliberal playbook. One part, as we shall see, was not.

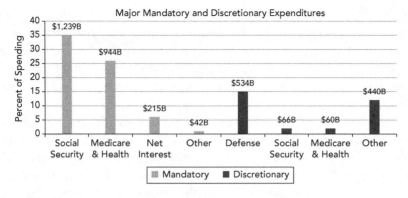

Figure 5.1:
US federal budget expenditures, 2016.
Source: US Office of Management and Budget 2017.

Some wondered if this was too good to be true. Could we really expect growth rates that high? And why wouldn't his huge tax cut, which outweighed his proposed budget cut more than four to one, translate into huge budget deficits? Deficits were anathema to virtually all Republicans and many Democrats who believed that they were a sign that government was out of control and getting too big, something that neoliberals despised. Republican House Speaker Paul Ryan had railed against deficits. And Obama's bipartisan National Commission on Fiscal Responsibility and Reform, the so-called Simpson-Bowles Commission, issued a strongly worded report in 2010 with support from some on both sides of the aisle calling for fiscal restraint and deficit reduction to pay down the national debt.[†] Experts on both the left and right estimated that Trump's economic proposals would increase deficits and add between $5 trillion and $10 trillion to the national debt over the next ten years. *Forbes Magazine*, for instance, concluded that his tax cuts would be of historic proportions. "[They] would make deficits worse. Much worse."[33]

Trump's defense against these charges was not exactly rock solid. To begin with, although he said he would cut the budget to compensate for some of his tax cuts, he promised in the same breath to preserve most federal spending including for defense and the three largest entitlement programs, Social Security, Medicare, and Medicaid.[34] But the numbers didn't seem to add up. The problem was, as Figure 5.1 shows, that roughly 70 percent of major federal spending was mandatory, not discretionary, and therefore off limits to budget cutting. This meant that he would have had

---

+ There was, however, not enough support in the commission to send the report to Congress—seven of the committee's eighteen members opposed the plan (Bartels 2016, p. 285).

only a small slice of the budget available for spending cuts, which left him little leeway for avoiding a massive deficit. The Office of Management and Budget estimated the deficit for 2016 to be about $550 billion (3.3 percent of GDP), which meant that if Trump's plan had been in place, he would have had to cut about half of all discretionary spending to balance the budget. Take another look at Figure 5.1. To achieve that goal without touching the programs he put off limits, he would have had to eliminate all spending in the "other" discretionary category—about $440 billion. This would have wiped out *all* expenditures for the following: veteran benefits and services; education, training, employment, and social services; transportation; administration of justice; natural resources and the environment; and general science, space, and technology. But even after doing all that, he would still have fallen short by about $110 billion.

Nevertheless, according to Trump's plan, we didn't have to worry. Why not? Because the most important thing mitigating deficits would not be his budget cuts but the tremendous economic growth that his policies would generate—growth that would yield more tax revenue than his tax cuts would cost. This too was classic neoliberal supply-side economics. But given the enormous gap between tax and spending cuts in his plan, this was something that even conservative economists questioned.[35] Still, when quizzed about this during one of the presidential debates, he told viewers that deficits wouldn't be a problem because "we will create a tremendous economic machine" that could generate as much as 5 or 6 percent annual economic growth. Virtually all reputable economists thought this estimate was even more far-fetched than his initial 3.5 percent claim.[36] Again, the math didn't seem right.

Moreover, history wasn't on Trump's side. The historical record suggested that Trump's neoliberal road map for making America great was likely to be about as effective as the maps the Germans would have used during World War II had they invaded Britain. Anticipating an invasion, the British removed many of their road signs to make those maps virtually useless. In other words, there was little evidence that neoliberalism worked. One of the best accounts of the vast research on this question was published by economist Jon Bakija and his colleagues, who studied many countries and reviewed dozens of research studies.[37] What did they find? First, higher levels of taxation are not always bad. In fact, they are not significantly associated with economic growth one way or another, either in the United States or abroad. This is because higher taxes are sometimes associated with government spending that stimulates rather than retards economic growth, such as investments in infrastructure, education, resolving market failures, and contributing to the general welfare of the population in ways that improve worker productivity. Indeed, many, many things affect economic growth besides taxes. Second, higher levels of government spending on social welfare programs do not necessarily hurt economic growth. They also tend to be associated with less government corruption and smaller government budget deficits. This is because countries with more extensive taxing and spending often learn how to manage fiscal policy more efficiently than other countries. Third, more taxing and spending tends to reduce inequality, which seems to improve economic performance. Less inequality is also associated with more revenue for the government. Finally, as political economist Mark Blyth has shown, in the wake of the financial crisis several European countries resorted to draconian neoliberal cuts in government spending to extricate themselves from the depths of serious economic recessions. The results were often terrible and quite the opposite from what was intended in terms of improving economic growth and reducing unemployment.[38]

The question, then, is, if Trump's economic plan sounded like pie in the sky, why did so many voters believe it? One reason was that this was a familiar story that politicians had been preaching for decades as they came to accept the neoliberal paradigm. By the time Trump arrived on the political scene, the paradigm had become so taken for granted by most Americans that he didn't have to do much to convince his supporters that he knew what he was talking about. Indeed, psychologists have shown that people tend to believe things if they hear them repeatedly, including things that are clearly wrong.[39] In other words, Trump's plan gained political traction because it fit an ideological trend that began in the 1970s—the rise of neoliberalism. However, there was one important exception—Trump's view on trade, particularly his idea of reconsidering NAFTA and some of America's other free trade agreements. This was an idea that appealed particularly to members of the working and middle classes who believed that their jobs had been lost to foreign competition. But let's put the free trade issue aside until later.

There were likely two additional reasons people bought Trump's plan. One was that they were simply ignorant of the facts and historical record either because they were working so hard to make ends meet that they didn't have time to keep up with the news or because they succumbed to the so-called fake news and alternative facts surrounding Trump's campaign and perpetuated by the right-wing media like Fox News. According to a study from the University of Maryland, when it came to political issues, Fox News viewers, the vast majority of whom were conservative, were the most misinformed audience of any major news network.[40] Trump supporters were also probably misinformed given his record of bending the truth. As Figure 5.2 shows, an independent fact-checking

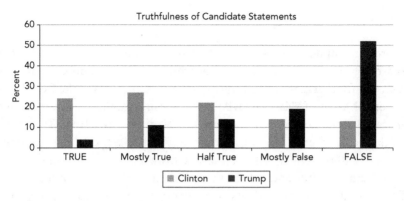

Figure 5.2:
Independent fact-checking of candidates' statements.
Source: PolitiFact 2017.

organization found that 71 percent of Trump's campaign statements were false or mostly false, as compared to 27 percent for Clinton. It was widely reported during the campaign that Trump had told *People Magazine* in 1998, "If I were to run, I'd run as a Republican. They're the dumbest group of voters in the country. They believe anything on Fox News. I could lie and they'd still eat it up." A number of reputable fact-checking organizations quickly debunked this quotation as a fake—he never said that and nobody was able to figure out who started the rumor. Nevertheless, given how loosely he played with the truth during the campaign and the apparent gullibility of Fox News viewers, he may very well have believed it and acted accordingly.[41]

The other reason so many people liked Trump's plan was that it was simple and easily understood, especially compared to Clinton's economic plan. Trump lived by the KISS Principle—Keep It Simple, Stupid. He was a pro at packaging his message in a few simple thoughts that resonated with crowds. She was not. Her ideas were not easy to grasp.[42] Her tax plan, for instance, was far more complicated than his, which was basically just about cutting taxes. She promised to impose a "fair share surcharge" on rich people, follow the "Buffett Rule," close loopholes for "corporate inversions," deploy a "Manufacturing Renaissance Tax Credit," and prevent multinational corporations from "earnings stripping."[43] And that was just for starters. I think it's safe to say that most Americans' eyes would quickly glaze over if they had to focus on the complexities of these things.

But there was still another reason Trump's plan was so appealing to people. It resonated with other firmly rooted ideological elements in American politics and society. He framed his plan effectively in ways that fit neatly with many people's public sentiments about government.

Before continuing, let's take a little test. Answer this question: what catchy phrases or slogans do you remember from the Trump and Clinton campaigns, or for that matter from any of Trump's opponents in the Republican primaries? When I asked my wife this question about three months after the general election, she immediately rattled off three from Trump but couldn't remember any from Clinton or anybody else. I couldn't remember any from Clinton either, although several from Trump came to mind. Then I asked some friends and got the same response. Finally, I quizzed a group of Dartmouth College students one evening who were particularly interested in politics and who had invited me to give a dinner talk about Trump and the election. Even among these politically well-informed students, the results weren't too much different. Overall, including my wife, friends, and students, everybody remembered Trump slogans like "Make America Great Again" or "Build a Wall." But for every three people who remembered at least one of Trump's catchphrases, only one person could remember any of Clinton's. In fact, Trump's slogans had so much pizzazz that they were mimicked on the signs people carried after his inauguration at women's anti-Trump rallies across America. Two frames were especially memorable and inspirational. One was "Make America Great Again," which gave rise to signs saying "Make America Nice Again," "Make America Think Again," "Make America Gay Again," "Make America Read Again," and "Make America Native Again." The other was "Build a Wall," which inspired "Build Kindness Not Walls," "Build a Wall Around Trump," and many more. My conclusion, based on this admittedly nonscientific evidence? Trump was great at framing issues in catchy and memorable ways; Clinton was not. Therein lies the talent of a great pitchman. This is important in politics.

But for frames to work, they need to resonate with something people are already familiar with, and in politics that's not only a taken-for-granted paradigm but also underlying public sentiments. For instance, one reason neoliberal reforms were passed on Reagan's watch was that conservatives framed them deftly in terms of Jeffersonian small-government ideals, which have been the bedrock of American ideology forever. That is, if you want to control big, centralized, and growing government, then you need to limit politicians' access to revenues by cutting taxes, just like you would cut off the food supply of mice in your kitchen if you wanted to get rid of them.[44]

Related closely to this is a part of American culture, discussed in earlier chapters, that holds individualism in high regard—people believe that whenever possible they should take care of themselves rather than rely on the government. Put differently, Americans reject collectivism in favor of individualism. This is one reason Reagan's image of the welfare queen resonated so vibrantly with the public. We also saw this earlier insofar as Americans think that people's economic situation is tied closely to how hard they work rather than the structural circumstances in which they find themselves. To a considerable extent, even poor Americans believe in individualism, particularly as a corollary of personal freedom.[45] The idea is that anything that restricts individual choice undermines freedom. For instance, higher taxes would reduce an individual's choices and therefore freedom in the market. Some went even further. During the Reagan years, some conservatives argued that high taxes jeopardized individual freedom by reducing net family income, which forced wives into the labor market, threatened their husbands' manhood, and fueled higher divorce rates, thus undermining the very fabric of the traditional American family.[46] Even in those days framing like this was strategic and sophisticated. Conservatives had substantially more money and other resources for monitoring public opinion to determine which frames resonated best with the public.[47] In the end, observers agree that an important reason that the neoliberal supply-side program became institutionalized was that its supporters were better at framing their arguments in ways that were appealing politically.[48]

Not much has changed since then. Generally speaking, since the 1960s, Americans have grown increasingly wary of big government, as opposed to big business or big labor, as a threat to the United States in the future. In the mid-1960s, about 48 percent of the public held this view, but by 2014, it had reached 72 percent, often because people felt that the federal government threatened individual rights and freedoms. And among Republicans, the numbers skyrocketed from 41 to 92 percent who believed this.[49]

More specifically, consider taxes. Americans' preference for the Jeffersonian ideal of small government has long been clear whenever they are asked about taxes. Since 1970, more Americans felt that their taxes were too high rather than either too low or just about right. And while the difference in opinion narrowed a bit from the mid-1990s through 2008, it expanded again after the financial crisis.[50] The story was similar for government spending. According to the Pew Research Center, since the mid-1970s, Americans have almost always favored small government with fewer services. During the late 1990s, that view was especially pronounced, but as recently as 2015 about half of those polled wanted smaller government in this regard, whereas only about a third wanted bigger government. The difference between Republicans and Democrats was pronounced and grew. By 2015, 80 percent of Republicans favored smaller government, as opposed to 31 percent of Democrats.[51] Why? According to Pew Research, the reason was that the public worried that big government was wasteful, corrupt, and inefficient. At least since the mid-1990s, many more Americans tended to view the government in this light than those who did not (57 percent vs. 39 percent in 2015). Again, the difference between Republicans and Democrats was substantial (75 percent vs. 40 percent).[52]

Pandering to these public sentiments and embracing the neoliberal creed, politicians on both sides of the aisle have often said they wanted to reduce the size of government.‡ Trump was no exception. In particular, he jumped on the tax-cutting bandwagon early, framing the problem in terms of neoliberal supply-side economics. In his 2011 book, *Time to Get Tough*, he wrote with respect to the capital gains tax: "When government robs capital from investors, it takes away the money that creates jobs—real private sector jobs that contribute to the health of our economy."[53] He also echoed people's concerns about government wasting the revenues it collected, accused the federal government of corruption, and promised that his administration would clean things up: "You have tremendous waste, fraud, and abuse. That we're taking care of. That we're taking care of. It's tremendous."[54] Trump's embrace of Jeffersonian ideals continued throughout his campaign and was often tied to his economic plan. In a speech on September 15, 2016, to the Economic Club of New York less than two months before the general election, he was crystal clear about this when he said, "My plan will embrace the truth that people flourish under a minimum government burden and will tap into the incredible, unrealized potential of our workers and their dreams." Again, there was resonance with public sentiments.

Corrupt government was a frame Trump invoked relentlessly during the campaign—and not just when it came to taxing and spending. For instance, as we saw earlier, he often complained that the election was "rigged" against him. At a Wisconsin rally, he was adamant about this: "Remember, we are competing in a rigged election. . . . They even want to try and rig the election at the polling booths, where so many cities are corrupt and voter fraud is all too common."[55] Similar charges continued after he was in the White House when he said that he would launch an investigation into what he claimed was rampant voter fraud where millions of votes had been cast illegally and often by undocumented immigrants for Hillary Clinton. And let's not forget Trump's frequent reference throughout the campaign to "Crooked Hillary," another popular frame suggesting that his opponent was a dishonest Washington insider—a former first lady, senator, and secretary of state who couldn't be trusted.

Trump's message of improving the economy by shrinking government had especially strong resonance because it tapped voters' mounting disgust with Washington politics. This was something that stemmed not only

‡ One notable example was the historic Reagan tax cut in 1981, the depth of which was exacerbated by a bidding war that broke out between Republicans and Democrats, each trying to outdo the other by repeatedly seeking to increase the size of the cuts.

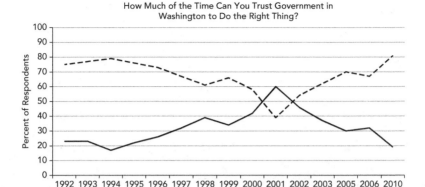

How Much of the Time Can You Trust Government in
Washington to Do the Right Thing?

Figure 5.3:
Public opinion on trust in government, 1992–2010.
Source: Gallup Polling 2017b.

from perceptions of corruption but also from the political polarization in Washington that had developed particularly since the mid-1990s, marked by several government shutdowns and especially since the 2010 midterm elections by the growing inability of Congress to agree on much of anything or work with the president. I'll have much more to say about this later in the book. But what's important now is that these perceptions of government dysfunction infuriated many Americans holding Jeffersonian values and primed them more than ever to support someone who promised to shake up the Washington political establishment. Trump seized the opportunity, proclaiming, for example, on his campaign website that "It is time to drain the swamp in Washington, D.C."[56] This became an especially popular phrase during the last month of the campaign as crowds often shouted it just as loudly as they had been shouting "Build the Wall!"[57] Why was this an effective fame? Trump supporters held these beliefs passionately. As one of them told an interviewer, "I'm anti-big government. Our government is way too big, too greedy, too incompetent, too bought, and it's not ours anymore."[58] Sentiments like these had been spreading nationwide. In 2014, Gallup reported that Americans complained that the government was the nation's number one problem, surpassing even problems associated with health care, the economy, jobs, unemployment, national defense, and the federal budget.[59] Moreover, as Figure 5.3 shows, Americans reporting that they trusted the federal government took a nose dive from 60 percent to only 19 percent between 2001 and 2010. Similarly, Figure 5.4 reveals that people's satisfaction with government plummeted between 2001 and 2015 from 53 percent to 18 percent. Of course, Trump's "Crooked Hillary" frame worked well here too insofar as it portrayed her as the epitome of the

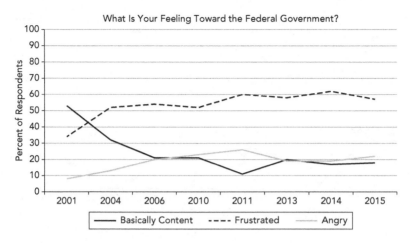

Figure 5.4:
Public frustration with government, 2001–2015.
Source: Pew Research Center 2015b.

Washington establishment, especially when contrasted with Trump himself, who had never run for or held public office in his life. Proof that this was another effective frame was that it often triggered chants of "Lock Her Up!" at Trump's campaign rallies.

This brings me to my final point about how Trump framed his economic plan so effectively. Remember that another cornerstone of that plan was to revisit America's commitment to open and free trade agreements. This was one thing in Trump's playbook that ran contrary to the neoliberal paradigm, which strongly favored free trade.[60] But there was more to this than first meets the eye. When it came to free trade, Trump was particularly hard on China, telling *The Economist,* for instance, that China is "killing us. . . . The money they took out of the United States is the greatest theft in the history of our country." He railed against the Trans-Pacific Partnership too, claiming that America had hired "stupid" negotiators who didn't pay attention to the details while foreign officials "know where every comma is," and that the agreement is a "total disaster."[61] But he saved his most scathing criticisms for NAFTA, which Trump called "the single worst trade deal ever approved in this country." According to Trump, NAFTA had cost the United States thousands of manufacturing jobs.[62] He directed most of his ire at Mexico both during and after the campaign. Echoing promises he made on the stump about punishing companies who outsourced jobs to Mexico, during the transition he threatened Toyota with stiff import tariffs if it opened a manufacturing facility in Mexico; he warned General Motors that it would incur a big border tax if it imported cars made in Mexico; and he praised Fiat Chrysler and Ford for expanding their operations in Michigan instead of Mexico.

So how did Trump square his anti–free trade position with the neoliberal paradigm he had tapped so effectively in the rest of his economic plan? He didn't. However, he did frame it in terms of another long-standing aspect of American ideology—racism. We need to recognize that public sentiments are not monolithic; they consist of lots of different beliefs. As I explained in previous chapters, one of Trump's concerns about Mexican immigration was that Mexicans were taking American jobs and driving down wages. By renegotiating NAFTA, he promised that he would solve these problems. However, it wasn't just free trade that was the problem, but free trade with Mexico. He rarely mentioned Canada, the third NAFTA partner whose population is over 80 percent white. In other words, he framed his anti–free trade plan by blending issues of race and jobs—dog whistle politics. The same could be inferred from his remarks about trade with China, and by extension many of the other comparatively low-wage countries involved in the Trans-Pacific Partnership including Malaysia, Singapore, Vietnam, and Brunei, which were all Asian countries to the west, and Peru, Chile, and Mexico, all Hispanic countries to the south.

The same was true of Trump's anti-immigration policy, which was also at odds with neoliberalism's belief in the benefits of the free movement of labor unfettered by government intervention. In fact, many business leaders supported immigration as a source of much-needed labor, either for low-skilled workers in agriculture and the service industries or for high-skilled workers in information technology, software engineering, biotechnology, and other sectors of the economy. Yet, as was true of his trade policy, Trump framed his anti-immigration policy in terms of race and protecting work-ing- and middle-class jobs.

There are three important takeaways in this. First, political plans and rhetoric are sometimes inconsistent or contradictory across policy areas. Second, resolving these inconsistencies requires crafting multidimensional frames that appeal to more than one aspect of the public's sentiments. Trump was a pro at this. But, third, the broader and most important lesson is that Trump's success was not cut from whole cloth. It was made from an old tap-estry of ideas and ideology that he inherited. He used it to sell his economic plan of tax, spending, and regulatory cuts, and revised trade agreements to enough Americans to get elected. It fit the neoliberal paradigm voters had become used to since the Reagan era. It resonated with many people's val-ues and sentiments regarding the dangers of big government, immigration, and more, which had also been on the rise. And in doing so, it hit emotional hot buttons more effectively than any other presidential candidate in a long time.[63] That's why "draining the swamp" was such a great frame. It was a metaphor that wrapped concerns about high taxes, wasteful spending, excessive regulation, exorbitant deficits, and distrust with establishment

Washington—as personified by Hillary Clinton—into a neatly framed package conjuring up vivid images of politicians, lobbyists, political operatives, and other dangerous creatures preying upon the American public. That Trump—the consummate pitchman—could sell himself as the one and only candidate capable of killing the vicious predators slinking around Washington helped pump up his image as a fearless advocate of the people ready to tackle the nation's problems—the Crocodile Dundee of American politics. Crocodile Dundee, of course, is the main character in the 1986 blockbuster film by the same name—a macho yet humorous, knife-wielding rough neck from the Australian Outback who manages not only to dispatch an aggressive crocodile and various other troublemakers during the movie but also to win the heart of the beautiful female reporter from New York City who wants to do a story about him.

Trump's economic plan stood in stark contrast to Clinton's plan, which, as noted, was far more complicated and difficult to understand. Her plan also lacked the snazzy frames that Trump was so good at inventing. And hers sounded like Keynesianism rather than neoliberalism because it talked more about raising taxes than cutting them, and promised to spend more, not less, money. For example, she pledged to immediately make four-year universities tuition-free for families earning less than $85,000 a year, set up a $25 billion fund for historically black colleges and universities, spend $10 billion on public–private partnerships designed to strengthen American manufacturing, and expand apprenticeships and training to improve the quality of the workforce.[64] In other words, her plan favored bigger not smaller government, which was another ideological strike against her.

One last bit of framing was important in Trump's campaign and resonated clearly with another long-standing set of American values—populism.[65] Recall from chapter 1 that populism could involve hostility toward moneyed or intellectual elites.[66] With respect to the latter, Thomas Frank observes that "anti-intellectualism is a central component of conservative doctrine" in America today, particularly among Republicans, who have great contempt for sophisticated ideas and who "rail against obnoxious Ivy League stuffed shirts."[67]

Trump appealed to populist sentiments all the time.[68] For one thing, he constantly attacked Hillary Clinton as an establishment elite, criticizing her, for example, of being pals with Wall Street bankers and giving speeches at Goldman Sachs for six-figure honorariums. For another thing, Trump did not resemble the intelligentsia. As one veteran journalist noted, "There's nothing 'elite' about him. There's nothing elite about the way he sounds. He sounds like the rest of us. Unfortunately, he sounds like the rest of us after we've had six drinks."[69] Trump's anti-intellectualism was evident as well in his statements about how he makes decisions. He did so, he said, "with very little knowledge other than the knowledge I [already] had, plus the words 'common sense,' because I have a lot of common sense and I have a lot of business ability." And on experts, he remarked, "They can't see the forest for the trees. . . . A lot of people said, 'Man, he [Trump] was more accurate than guys who have studied it all the time.'"[70] The irony in all this, of course, was that Trump received a bachelor's degree from the University of Pennsylvania—one of the elite Ivy League universities—and was firmly ensconced in the richest 1 percent of American society, often seen at black-tie galas and fundraisers rubbing shoulders with East Coast blue bloods and the jet set. Nevertheless, playing the populist card helped Trump appeal especially to middle- and working-class voters.[71] Finally, let's not forget the nationalist side of Trump's populism—his repeated promises to make America first, keep out dangerous foreigners, and stop kowtowing to foreign governments in trade and other things.

Clinton may have been vulnerable when it came to stories of her courting Wall Street bankers, her Wellesley and Yale diplomas, or her overly intellectual approach to policymaking. In contrast to Trump, she relished talking about the details of policy much more than pressing the flesh out on the campaign trail. But she did apparently have one thing going for her that Trump did not—she was a woman. And that should have given her a huge advantage over Trump when it came to women's issues. But it didn't.

THE PITCH TO TRADITIONAL FAMILY VALUES

Women's issues were not the main thrust of Trump's campaign—economic issues were. That's why "Make America Great Again" was such a big deal. But women's issues eventually became prominent and revealed something about how effectively Trump tapped deeply held conservative values. I suggested earlier that Trump was the Crocodile Dundee of politics—a manly character poised to save America from peril. His macho persona spilled over into women's issues. This is a two-part story.

The first part is about Trump's sexism. He was hounded throughout the campaign by allegations from various women about his sexual improprieties. His sexist comments about Megyn Kelly, one of the moderators of the first television debate with Clinton, were also widely reported. But the ultimate demonstration of his misogyny was his taped comment to a television entertainment show host discovered about a month before the general election. Trump bragged that because he was such a huge television celebrity, having starred in the hit show *The Apprentice*, he could have his way with women. As Trump explained, "And when you're a star, they let you do it. You can do anything. Grab 'em by the pussy. You can do anything."[72]

When the tape was leaked to the press and went viral on the Internet, women were outraged. Yet, as we will see in chapter 8, Trump didn't do too badly among women, especially white women with less than a college education, 62 percent of whom voted for him despite his sexist remarks and behavior. Furthermore, a whopping 87 percent of Trump supporters said his treatment of women did not bother them.[73]

The second part of the story is about abortion. Trump won the overwhelming majority of the white born-again evangelical Christian vote and over half of the Protestant vote overall. He also won a larger percentage of the Catholic and Mormon vote than Clinton. What these religions all shared, of course, was a vehement opposition to abortion.[74] The antiabortion crusade had galvanized conservative Christians for decades. In 1999, Trump had advocated that a woman should have the right to choose whether she wanted an abortion. But by the time he threw his hat into the political ring, he had switched to a prolife position. His campaign reported that once he became president, "Then he will change the law through his judicial appointments and allow the states to protect the unborn," a position that would have appealed not just to religious prolife voters but also to conservative states' rights voters—the latter typically viewing states' rights as an antidote for big government.[75] This was a shrewd way to pose the issue because it simultaneously appealed to both sets of values. And it was another example of the importance of being able to craft multidimensional frames from different public sentiments.

Furthermore, by siding with the antiabortion crusade, Trump not only capitalized on traditional conservative family values but also jumped on a powerful and well-funded religious bandwagon that had been rolling for years in American politics. Following the tumultuous 1960s and early 1970s, which ushered in more-tolerant attitudes toward sexual freedom, abortion, and homosexuality, evangelicals turned increasingly toward the Republican Party and became more active in politics. Led initially during the 1980s by the Reverend Jerry Fallwell's Moral Majority, this movement pushed conservative social issues, particularly abortion, on to the political agenda.[76] To be sure, according to Gallup, since 1975, less than a quarter of the public opposed abortion under all circumstances, and since 1996, a majority of Americans identified themselves as being prochoice.[77] But conservatives were undeterred by these numbers and had pushed hard for prolife legislation ever since the Supreme Court's landmark 1973 decision in *Roe v. Wade* affirmed a woman's right to an abortion. And they had scored many victories at the state level, where dozens of abortion clinics had been closed and doctors faced tougher restrictions on providing such services. Nowadays, for example, forty-three states prohibit abortions after a specified point in the pregnancy (except when the woman's life or health is in danger), thirty-eight states require an abortion to be performed by a licensed physician, and thirty-seven states require parental involvement in a minor's decision to have an abortion.[78] Trump's antiabortion view gave him the support of a powerful political machine, which undoubtedly helped his ground game during the campaign.

Two things are interesting about these stories. First, Trump's prolife position and his sexist persona spoke to traditional family values where men were dominant if not superior to women and life was sacred from the moment of conception. For decades, conservative politicians had appealed to these sentiments in voters.[79] This helps explain why so many women voted for Trump despite his reported sexism; despite his decision to pick Indiana Governor Mike Pence, a staunch antiabortion advocate, as his vice presidential running mate; and even though he promised to eliminate federal funding for Planned Parenthood, an organization that provided health care services for women. Only 3 percent of Planned Parenthood's services were abortions—the rest were things like breast exams, gynecological exams, Pap smears, and contraceptives.[80] But that didn't matter. The point is that many women who supported Trump likely did so because he embraced their traditional family values. Indeed, white working-class women often resented Clinton for accusing Trump of sexism.[81] As it turned out, half of Trump voters believed in the traditional American family model.[82]

Second, Trump doubled down on those traditional family values by railing against Muslim immigration. After all, there was some common ground between the people who supported him because he took a strong stand against radical Islam and the people who supported him because he affirmed traditional family values. Both groups feared that the moral fabric of America was in grave danger. Remember that people worried that Islamic Shari 'a law would eventually destroy America's most basic values. The prolife movement worried that the loose sexual mores of the 1960s and 1970s posed a similar threat, particularly because they had opened the door for legalized abortion thanks to the Supreme Court's landmark ruling, which they detested. Wielding the family values frame, Trump killed three birds with one stone— he justified his prolife position on abortion, his sexism, and his Islamophobia. That said, although the family values framing may have helped him win the election, it did not appease women's rights advocates, as the women's anti-Trump demonstrations proved the day after his inauguration.[83]

CONCLUSION

To wrap up, Trump's economic plan resonated with the dominant policymaking paradigm of the day, neoliberalism. And the ascendance of neoliberal ideology was in part a response to some of the economic changes associated with the end of the Golden Age of American prosperity—the red thread running through my argument. Moreover, Trump was a master at framing that plan in ways that echoed many deeply held public sentiments. So even if the mathematics or logic of his plan might have raised doubts, he still managed to sell it well enough to capture his party's nomination and then the White House. Something similar happened with respect to women's issues, where he managed to build frames that appealed to conservative Christians and other advocates of traditional family values.

One caveat is necessary. Trump's ability as a pitchman was not entirely of his own doing. It appears that Trump had help from two very high-powered data analytic companies, Cambridge Analytica and SCL, which specialized in collecting enormous amounts of data from places like people's Facebook accounts and using it to develop messaging and information strategies for their clients. They worked for Ted Cruz before he dropped out of the Republican primary race. Apparently, Trump's team hired Cambridge Analytica and SCL to identify words and phrases that were currently trending on social media and resonated with people's emotions about various topics. The technique even had a name—biopsychosocial profiling. Trump's campaign would then incorporate these words into his speeches and press conferences to trigger people's emotions on various topics in ways favorable to his pitch. Andy Wigmore, who worked with these firms on the British referendum campaign to leave the European Union, provides an example: "So with immigration, there are actually key words within that subject matter which people are concerned about. So when you are going to make a speech, it's all about how can you use these trending words. . . . It's all about the emotions."[84] As I mentioned earlier, Republicans had been doing this for years, albeit in less technologically refined ways, and I am sure Democrats had been too. But it appears that Republicans had taken this to new heights in the 2016 campaign in what was probably the most sophisticated propaganda campaign in US electoral history.[85] It was nothing short of cognitive warfare that helped polarize American politics.

CHAPTER 6

Polarization and Politics

I was in Washington, DC with a colleague interviewing people at think tanks and government research agencies in April 2008, just a few months before Barack Obama was elected president. Nearly everyone told us that since the 1980s, the political atmosphere in the city had grown more and more polarized, and that partisanship had gotten worse than anyone could remember. One person at the Heritage Foundation, a conservative think tank, explained that it had reached a point where colleagues at think tanks on the left and right were now reluctant to walk together on the Washington Mall for fear of being spotted, photographed by someone with a cell phone camera, and reported to their superiors for fraternizing with the enemy. In some cases, the level of paranoia bordered on the ridiculous. One day we were scheduled to interview someone at the Council of Economic Advisors, but when we arrived, he refused to talk to us until we proved that we were the academics we claimed to be and not journalists or undercover political operatives digging up dirt on the Bush administration. Someone else, a Republican at another conservative think tank, told us that her Democratic friends no longer invited her to their dinner parties simply because she was a conservative—and that this sort of thing had become common now in Washington. Things were bad, but nobody could have predicted then how much worse they would soon become.

How did this happen? The economic, racial, and ideological trends I have been discussing flowed together forming a fourth trend—rising political polarization. By the time of the election in 2008, the political differences between Democrats and Republicans and the level of acrimony between them had reached a tipping point. If the right catalyst came along, polarization could suddenly turn into full-blown political gridlock—politicians would be at each other's throats and the wheels of policymaking would slow to a dysfunctional crawl. That catalyst was the financial crisis, Obama's election as president, and his efforts to manage the crisis and the nation's health care problems. This chapter explains how polarization reached that critical threshold. The next chapter tells how the catalyst turned polarization into gridlock and how Donald Trump took advantage of it all.

THE CONTOURS OF POLARIZATION

The ideological gap between Republicans and Democrats had been widening gradually for decades. Studying this sort of thing is bread and butter for political scientists, who have produced scads of studies trying to figure out how much polarization there is in America—both among the public and among the political elite. Let's start with the public. In countless surveys, researchers have asked people to describe whether they consider themselves to be liberal, moderate, or conservative and to express their opinions on a host of policy issues. Figure 6.1 shows how people's political ideologies changed since the onset of stagflation. In 1972, 26 percent of the electorate reported that they were conservative, while 18 percent reported being liberal. Things fluctuated after that, but by 2012, the numbers had risen to 36 percent for conservatives and 24 percent for liberals, indicating that people's ideological positions were shifting away from the center toward either the right or left. Note as well that the increase in conservatives was nearly twice as large as the increase in liberals, an indication that the country was becoming more conservative overall—and that neoliberalism was setting

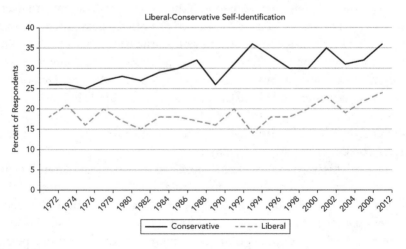

Figure 6.1:
Changing political ideology in the electorate, 1974–2012.
Source: Author's calculations based on data from the American National Election Studies 2017.

into the American psyche. Polarization becomes clearer when people are asked whether they consider themselves to be either a strong Republican or Democrat. Figure 6.2 shows that in 1972, only 26 percent of conservatives and 28 percent of liberals said that they identified strongly with their parties, but by 2012, the numbers jumped to 41 percent and 45 percent, respectively. Perhaps most telling, according to Pew Research's composite index of forty-eight political values, by 2012, partisan polarization among the public soared to its highest point in the past twenty-five years, nearly doubling since 1987.[1] According to some researchers, rising polarization was driven by the fact that ideology rather than membership in a particular economic, racial, or religious group had become the more important determinant of party identification.[2] Indeed, Republican contempt for Democrats and vice versa has been growing at least since 1994. Seventy-four percent of Republicans held unfavorable or very unfavorable attitudes toward the Democratic Party in 1994, but by 2016, that number had risen to 91 percent. For Democrats viewing the Republican Party in a similar light, the numbers increased from 59 percent to 86 percent.[3] This helps explain why Republicans and Democrats didn't invite each other to their dinner parties much anymore.

James Campbell (no relation to me) provides an extremely thoughtful and thorough assessment of the vast polarization literature and offers some convincing conclusions. To begin with, everyone agrees that most Americans share a set of basic values—I called them public sentiments in the previous chapter—such as wanting good jobs, equal opportunities, safe streets, efficient government, fair elections, some sort of safety net for those

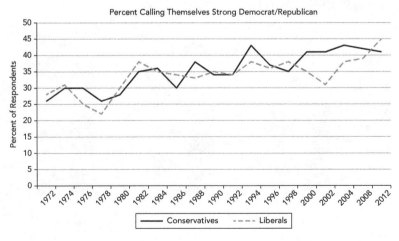

Figure 6.2:
Rising partisanship, 1974–2012.
Source: American National Election Studies 2017.

who cannot fend for themselves, and national security. And until the 1960s, most people were fairly moderate in their political views. But then things started changing. He explains that the issues raised by the civil rights, Black Power, anti–Vietnam War, and countercultural movements, and later the feminist movement, began polarizing the nation. Nevertheless, according to Campbell, moderates still constituted about half of the electorate by the early 1970s, the rest being either liberal or conservative. But polarization continued to rise. One indication he says is that people's general ideological views, their positions on specific policy issues, and their party affiliations became more tightly correlated over the years—that is, people became more consistently liberal or conservative. Another is that there was a gradual decline in split-ticket voting and an increase in voter turnout. He argues that today only a plurality of Americans call themselves moderates, while the majority—roughly three-fifths—call themselves either conservative or liberal.[4]

Figure 6.3 reports the percentage of Democrats whose ideological views are more liberal than the average (median) view of Republicans and the percentage of Republicans whose ideological views are more conservative than the average view of Democrats. During the 2000s, Democrats shifted in a liberal direction relative to Republicans, and Republicans shifted in a more conservative direction relative to Democrats. And ideological thinking is now much more closely aligned with partisanship than in the past.[5] As a result, ideological overlap between the two parties has diminished: today, 92 percent of Republicans are to the right of the median Democrat, and 94 percent of Democrats are to the left of the median Republican. As noted earlier, many more Americans are conservative today than liberal, an important point to which we will return soon.

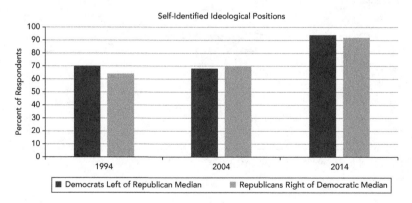

Figure 6.3:
Ideological polarization among the public, 1994–2014.
Source: Pew Research Center 2014a.

However, how liberal or conservative someone is can vary depending on which policy issue we are talking about. Increasing polarization since the 1970s is evident between Democrats and Republicans, especially when it comes to the government's role in society, such as how much it should regulate, how much it should spend, how heavily it should tax, and how generous its welfare programs should be.[6] According to Pew Research, Democrats and Republicans drifted particularly far apart on economic issues, the primary concern of this book, over things like whether business regulation does more harm than good, whether stricter environmental laws cost too many jobs and hurt the economy, and whether corporations make a fair and reasonable amount of profit. Republicans became more likely to find business and environmental regulations distasteful, and less likely to worry about corporate profitability. Democrats moved in the opposite direction. Republicans also grew increasingly wary of helping the needy and, as discussed in chapter 4, became more likely to blame the individual rather than society for the difficulty many African Americans have had getting ahead in life.[7] Not surprisingly, then, polarization between whites and nonwhites also increased significantly.[8]

But what about the political parties and their leaders—the political elite? After all, what matters ultimately is that polarization got so bad between the two parties that it eventually led to gridlock, where legislating in Washington ground to a virtual halt. Based, for example, on the analysis of roll-call voting in Congress, Campbell shows that both parties have become more cohesive internally and consistent ideologically, and that the ideological gap between them has widened. Put differently, both parties have closed ranks and hunkered down in opposition to each other, especially since the mid-1990s. By some accounts polarization nowadays is greater than it has ever been since post–Civil War Reconstruction over a century ago. Campbell concludes that the situation has deteriorated to such a low point that

> many on both sides now find it difficult to fathom how reasonably intelligent people can reside at the other end of the ideological spectrum. Those on the other side are often dismissed as insincere, misinformed, stupid, delusional, or worse. Their views are derided as impervious to evidence and immune to reason. This cuts both ways. Many liberals vilify conservatives and many conservatives disparage liberals.[9]

Thomas Edsall, a particularly astute observer of American politics, agrees, noting, "Partisan disagreements are now so wide, and the ideological outlooks of activists and elected officials so antithetical, that there is not agreement on the facts, on what is true and what is false."[10] How polarization got this bad requires some explanation.

The gist of the story is that both Democrats and Republicans moved in a conservative direction on many issues, but the Republicans moved far- ther to the right than the Democrats. There were, of course, a few excep- tions where Republicans and Democrats tended to move closer together on some social issues and even shifted a bit to the left. This was true, for example, for the legalization of marijuana and gay marriage. However, it was not true for the all-important economic issues that I have been discuss- ing. So, exceptions aside, the political center of gravity shifted to the right and the ideological distance between liberals and conservatives got wider, especially between the two parties. For the record, others have somewhat different interpretations of the polarization of American politics, which I discuss in the appendix at the end of the book for readers who are inter- ested. More important, however, polarization boiled down largely to the combined effects of the economic, racial, and ideological trends described earlier in the book. A good place to start is with the uneven rightward drift in ideology.

Ideological Trends

Since the 1970s, both political parties shifted to the right thanks in part to the rise of neoliberalism. But the Republicans embraced this ideology much more fervently than the Democrats and, as a result, moved farther to the right. For example, Americans have long tended to favor smaller government and fewer services, but since the 1990s, that tendency has become more pronounced and the difference between Republicans and Democrats on this issue has grown. In 2015, an overwhelming 80 percent of Republicans but only 31 percent of Democrats held these views.[11]

During the Golden Age, the Republican Party's moderate wing, home to people like Dwight Eisenhower and Nelson Rockefeller, saw an important yet restrained role for government. But they were gradually pushed aside by more conservative Republicans, including Ronald Reagan, who famously said that government was the problem, not the solution. In fact, by today's standards Reagan was pretty moderate. He cut taxes but then raised them when budget deficits ballooned. He cut welfare spending but did not elimi- nate programs entirely. In fact, although Reagan was an arch conservative in his ideological rhetoric, he was a pragmatic politician in practice, not averse to compromise to get things done.[12] Similarly, his successor, George H. W. Bush, was a fiscally conservative president who did not avoid raising taxes if needed.

Part of the turn to the right involved the Watergate scandal and Nixon's subsequent resignation from the presidency, which alienated many moderate Republicans enough for them to switch allegiance temporarily to the Democratic Party.[13] This created an opportunity—a vacuum of sorts—for more extreme conservatives to take control of the Republican Party. Then in 1994, Newt Gingrich, a die-hard neoliberal and eventual adviser to Donald Trump, helped engineer a stunning electoral victory where Republicans won the House of Representatives for the first time in forty years. This also marked the beginning of what one US senator calls the politics of personal destruction—saying whatever it takes to denigrate your opponent including character assassination, deceit, and outright lying.[14] Six years later George W. Bush, another hard-core neoliberal, won the presidency. This pushed the Republican Party even farther to the right. As noted in chapter 5, the neoliberal shift was driven by more conservative money flowing into political campaigns and by increasingly conservative political rhetoric and policy ideas coming from the think tanks, talk radio, and cable news programs, such as Fox News. One of the most important examples of this since 2002 was a vast network of political organizations including political action committees, think tanks, and issue advocacy organizations, as well as very wealthy funders coordinated by the billionaire Koch brothers, whose libertarian political agenda zeroed in almost exclusively on economic issues. We will see later that this network played a key role in the rise of the ultra-conservative Tea Party Movement during the Obama years.[15]

Religious ideology also came into play. The Christian coalition, initially mobilized by Jerry Fallwell's Moral Majority in the 1980s, helped move the party to the right on social issues like abortion, school prayer, and for a while homosexuality and same-sex marriage.[16] This was a move to defend traditional family values, initially from what the religious Right viewed as corrosive liberal forces within the country like hippies and pro-choice feminists, and later from dangerous religious forces outside the country, notably Islamic fundamentalism and Shari 'a law. As one conservative pastor exclaimed in 2016 at a national meeting of Southern Baptists, "I would like to know how in the world someone within the Southern Baptist Convention can support the defending of rights for Muslims . . . when these people threaten our very way of existence as Christians and Americans?"[17] But the religious Right also pushed the Republican Party in a more conservative direction on economic issues. The Fallwell crowd feared that exorbitant taxes and welfare spending also threatened the traditional family by forcing women to give up their homemaker role and go to work to help pay those taxes, and by creating incentives for women to have abortions and kids out of wedlock.

On the Democratic side the story is a bit more complicated. To begin with, the party initially became more liberal during the 1960s, moving to the left, not the right. The baby boomers came of age during a time when protests, race riots, and sex, drugs, and rock 'n roll were on the rise, and when "Question Authority" was a popular bumper sticker. They tended to be liberal and vote for Democrats. After Johnson signed civil rights legislation, African Americans, who also typically supported liberal causes, flocked to the Democratic Party. So did the feminists.[18] All of this culminated in George McGovern's 1972 nomination as the party's presidential candidate. But McGovern's nomination was a liberal high-water mark—the most liberal candidate in the party's history—after which it started becoming more conservative, although by no means as conservative as the Republicans.[19] Nixon clobbered McGovern in the election, winning every state except liberal Massachusetts. That crushing defeat slammed the brakes on the party's liberal momentum. However, there was more to the story than this.

The defection of moderate Republicans to the Democratic Party mentioned earlier created a split within the Democratic Party. Many of these so-called New Democrats were relatively affluent, middle-class, well-educated professionals, not to mention white and moderately conservative, which put them at odds to a significant degree with the more ethnically and racially diverse working-class voters that formed the base of the liberal New Deal coalition upon which the party's electoral fortunes had rested for decades. As a result, the party started drifting to the right, especially on economic issues, as Democratic politicians courted this so-called yuppie (young, urban, professional) vote and won seats in Congress.[20] The trend continued thanks to the Democratic Leadership Council (DLC), a nonprofit organization founded in 1985 whose purpose was to attract white middle-class voters through a less liberal, more centrist "Third Way" approach to Democratic Party politics. According to journalist Thomas Frank: "The Democratic Leadership Council . . . has long been pushing the party to forget blue-collar voters and concentrate instead on recruiting affluent, white-collar professionals. . . . As for the working-class voters who were until recently the party's very backbone, the DLC figures they will have nowhere else to go." This, he complains, is "the criminally stupid strategy that has dominated Democratic thinking off and on" ever since the early 1970s.[21] Stupid or not, it worked, at least insofar as the party's more conservative approach continued to attract middle-class and professional voters, especially when it came to economic issues.[22]

This went hand in hand with the general rise of neoliberalism, which also pushed the party to the right, particularly when it came to tax policy. The yuppies favored more regressive tax reforms than the party's traditional constituents. In other words, the yuppies were inclined to favor tax cuts for the more affluent members of society, including themselves. So, although Democrats controlled both chambers of Congress and the White House, in 1978, President Jimmy Carter signed the first major tax bill of the post–Golden Age that didn't skew benefits toward middle- and lower-income groups. He lowered the capital gains tax rate too, which also benefited the more affluent taxpayers. This was a neoliberal move and a complete reversal of traditional Democratic tax policy.[23] It was a clear case of shifting ideological winds blowing the party in a new, more conservative direction on a key policy issue. Journalist John Judis summarizes this as follows:

> By the late 1970s the Carter administration had acquiesced to supply-side business tax cuts and to a monetarist strategy of using high interest rates and rising unemployment to curb inflation. Over the next 12 years, Democrats, led by the "New Democrats," would accept other key aspects of the neoliberal agenda, including trade pacts like NAFTA that eased foreign investment, deregulation of finance, and immigration measures to accommodate unskilled and later highly skilled guest workers.[24]

However, the New Democrats were more moderate than the Republicans they had abandoned because they advocated some policies that ran against the neoliberal grain. One example was their support of environmental regulation. Another was their support for programs benefiting working women, such as all-day kindergarten, educational assistance for people going to college, and affirmative action in the labor market.[25] So although they helped move the Democratic Party in a more conservative ideological direction on some issues, they helped anchor it to more liberal positions on others.

Overall, then, although the party drifted toward the right ideologically, it did not drift as far as the Republicans, which is one reason the parties became more polarized. But there was more to it than that. Ideological positions on these and other issues were connected to the red thread in my story—changes in the economy and the demise of America's Golden Age. So, let's take a closer look at the economic side of polarization.

Economic Trends

Organized labor had been a steadfast Democratic Party supporter since the 1930s. Remember that since the late 1950s, the labor movement had been getting weaker thanks to the decline of manufacturing, the rise of outsourcing, and other economic trends. This meant that the unions' ability to help finance Democratic candidates favoring liberal working-class interests and turn out the vote for them was waning. This was one economic reason the party began shifting to the right. Making matters worse, organized labor was appalled at McGovern's strident anti–Vietnam War position, perceived by many union members as tantamount to supporting the spread of communism.[26] The American Federation of Labor and Congress of Industrial Organizations (AFL-CIO) Executive Council voted not to endorse either McGovern or Nixon in the 1972 presidential election. At the state level, organized labor's support for McGovern was only lukewarm. And to top it all off, the teamsters, construction trades, and longshore unions backed Nixon, not McGovern, in the election.[27] The unions had long anchored the party to the left of the Republicans. Now that anchor was slipping. It was slipping as well because the yuppie wing of the Democratic Party was not inclined to stick up for organized labor or working people's issues. Indeed, Bernie Sanders, among others, blamed Clinton's loss to Trump and earlier Democratic losses in countless other elections at the national and state levels on the Democratic Party leadership's neglect of working-class economic issues.[28]

The flip side of the unionization coin is a tale about business interests getting more conservative. Here again, the economic changes discussed in chapter 3 came into play. Two are important. First, during the Golden Age, the business community was somewhat divided in its support for the two parties. Small business generally supported Republicans, while big business, such as internationally oriented banks and major manufacturing companies, was not averse to supporting moderate Democrats. Why? Whatever tax increases were necessary to pay for the Democrats' military spending and liberal social programs—guns and butter—did not bother big business too much so long as they could pass the costs of higher taxes along to consumers in the form of higher prices, which they did rather easily because these firms faced relatively little competition. This wasn't as easy for small business operating in much more competitive markets. However, beginning in the 1970s, as the Golden Age receded and economic globalization advanced, it became harder for big business to do this because foreign firms, such as Toyota and Volkswagen in automobiles and Sony in consumer electronics, had emerged as formidable competitors and were already selling their products at low prices thanks to their technological and production advantages. Big business began to shift its support to the Republicans or conservative Democrats, who were less likely to raise taxes—especially to pay for social programs. They did so as well to roll back what they considered to be onerous and expensive business regulations put in place during the 1970s by agencies like the Environmental Protection Agency and the Occupational Safety and Health Administration, and by the Clean Air and Water Acts—programs often advocated by those newly minted yuppie Democrats.[29]

But a second change in the business community was also important. During the Golden Age, the corporate elite—top executives from big business—tended to hold moderate and pragmatic political views regardless of the political party they supported. During the 1970s, they grew more unified around those views and, as a result, often exerted pressure on Republicans and Democrats in Washington to come together and compromise to fix the nation's most pressing problems.[30] But, as sociologist Mark Mizruchi shows, as the Golden Age slipped away, competition increased and, in turn, the incentives for political unity and cooperation within the business community slowly deteriorated. They weakened as well because by the 1990s, corporate America was winning the fights against both regulation and organized labor, which had been another impetus for firms to close ranks politically. As a result, solidarity among the corporate elite diminished and they began to pursue more fragmented and narrowly self-interested lobbying rather than farsighted collective action geared toward solving big national problems like soaring debt, trade deficits, health care, and a looming fiscal crisis for the big entitlement programs. As Mizruchi puts it:

> The decline of the American corporate elite has played a major role in the crisis of twenty-first-century American democracy. . . . The gridlock in Washington, the prominent role of extremist elements who in earlier decades would have been considered outside the realm of legitimate political discourse, the inability to address serious problems . . . are all due in part to the absence of a committed, moderate elite capable of providing political leadership and keeping the destructive sectors of the American polity in check.[31]

In sum, changes in the labor movement and business community helped push politics to the right, but with less pressure on the Democrats than on the Republicans, which exacerbated polarization. However, two caveats are in order—one about the generations and another about gender.

Economic trends also polarized the generations in ways that helped move politics in a more conservative direction. As private pensions began to disappear—thanks to the decline of traditional manufacturing industries—people had to learn to save for retirement in their individual retirement accounts. Not everyone did so. Why? In part, as chapter 3 explained, wage stagnation made it harder and harder to save money in the first place. As a result, people approaching retirement were increasingly in danger of not having enough money to sustain them through their old age. And since they are generally on fixed incomes, they are susceptible to conservative calls for either holding the line on taxes or reducing them. All else being equal, older Americans tend to be more conservative anyway, but this compounded the rightward shift in American politics, particularly as the numerically large baby boom generation moved toward retirement.[32] As a result, both Republicans and Democrats catered increasingly to the interests of the elderly as represented frequently by the American Association of Retired Persons—one of the most powerful lobbies in Washington. In turn, Social Security and Medicare, two gigantic entitlement programs for the elderly, were off limits politically to budget cutters, as was most military spending. When conservative calls for reducing budget deficits got louder, budget-cutting politicians did not have much left from which to choose. This created the possibility for intergenerational polarization insofar as programs for the elderly were spared, but those for younger people were sitting ducks.

Consider education. State and local government appropriations for public universities dropped steadily after 2000. To compensate, universities raised tuition and fees beyond the rate of inflation. And to manage these higher costs, students borrowed more money—debt that many of them had trouble paying off later.[33] Insofar as programs like this for younger people were those advocated typically by Democrats but opposed by Republicans, the intergenerational split spilled over into politics, pushing the two parties even farther apart. It makes sense, then, that between 1992 and 2016, according to Pew Research, whites fifty-two years of age and older, and especially those over seventy years, drifted to the Republican Party while younger people did not.[34]

The economics of gender also came into play in the polarization story. Women tend to support liberal policies and vote for Democrats more than men do. The gender gap first emerged in presidential elections in the early 1950s and grew through the mid-1980s, more or less leveling off after that, with most women solidly in the Democratic camp and most men in the Republican camp. The gap stemmed largely from the rise in female labor force participation, which as mentioned in chapter 3 was partly because women needed to help their families make ends meet economically as the Golden Age faded. This exacerbated political polarization too because working women—especially those with kids—relied on government programs typically supported by liberals, such as day-long kindergarten, child care subsidies, and school lunch programs, not to mention affirmative action labor market policies.[35] The gender gap spiked in the 2012 presidential election when women turned out in droves for Obama. The gap that year was the largest ever recorded by Gallup Polling since it began measuring it in 1952.[36]

Insofar as the rightward shift and polarization of politics involved shifting labor, business, generational, and gender interests, much of the action was driven by changes in the economy and the decline of the Golden Age in America. This, of course, is the red thread in my argument, which also continued to weave its way through the story when it came to polarization around issues of race and ethnicity.

I explained in chapter 4 that Richard Nixon played the race card deftly. He used the Southern Strategy to attract white working-class voters to the Republican Party, implying, among other things, that their taxes were financing social programs for lazy people on the dole, particularly African Americans. These were the same workers who would soon fear losing their jobs and having their wages depressed thanks to automation, globalization, and the decline of traditional US manufacturing industries. They would eventually blame it partly on Hispanic immigration and trade policy. Other Republicans followed Nixon's lead and used this strategy with some success on middle-class constituents too. I remember, for instance, having a heated conversation about this with my Republican brother-in-law, a white middle-class pharmacist who worked two jobs in rural Pennsylvania—a depressed region of the state that never recovered fully from the Great Depression and the decimated coal mining industry. He was raised in an Irish Catholic working-class family where his father had been a union member and everyone voted Democratic. However, he was upset that he had to pay taxes for programs that in his view simply encouraged some of his poor, unemployed customers—often people of color—to take advantage of the government's largesse, in this case Medicaid, instead of getting a job. As a result, he switched allegiance to the Republican Party—and he was not alone. In the face of an increasing white backlash, Democrats started losing more of their white middle-class supporters, who grew disenchanted with the party's liberal wing. As noted, the DLC was created to counter this trend. However, the point is that the two parties became increasingly polarized racially.

By the early 2000s, conservative, white, married people viewing themselves as paying taxes to finance programs for downwardly mobile and culturally subversive minority groups constituted much of the Republican Party's base. Meanwhile, racial and ethnic minorities, women, poor people dependent on government services, and liberal whites made up the Democratic Party's base.[37] Public opinion polls reflected this in questions about discrimination and supporting affirmative action. By 2014, there was a sharp partisan divide between Republicans and Democrats on this issue. Sixty-one percent of Republicans believed that discrimination against whites was at least as big a problem as was discrimination against blacks. Just as many Democrats disagreed. Tea Party Republicans felt particularly strong about this, with 76 percent believing that whites were discriminated against at least as much as blacks. Moreover, white Republicans outnumbered white Democrats three to one in believing that too much attention is paid nowadays to issues of race.[38] As sociologists Doug McAdam and Katrina Kloos astutely observe, "One of the central sources of continuity linking the Republican Party that emerged under Nixon in the late '60s and early '70s with the GOP of today is a sustained politics of racial reaction."[39] In other words, the white backlash discussed in chapter 4 assumed a politically partisan flavor that further polarized the two parties.

Immigration helped fuel racial polarization in American politics too. Rising immigration, facilitated partly by looser immigration laws passed in the 1960s, meant that by the late 1970s, there was a growing population of new immigrants seeking educational and economic opportunities, which intensified the competition for college admissions, jobs, and promotions. The problem was that this was happening just as the economy was beginning to suffer from the effects of stagflation, globalization, and rising international competition, so the supply of opportunities did not keep pace with increased demand. This was another reason many people perceived that their racial group was now pitted against others. In particular, conservative white men saw themselves competing against minorities.[40] Both explicit and implicit anti-Hispanic and antiblack attitudes increased among Americans.[41] Rising anti-Muslim sentiment also emerged in the wake of the 9/11 attacks. Racial and ethnic scapegoating was on the rise. The important point, however, is that all of this further exacerbated racial and ethnic polarization between the Republican and Democratic Parties as the Democrats attracted a growing minority population and the Republicans became increasingly white.[42]

Social movements were a polarizing force in American life during these years, particularly in race relations. As I explained earlier, during the 1960s, the Democratic Party shifted to the left for a while thanks to the civil rights, antiwar, and women's movements. But this started coming to an end in the 1970s, about when the yuppies were defecting from the Republican Party and neoliberalism was emerging as the dominant economic ideology. On the right, the Christian conservative movement of the 1970s and 1980s pulled the Republican Party to the right, as did the Tea Party Movement during Obama's presidency.[43]

In any case, by 2008, escalating polarization had reached a tipping point where if the right catalyst came along it could easily transform polarization into full-blown gridlock. But before getting to that we need to pause briefly, take a step back, and look at the institutional environment within which all of this unfolded. Arguably, had that environment been different, things might not have turned out as they did and Trump might not have become president.

INSTITUTIONS MATTERED TOO

I argued in chapter 1 that institutions played an important role in shaping the four trends upon which Trump capitalized to win the White House.

This is clear insofar as institutional changes increased the level of conservatism and polarization in Washington. To begin with, recall that campaign finance laws changed in ways that facilitated the flow of more outside money into elections beyond the control of the political parties themselves. As outside money became more important, both parties became more responsive to these influences. This was another reason Democrats became more attuned to the conservative interests of middle- and upper-income voters at the expense of their traditional working-class constituents.[44] Similarly, corporate operatives and lobbyists became ubiquitous in Washington, plying their trade on Republicans and Democrats alike. According to McAdam and Kloos, "In this new environment, Democratic members of Congress were, if anything, only slightly less susceptible to the influence and blandishments of the business community than Republicans."[45] Again, pressures developed pushing both parties to the right, albeit at different speeds, which contributed further to polarization. Even researchers who think that things besides political contributions are more important in the polarization story agree that campaign contributors and lobbyists, not to mention media commentators and activists, have helped push politics in a more conservative and polarizing direction.[46]

Gerrymandering played a role too. Every ten years after the national census has been taken, population shifts from one state to another are documented. This leads to redistricting for seats in the House of Representatives. States whose population increases significantly gain seats, while states whose population decreases significantly lose them. And when this happens, whichever party controls the state government gets to redraw the district lines in their state. Often this is done in ways that create electoral advantages for the incumbent party. As it turned out, this was often the Republican Party, because it gained more control over state legislatures as the population shifted away from Democratic Rustbelt states to Republican Sunbelt states thanks to changes in the economy. This frequently involved redrawing district lines to undermine the electoral clout of African American and Hispanic communities, which tended to vote Democratic, thereby helping to push politics in a more conservative direction.[47] The practice became more prevalent and sophisticated, especially since 2000, thanks to the Republican State Leadership Committee (RSLC), founded in 2002 with a $30 million budget from the US Chamber of Commerce. The RSLC played a key role in organizing the first nationally coordinated gerrymandering effort—the Redistricting Majority Project otherwise known as operation REDMAP—that helped boost the number of Republican-controlled seats in the House in the 2012 election.[48] This sort of partisan redistricting got so bad that in a few states the courts ordered the new district lines to be redrawn. These conflicts were one way in which gerrymandering also exacerbated racially polarized politics. But there was another way gerrymandering polarized politics too.

Because of gerrymandering, there were fewer seats in the House, with truly competitive races between a Republican and a Democrat. This encouraged incumbents to embrace more ideologically extreme policies during the primaries because their party would likely win the general election anyway. They took more extreme positions to appeal to their party's electoral base, which tends to be more adamant ideologically and more likely to vote in the primaries. The defeat of US Representative Eric Cantor from Virginia in 2014 is a case in point. Cantor was a rising star in the Republican Party and a darling of the conservative Tea Party Movement but lost the primary to an even more conservative challenger. In cases like these, gerrymandering contributed to political polarization as more ideologically dogmatic and conservative politicians won these so-called safe seats.[49]

Nationwide, the effects of gerrymandering have been clear. The Associated Press conducted a statistical analysis of all 435 US House races in 2016, as well as thousands of state-level House and assembly races. The results showed that Republicans enjoyed a major advantage thanks to gerrymandering. Without going into methodological details, the AP devised a test designed to detect cases where one political party may have won or widened or retained its grip on power through gerrymandering. There were four times as many states with Republican-skewed state House or assembly districts as there were Democratic ones. "Among the two dozen most populated states that determine the vast majority of Congress, there were nearly three times as many with Republican-tilted US House districts." This included traditional battleground states, all of which had districts redrawn by Republicans since the 2010 census. The Princeton University Gerrymandering Project confirmed these results, which were consistent with analyses of earlier congressional elections conducted by the Brennan Center for Justice at the New York University School of Law. The point is that gerrymandering helped give the Republicans a clear advantage in gaining and increasing their control over the House and, in turn, pushing it in an increasingly conservative and polarizing direction.[50]

By some accounts, pro-Republican gerrymandering after the 2010 census was the most extreme in modern history.[51] In North Carolina, for example, thanks to Republican redistricting in 2011, state politics took a sharp conservative turn and transformed the state's US House delegation from a slight Democratic to a solid Republican majority. It also polarized North Carolina's state politics. According to Carter Wrenn, a veteran North Carolina Republican political consultant, "It's more polarized and more acrimonious than I've ever seen. . . . And I've seen some pretty acrimonious politics. I worked for Jesse Helms." Helms was a long-time US senator from

North Carolina and a segregationist on par with Alabama Governor George Wallace.[52] The politics in North Carolina became so partisan and divisive that when a Democratic governor was elected in 2016, the Republican-controlled legislature moved to strip him of many of his constitutionally given powers.

Five other institutional features of American politics had significant effects on rising conservatism and polarization too. First was the Republican move, discussed in chapter 4, to restrict voting by minorities and college students who tended to vote for Democrats. This enraged Democrats, who often tried to stop it in the courts. Again, North Carolina was an example, but so was my state, New Hampshire, where the Republican legislature bent over backward trying to limit the ability of out-of-state college students from voting.

Second was the expansion of the whipping system in the House and Senate since the 1970s whereby party leaders used their congressional underlings—the whips—to count votes in Congress for legislation and then pressured hesitant party members to vote the party line rather than seeking compromise with the opposition.[53] Failure to toe the party line could have serious consequences for a legislator. For example, the party leadership might deny the legislator a plum committee appointment. It might also result in a loss of party funding or infrastructural support the next time the legislator ran for office.

Third, the US political system is based on federalism. The possibilities for gerrymandering, eviscerating voting rights, and pursing the Southern Strategy, among other things, would have been diminished significantly were a more centralized form of government in place. Neither North Carolina nor New Hampshire could have imposed arbitrary voter ID laws had national legislation specified who could and could not vote in national elections. And when it comes to gerrymandering, if the US Supreme Court overturns some of the gerrymandering currently under appeal, it will be another indication that things might have turned out differently if the political system had been more centralized in the first place.

Fourth, the advent of the primary system by which the two parties select their presidential nominees drove another polarizing wedge between them. Beginning in the early 1970s, the Democrats and then the Republicans instituted state-level primary or caucus systems, which gave party activists, who as mentioned earlier often held more extreme ideological views than most voters and party leaders, greater influence over the nominating process.[54] This was one reason McGovern won the Democratic nomination in 1972, did so well with the party's yuppie contingent, and alienated its traditional blue-collar base. Before this the nominees were selected at the party national conventions, with much of the action taking place behind closed doors in smoke-filled rooms where party bosses called the shots, often picking more moderate candidates.[55]

Finally, I mentioned in chapter 1 that America's two-party winner-take-all electoral system is more prone to polarization than many European systems based on proportional representation. In Europe, where several parties compete in elections, it is often the case that no party wins a clear majority. As a result, two or more parties need to agree to work together to form a governing coalition. Similarly, parties gain seats in parliament according to what percentage of the vote they win. Again, passing legislation requires lots of deal making. The horse trading involved tends toward compromise and moderation. The odds of growing political polarization would have been reduced in America had there been a system of proportional representation in place.

In short, if the institutions had been different, then American politics might not have shifted so far to the right, political polarization would not have reached the epic proportions it did, and, as we shall see in the next chapter, Donald Trump would have been deprived of one of his most appealing campaign promises—to rectify the polarization and gridlock in Washington with which many Americans had become disgusted.

CONCLUSION

One question remains that is worth a moment of our time. Why didn't polarization occur earlier? Why was it only in the mid-1990s that things started to become especially nasty? The short answer is simply that things take time to unfold. The economic, racial, and ideological trends I have been discussing didn't happen overnight. Nor did the institutional changes just reviewed.

But there is one more reason polarization didn't start getting bad until then—and it is steeped in irony. American hegemony was solidified with the fall of the Berlin Wall in 1989 and the demise of the Soviet Union soon thereafter. Without a clear foreign threat, there was less incentive for politicians to come together and form coalitions and compromises in the national interest. After all, Franklin Roosevelt managed to forge historic compromises in the 1940s when fascism was on the rise in Europe and Japan and the country was at war. Lyndon Johnson did much the same during the 1960s when the specter of communism loomed large over Southeast Asia and the Cold War was in full swing. Without that unifying force, political fragmentation became much more likely. This was even true *within* the two main political parties. For instance, during the 1950s and 1960s, William F. Buckley Jr. and his colleagues at the *National Review* helped unite libertarian, religious, and other Republican factions by arguing that communism threatened both individual freedom and Western civilization. Without that foreign threat, Republicans would have been less likely to work together.[56] Therein lies the irony—an increase in America's hegemonic strength abroad thanks to the demise of communism weakened its capacity for political governance at home.

We will return to the issue of American hegemony in the final chapter. But first we need to see how polarization turned into political gridlock, and how Trump exploited it. That requires an understanding of how the economic, racial, ideological, and political trends we have been discussing were transformed suddenly by an unprecedented and very powerful catalyst.

CHAPTER 7
Gridlock, Crisis, and Obama

Traffic on the major highways in and out of Boston begins getting heavy during the week around 4:00 PM, gradually slowing to a crawl within an hour or so, especially on Friday when people are fleeing the city to ski up north during the winter or visit the beaches on Cape Cod to the south during the summer. It's worst where three or four lanes of traffic are forced to merge. It doesn't take much before gridlock sets in and traffic grinds to a halt. A serious accident—a catalyst—can do the trick. And when that happens, people's tempers, already on edge, flare and road rage can result where people get so angry that they yell, swear, shake their fists at other cars, pound the steering wheel, and do other crazy things that only make matters worse—sometimes dangerously so.

Something similar happened in Washington where the economic, racial, and ideological trends I have been discussing merged, creating political polarization, which over the years grew worse and worse and finally reached a tipping point. When the right catalyst was introduced, the situation suddenly turned into full-blown political gridlock where policymaking was engulfed in obstructionism, delay, and dysfunction. The catalyst that finally triggered gridlock involved four things. One was the government's decision not to rescue one of Wall Street's most hallowed investment banks, Lehman Brothers, when it got into trouble in the subprime mortgage market. This triggered a financial crisis unlike any since the Great Depression. Second was Barack Obama's election as the first African American president of the United States, which exacerbated racial tensions. Third was his handling of the financial crisis and its aftermath, which involved massive government bailouts for several big banks, a huge insurance company, and the US automobile industry, as well as a radical overhaul of the nation's financial regulations. Fourth, on top of that, he revolutionized the nation's health care system. All of this amounted to an enormous government intervention into the economy that flew in the face of neoliberalism, which by then had become the received policy wisdom. The working and middle classes were hurting badly. The situation exploded. Congressional decorum broke down, partisanship hit new heights, and polarization in Washington suddenly turned into political paralysis. Across the country the public was outraged. And Trump turned the situation to his advantage. This chapter explains how it happened.

GRIDLOCK ARRIVES

By some measures, gridlock developed slowly and steadily in Washington, reaching a zenith during Obama's presidency. An analysis from the Brookings Institution found that in the mid-1970s, only about 40 percent of important legislative issues were left unresolved by the end of a congressional session—a number that grew gradually thereafter. By the middle of the Obama presidency it reached about 60 percent, with a few years surpassing 70 percent.[1] However, by other measures gridlock emerged much more abruptly on Obama's watch, indicating that a tipping point had been reached and that events surrounding his presidency served as the catalyst ushering in a qualitatively new and decidedly worse era of legislative dysfunction.[2]

For example, the number of vacancies in the administration and judiciary soared during Obama's presidency, especially during his second term. Members on both sides of the aisle agreed that they had never seen things this bad, largely because the confirmation process had become a political football. The Republicans were prone to stalling or blocking administrative confirmations wherever possible, often by requesting nominees to answer hundreds of questions in writing. Notably, following Obama's re-election, his nominee for the Environmental Protection Agency received 1,000 written questions from the Senate as part of the confirmation process. Jacob Lew, the Treasury secretary nominee, got 444 questions prior to his confirmation hearing—more than all those received by the seven previous Treasury secretary nominees combined. In turn, the White House took longer to prepare nominations in the first place because it realized that it had to put candidates through an excruciating vetting process to make sure they could pass muster in the confirmation hearings.[3]

As for judicial appointments, compared to his three 2-term predecessors (Reagan, Clinton, Bush), there was nothing special about how many nominations Obama made to the federal district court bench through his seventh year in office or how many were confirmed. But in his last year in office, the number of nominations confirmed fell far short of his predecessors. The Senate confirmed only 30 percent of his eighth-year nominees, much fewer than it did for Reagan (66 percent), Clinton (50 percent), or Bush (68 percent). As a result, on Obama's watch, district court vacancies nearly doubled from thirty-three to sixty-five between mid-April 2015 and mid-April 2016, which was far worse than his predecessors. Why? Although all of these presidents had to contend with Senate confirmation hearings controlled by the opposition party, Republicans dug in their heels and refused to confirm many of Obama's nominees, or in some cases even bring them forward for hearings.[4] Even when they did confirm someone, the process dragged on forever. For instance, it took more than a year before the Republican-controlled Senate confirmed Lawrence Vilardo in October 2015 to the US Western District Court in New York State, whereas when the Democrats still had a majority in the Senate, it only took about three months to confirm Geoffrey Crawford to the US District Court in Vermont.* Of course, Republican Senate Majority Leader Mitch McConnell's refusal to meet with let alone convene confirmation hearings for Merrick Garland, Obama's nominee to the Supreme Court and a judge whose record was impeccable by all accounts, epitomized gridlock.

Furthermore, the use of the filibuster—speaking on the floor of Congress to prolong debate and delay voting on a piece of legislation—became more common as polarization increased in Washington. Historically, the filibuster was used to kill legislative proposals that didn't have strong bipartisan support, but on Obama's watch McConnell used it to slow down or torpedo things that *did* have bipartisan support so that Obama wouldn't get credit for it. Indeed, the use of the filibuster skyrocketed during Obama's first year in office. So did the number of cloture votes, which ended debate, stopped a filibuster, and brought legislation to a vote—but only after several days had passed. Four out of every ten cloture votes taken in the entire history of the US Senate up to 2014 occurred during McConnell's tenure as minority leader.[5] Michael Mann and Norman Ornstein, two keen observers of national politics, argue that the filibuster became a stealth weapon used by Republicans during the Obama years to obstruct even legislative matters that used to be routine and widely supported. In their words, "It is fair to say that this pervasive use of the filibuster has never before happened in the history of the Senate."[6]

* My thanks to Judge Crawford for this information. Even though his confirmation process was comparatively short, it was still intense and thorough: an FBI background check; reviews of all his public addresses, decisions from the Vermont bench, and personal finances; written answers to a slew of questions from the Senate Judiciary Committee; and two grueling interrogations by White House and then Justice Department lawyers.

Some of the most egregious examples of gridlock involved budgetary matters. For years Congress had passed continuing budget resolutions and raised the debt ceiling when necessary with no strings attached and little hesitation. That all changed under Obama as Republicans tried to squeeze out a variety of concessions from the White House in exchange for their cooperation. As a result, the budget resolutions covered shorter periods of time, an indication of how difficult it was for Republicans and Democrats to agree on them. More significant, however, in 2011, House Republicans demanded concessions before agreeing to raise the debt ceiling—the cap on how much money the federal government was allowed to borrow. A dramatic game of chicken ensued between Republicans and Democrats with threats of a major government shutdown. Finally, Congress raised the ceiling with only hours to spare before the government would have started defaulting on its debt. The episode was unprecedented, unnerved the international financial community, and caused Standard and Poor's to downgrade the federal government's credit rating for the first time in history. Nevertheless, Congress fought over the debt ceiling again in 2013, this time with House Republicans trying to hold the Affordable Care Act hostage— an effort that ultimately failed. Such partisan political brinkmanship was unparalleled in US history.[7]

It's no surprise, then, that people became fed up with Washington politics. Remember from chapter 5 that public trust and satisfaction with government declined significantly after 2001. The public's approval rating of Congress also plummeted during that time from about 50 percent agreeing that it was doing a good job to just 17 percent by 2016.[8] And Obama's approval rating (48 percent) was lower on average than any president in over thirty years.[9] What went wrong?

THE FINANCIAL CRISIS

The first part of the catalyst was the 2008 financial crisis. Far from a normal business cycle slump, the crisis was a perfect storm that took decades to unfold. The story was driven in part by incentives in banks and mortgage companies that encouraged predatory lending and exceedingly risky investments. But the government was also to blame, motivated to a considerable degree by the rise of neoliberalism as it applied to the deregulation of the banking and financial services industry.[10] The trouble started in the subprime mortgage market where people with lousy credit ratings were sold adjustable rate mortgages that, as it turned out, they couldn't afford. But given the wage stagnation and other economic problems facing middle- and working-class families that I described in chapter 3, this was their only hope for achieving the centerpiece of the American Dream—home ownership. When interest rates began going up, many of them couldn't pay their mortgages, the housing market crashed, and millions lost their homes through foreclosure.

Some of Wall Street's largest banks got caught up in the collapse because they held billions of dollars of these mortgages in asset-backed securities—bonds consisting of bits and pieces of subprime mortgages and perhaps credit card debt, auto loans, and other consumer liabilities. When the housing market started to crash in 2007–2008, so did the banks holding these bonds. The first casualties were Bear Stearns and then Washington Mutual, which the government helped liquidate at considerable public expense. But when Lehman Brothers went bankrupt after the government refused to help, all hell broke loose. This was the straw that broke the camel's back. Now it was apparent that nobody knew who was holding the toxic subprime mortgages, who might go belly up next, and whether the federal government would bail them out. As a result, banks were afraid to lend anybody money, so the credit markets froze. At the same time American International Group (AIG), the world's largest insurance company, was suddenly in serious trouble too because it had insured billions of dollars of these asset-backed securities against default. It was almost as if AIG had sold fire insurance to everyone in town and everybody's house had suddenly burned to the ground the same night so the company had to pay everyone all at once for their losses—and might not be able to do so. Those holding asset-backed securities including institutional investors like gigantic mutual funds and hedge funds couldn't be sure whether their insurance was worth the paper it was printed on. In such an uncertain financial climate, even businesses that were in good shape couldn't get credit and had trouble refinancing loans.[11]

For example, National Public Radio ran a story during the first year or so of the crisis about Crate and Barrel, a midpriced furniture and housewares chain with a store in Cambridge, Massachusetts. The business was doing well enough, but then sales began slipping as the crisis unfolded. In turn, the owner had a hard time making his payroll and turned to his local bank for a short-term loan to cover this and a few other expenses. He had done business with the bank for years and never had financial troubles before, but the bank refused to help simply because the economic situation in general was so unsettled. He had to begin laying off workers, working longer hours himself, and eventually went out of business through no fault of his own.

As the crisis metastasized, millions lost their jobs, retirement accounts evaporated, and the economy plummeted toward what many feared might become a crisis worse than the Great Depression of the 1930s. The Great Recession was on. Unemployment doubled from 4.6 percent in 2007 to nearly 10 percent by 2010. People blamed the federal government, Wall Street banks, and unscrupulous mortgage lenders for the crisis. Exacerbating trends discussed in chapter 4, they also began blaming immigrants from Mexico and Latin America for taking their jobs. Economic and racial issues converged again, but this time energized by the crisis and in an atmosphere further charged racially thanks to the 9/11 terrorist attacks that had put Muslims in the crosshairs of many Americans. That was bad enough, but people got even madder about how the government started handling the situation.

The Bush administration moved to bail out Wall Street. In September 2008, Henry Paulson, Bush's Treasury secretary, got Congress to approve a $700 billion bank bailout package, the Troubled Assets Relief Program (TARP), but not before his first request was rejected in a close partisan vote by the House, throwing the stock market into a one-day tailspin, losing 778 points. Paulson used about $100 billion of TARP money for the government to buy preferred stock in eight big banks. The plan was to thaw out the credit markets by injecting liquidity into the banking system. But in many people's minds this was a step toward socialism—state ownership of the means of production—even though the idea was for the government to sell back these shares a few years later, hopefully breaking even on the deal if not making a little money. Nevertheless, the joke at the time was that Bush came into office as a social conservative but left as a conservative socialist. The government used TARP funds the same way in lending AIG $85 billion in exchange for a temporary 79.9 percent equity stake in the company—a bailout that eventually totaled $182 billion by March 2009. In the meantime, Barack Obama was elected president.

OBAMA'S ELECTION

The second element of the catalyst was Obama's election in 2008. The mere fact that an African American was elected president of the United States was remarkable given the country's history of racism. Many hoped that Obama's victory would mark a turning point in race relations in America. Some envisioned a "postracial America." They were sadly mistaken. For one thing, Obama's racial identity had been called into question during the 2008 campaign by those who demanded to see his birth certificate suspecting that he was born in Kenya and, therefore, might be ineligible to be president. He produced the document, but that wasn't enough to allay people's concerns. The percentage of people polled who believed that Obama was foreign born and/or a Muslim increased dramatically, especially among Republicans, between the 2008 election and 2011.[12] Even Donald Trump raised the so-called birther issue, telling the *Today* show in 2011, for example, that "I have some real doubts. . . . I have people that actually have been studying it and they cannot believe what they're finding." On another show, *Good Morning America*, he made the same charges but added, referring to Obama's birth certificate, that "Maybe it says he's a Muslim."[13]

Furthermore, according to detailed statistical analyses of the 2008 election by UCLA professors Michael Tesler and David Sears, "Barack Obama's candidacy polarized the electorate by racial attitudes more strongly than had any previous presidential candidate in recent times."[14] Even within the Democratic Party during the primaries, there was a deep division over who supported Obama or not between people who were liberal on racial issues and those who were conservative on them. The former supported him but the latter did not. Moreover, Tesler and Sears found significant spillover effects—all else being equal, any policy issue for which Obama took a public stand could become polarized according to people's racial predispositions. For instance, during the campaign Obama favored raising taxes on the wealthy, but people's support for his position was significantly affected by whether they were conservative or liberal on racial issues, with racial liberals being more inclined to support it than racial conservatives. Tesler and Sears did their analysis early in Obama's first term in office, but their conclusion was prophetic:

> Race is probably the most visceral issue in American public life. As such, increased polarization of the electorate according to racial attitudes could make the contemporary political discourse even more vitriolic than the earlier rancorous atmospheres under Presidents Bill Clinton and George W. Bush. Such a racialized environment would have the potential to make reaching common ground on public policy an even more difficult task in the age of Obama.[15]

Truer words were never written. Postelection surveys and panel data showed that the impact of racial resentment did not diminish once Obama took office. One indication was that the highly racialized voting in the 2008 presidential election was repeated four years later.[16] Another indication was that thirty-eight states soon introduced legislation, such as the voter ID laws mentioned in chapter 4, that many people believed was intended to inhibit voting by minority groups.[17] Finally, over the course of Obama's presidency, the percentage of all Americans who believed that racism was a big problem in their country doubled from 26 to 50 percent. Nearly three-quarters of African Americans and more than half of Hispanics agreed.[18]

The combination of the financial crisis and Obama's election helped bring polarization to the boiling point in another way too—by turning up the heat another notch on the immigration issue. During the early 2000s,

Democrats and a few Republicans had tried to cobble together legislation creating a path to citizenship for undocumented immigrants. But in the wake of the financial crisis, the Great Recession, and Obama's election, this effort collapsed as racial hostility toward immigrants soared. Recall that many conservatives viewed immigrants as a financial burden on Americans, who had to pay for their treatment in hospitals, their kids' education and other social services. Moreover, many people believed that immigrants were competing with Americans for jobs in an economy where the unemployment rate had suddenly jumped. The Republican Party, urged on by its stridently conservative electoral base, saw a wedge issue and took full advantage of it, suddenly rejecting all discussions of a path to citizenship. The issue stalled in Congress—one of many examples of gridlock.

The toxic relationship between race, immigration, and the financial crisis was especially clear in Arizona, a state with lots of Mexican immigrants, a state that had been hit especially hard by the housing crisis and Great Recession, and a state that took a very hard line on immigration.[19] The most notorious example of this was Sheriff Joe Arpaio, known as "America's toughest sheriff," who made national headlines by running aggressive patrols that engaged in racial profiling to round up suspected undocumented Hispanic immigrants. Once in custody, these people were often housed in canvas tents in triple-degree temperatures under the broiling Arizona sun and forced to wear pink underwear. Arpaio eventually lost his job, was found guilty of civil contempt of court, and was later convicted of criminal contempt as well. Trump soon pardoned him.

Of course, it was not inevitable that Obama's election would trigger gridlock.[20] Mitch McConnell said as much in a 2010 interview just before the midterm elections: "If President Obama does a Clintonian backflip, if he's willing to meet us halfway on some of the biggest issues, it's not inappropriate for us to do business with him."[21] However, there were no backflips and McConnell dug in his heels after the election, refusing to do much of anything with either Obama or congressional Democrats.

In fact, congressional Republicans had started conspiring to obstruct Obama and the Democrats' agenda two years earlier. Even before Obama's inauguration, McConnell explained to his caucus in 2008 that the plan was to make the new president less popular by preventing him from accomplishing anything.[22] And on the evening of the inauguration, leading Republicans gathered at an upscale Washington restaurant to plot their next moves. Planning a gridlock strategy was the first order of business. Representative Kevin McCarthy from California declared, "If you act like you're the minority, you're going to stay in the minority. . . . We've got to challenge them on every single bill and challenge them on every single campaign." They also agreed to attack Obama's nominees for top positions in the government, and attack vulnerable Democrats in the media and on the airwaves. McConnell demanded unwavering cooperation from his Republican colleagues to ensure that the administration didn't succeed in anything.[23] He got it—but he had already been enjoying it to a degree. Since the 1980s, Republicans had displayed far more unity in Congress than Democrats, and were far more aggressive than Democrats in inflicting losses on losers of policy fights, such as cutting the opposition's favorite social programs to the bone wherever possible.[24] As noted earlier, their whipping system was superb. This became even more evident once the Republicans finally controlled both houses of Congress in 2015 and refused to give an inch on any Democratic proposal, not to mention judicial or administrative nominees. Governing, which had become more sluggish over the years, now ground to a virtual halt, policy ideas got stuck in legislative limbo, and the level of rancor and incivility in politics hit the roof.[25] Shortly after Trump came to power, Republican Speaker of the House Paul Ryan confessed his party's culpability in all this: "We were a 10-year opposition party, where being against things was easy to do. You just had to be against it." All they had to do was say "no" to everything—and they did.[26] However, Obama's election and the politics of race are not the end of the story.

OBAMA AND THE CRISIS

How Obama handled the financial crisis and Great Recession was the third part of the catalyst that transformed polarization into gridlock. Obama doubled down on his predecessor's crisis management plan. In February 2009, he approved a $787 billion stimulus package to revive the economy by cutting taxes, extending unemployment benefits, and funding public works projects. He also signed the American Recovery and Reinvestment Act, which pumped another $260 billion into the economy through a combination of tax cuts and credits, infrastructure improvements, small-business loans, and more. He also nationalized Fannie Mae and Freddie Mac, two huge federally chartered mortgage companies that got into trouble during the crisis. Finally, to save the US automobile industry and the seven million jobs associated with it, the government temporarily took over General Motors and Chrysler at a cost of $80 billion, and lent Ford another $6 billion.[†]

† Many accounts are available of the government's efforts to save the banks, AIG, the automobile manufacturers, Fannie Mae, and Freddie Mac and avoid an even worse recession. For a helpful overview, see Amadeo 2017a, 2017b.

On top of all this, with the Obama administration's help, Democrats in Congress introduced legislation in March 2010 to improve regulation of the banking and financial services industries. Obama signed the Dodd-Frank Wall Street Reform Act four months later—the most sweeping regulatory reform in banking since the 1930s.[27] This was a huge incursion of government into the financial services industry. It was designed to prevent a crisis like this from ever happening again.

The upshot of all this was fourfold. First, it looked like neoliberalism had suddenly been laid to rest and Keynesianism—pump priming extraordinaire—was back in business. Robert Skidelsky, an eminent political economist who had written the definitive three-volume biography of Keynes, led the cheers with his well-received book published only a year after the crisis hit entitled *Keynes: The Return of the Master*. All of this was particularly infuriating to many conservative policymakers who still believed in neoliberalism.

Second, many of the government's policies didn't sit well with the public either. In part, this was because many of them had come to believe in neoliberalism too. But more generally, people were angry that the Obama administration had apparently bent over backward to save Wall Street but had forgotten Main Street, where people had lost their businesses, homes, jobs, and retirement accounts—and whose taxes, they believed, had paid for the bank, AIG, and auto industry bailouts. Many seemed to forget that some of the bailouts originated on Bush's watch. But never mind. Joseph Stiglitz, a Nobel laureate in economics, captured the public mood when he wrote that many Americans across the political spectrum were feeling that this was socialism for the rich and capitalism for the poor.[28] These concerns surfaced early when the House refused to pass the first version of TARP in the partisan vote mentioned earlier that had sent the stock market tumbling. However, the public was at loggerheads over the issue too. As late as 2013, about half of those surveyed thought that the government was more concerned with making Wall Street firms profitable than making sure that the financial system worked well for all Americans; the other half said it was fine or were unsure.[29] That same year Americans were also deeply split over whether there was too much or too little government regulation of financial institutions and markets (43 percent vs. 49 percent), with two-thirds of Republicans saying there was too much and two-thirds of Democrats saying there was not enough, results that held steady through 2015.[30] The automobile industry bailout was more popular.[31]

Third, there was profound pessimism about the economy. In 2015, long after the crisis began, a whopping 74 percent of those surveyed said the economy was still in only poor or fair shape, 20 percent said it would probably be worse next year, and over half expected no improvement. Again, opinions broke along partisan lines, with Democrats being more optimistic than Republicans.[32] People agreed that the economy was in serious trouble but disagreed vehemently about how the government had handled it. As political scientist Larry Bartels put it, there were "massive partisan differences" on Obama's economic rescue package years after it was implemented.[33]

Fourth, this economic pessimism was expressed most visibly by the Occupy Wall Street Movement, which started in September 2011 when a group of demonstrators took over Zuccotti Park in the middle of New York City's financial district. With chants and signs proclaiming that "We are the 99 percent," they protested growing inequality in America, exacerbated by the crisis, where the top 1 percent of the population held a huge amount of the country's income and wealth. One survey found that the vast majority (80 percent) of demonstrators were liberal, while only 6 percent were conservative. Yet, curiously, 73 percent said they disapproved of how Obama was doing his job, even though 60 percent reported having voted for him in 2008. They ranked unemployment as the most important problem facing the country. And foreshadowing Trump's rise to power, a plurality of 36 percent said they wouldn't vote for either Obama or the Republican nominee, whoever it turned out to be, in the next presidential election.[34] They were fed up with the status quo. Sister movements sprang up in hundreds of cities and towns across the country, including Hanover, New Hampshire, where I teach and where a small group of protestors set up tents and sleeping bags on a downtown corner, hunkering down through a frigid New England winter to protest against Wall Street and inequality. Figure 7.1 shows that by 2015—seven years after Lehman Brothers collapsed—most people believed that the government's rescue efforts had done little or nothing to help the middle class (72 percent), small business (68 percent), or the poor (65 percent).[35]

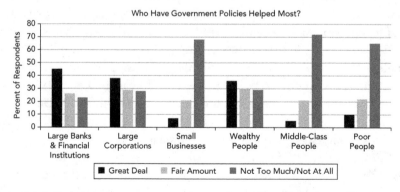

Figure 7.1: Public opinion on government performance in the Great Recession, 2015.
Source: Pew Research Center 2015c.

The financial crisis, the Great Recession, Obama's election, elevated racial tensions, and Obama's handling of the crisis all contributed to the Republicans' unwillingness to work with Democrats on pressing national issues. As we will see later, it also gave ammunition to the Trump campaign. However, the anger and gridlock that bubbled up over all this paled in comparison to what happened with Obama's health care reform.

OBAMA AND HEALTH CARE REFORM

The fourth and final part of the catalyst was Obama's major health care initiative. He delivered a nationally televised speech to both chambers of Congress on September 9, 2009, where he rolled out his health care reform plan. As he was explaining that the program would not cover undocumented immigrants, Representative Joe Wilson, a Republican from South Carolina, yelled "You lie!" from the back of the chamber. People were stunned. Wilson's outburst was an unprecedented breach of congressional decorum for which he was pilloried in the press and later admonished by a rare bipartisan vote in the House. However, it signaled how much Obama's initiative had infuriated the Right. But why were they so upset?

In 2009, Obama decided to tackle one of the thorniest problems facing America—reforming the health care insurance system to increase coverage and reduce costs for millions of Americans. Bill and Hillary Clinton had tried this in 1993 and failed in spectacular fashion. Obama's vice president, Joe Biden, and other close advisers warned Obama not to attempt it, worrying that it would be his Waterloo. But Obama insisted it was the right thing to do. Even before the administration went to work on health care reform, people were deeply divided over the issue. Things only got worse after the policymaking wheels began turning. Crafting a bill was complicated and required compromises, notably backing off from a government-funded insurance option—the so-called public option—to which the insurance industry had vehemently objected. Eventually, the Patient Protection and Affordable Care Act (ACA), nicknamed Obamacare, was signed into law in March 2010, but not before it had generated a firestorm of political controversy exacerbating an already deeply polarized electorate and Congress.[36]

People were spooked by the ACA. For one thing, Republicans ran ads and made speeches about how the ACA was a disaster that would cut $500 billion from Medicare, threaten the ability of seniors to choose their own doctors, raise taxes and fees to pay for coverage, and compromise the quality of health care people would receive.[37] For another thing, conservatives were incensed that Obama could even consider a public option, even though Medicare and Medicaid already provided publicly funded health care for the elderly and poor. They were also upset that the legislation included a mandate requiring people to buy insurance or pay a fine. This all ran very much against the grain of neoliberalism. And many objected to the federal government subsidizing insurance for low-income households and requiring insurance providers to cover things like contraceptives—something that rankled Catholics and the Christian Right, who advocated traditional family values. Finally, of special concern were the online insurance exchanges where people could buy coverage. If their state government didn't set one up, then customers could shop on the federal government's exchange. To the conservatives, all of this smacked of big, intrusive, expensive, liberal government spiraling out of control—a concern heightened when the federal exchange was opened with all sorts of technical glitches. In conservative circles this was emblematic of the inefficiency and incompetence of big government run amok.

Conservatives also portrayed this as another slippery slope to socialism, especially given all the talk about the public option. During summer 2009, when the plan was still being debated, economic angst and racial animosity, already simmering due to the financial crisis and other things I have discussed, suddenly boiled over. For instance, Republicans like one-time vice-presidential nominee Sarah Palin leveled a fusillade of accusations against the ACA, including the erroneous charge that it mandated "death panels" that would determine which sick people could get health care. Palin posted the following on her Facebook webpage: "The America I know and love is not one in which my parents or my baby with Down Syndrome will have to stand in front of Obama's 'death panel' so his bureaucrats can decide . . . whether they are worthy of health care." PolitiFact, a Pulitzer Prize–winning fact-checking organization, declared this to be utter nonsense—there was no such thing as a death panel in the ACA. Nevertheless, the death panel term caught on with many opponents and the public, as did other inaccuracies and misrepresentations, including the notion that the law covered the undocumented immigrants that Joe Wilson was yelling about during Obama's speech to Congress.[38] Here was a perfect example of alternative facts at their worst.

Accusations that the ACA, not to mention other Obama programs, was an insidious form of socialism continued long after it was enacted. For example, pundits and others on the right, including prominent media personalities like Rush Limbaugh, Eric Bolling, and Sarah Palin, accused Obama at various times on Fox News of pursuing a Marxist agenda and defiling American small-government, free market values.[39] But it wasn't just conservative political elites who hated the legislation; it was the conservative grassroots too who were seething and took to the streets.

In 2009, local Tea Party groups began forming around the country, eventually swelling to about a thousand in all. They often showed up at the summertime town hall meetings members of Congress held routinely in their districts to chat with constituents. People were furious about the plan. Many arrived at these meetings with signs portraying Obama in all sorts of disparaging ways—as a foreigner, a Muslim, a traitor, a black terrorist, a socialist, a communist, a fascist, and simply someone out to destroy the American way of life. The meetings often deteriorated into full-throated yelling and screaming. To be sure, the Tea Party Movement had other concerns too, but the ACA was at the top of their list. What is particularly interesting is how ill-informed many of the Tea Party members were about the policy, and how their opinions were often inconsistent and contradictory. For instance, they were fervently anti–big government and found socialism to be anathema, yet they loved Medicare and Social Security—the two huge government entitlement programs. They also tended to believe that racial and ethnic minorities were less hard-working than whites; that immigrants were freeloaders overburdening the welfare state; and that immigrants, Muslims, and minorities in general were undermining American culture and values.[40] Indeed, as political scientist Alan Abramowitz found, "Tea Party supporters displayed high levels of racial resentment and held very negative opinions about President Obama compared with the rest of the public and even other Republicans."[41] We have seen that many of these beliefs had been around for a long time, but now they got worse.

As we saw earlier, conservatives had long been concerned that low-income racial and ethnic minorities had been taking advantage of government social programs. This was the essence of the Southern Strategy. Now conservatives, and Tea Party members in particular, were angry at the prospect that yet another opportunity—a new "entitlement" program—was being created for these "undeserving" groups to game the system at the expense of white folks.[42] Statistical analyses reveal that after Obama was sworn in and became more vocal about the need for health care reform—especially the need to require people to buy coverage—opposition rose, particularly among those expressing high levels of racial resentment. In other words, as debate ramped up about what health care reform should look like, it became racialized.[43] In fact, the Tea Party often exemplified those dog whistle politics I mentioned in chapter 4—a profound dislike of welfare programs for "other people" but also great suspicion of undocumented immigrants and Arab Muslims. Of course, they occasionally abandoned the dog whistle when it came to Obama, who was sometimes portrayed at Tea Party rallies on placards as an African savage straight out of an old Tarzan movie.[44]

More important in terms of my argument, the Tea Party Movement personified the four trends I have been talking about all along. It was concerned with the declining economic prospects of most Americans. It held racial and ethnic minorities and immigrants accountable for a variety of the nation's ills. It believed deeply in neoliberal ideology's critique of big government, high taxes, and exorbitant spending on liberal social programs. And, finally, when it came to political polarization, the Tea Party believed that there should be no compromising with Democrats on the ACA—it should be abandoned entirely. As a result, the Tea Party Movement was an extremely important impetus—although certainly not the only one—pushing polarization over the edge into the gridlock upon which Trump eventually capitalized.

Sensing a political opportunity, professional advocacy organizations and the right-wing media, including Fox News, jumped on the bandwagon and began speaking for the Tea Party Movement, which soon garnered tremendous financial and other resources from conservative organizations funded directly or indirectly by wealthy individuals and well-heeled conservative nonprofit organizations.[45] I recall, for instance, watching a Fourth of July parade in little Beaufort, North Carolina, three years later when in the distance an elaborate-looking float, at least compared to the rest, appeared down the street. As the parade moved past me it became clear that it was a Tea Party float, all decked out in red, white, and blue bunting, with about twenty people sporting bright red Tea Party Patriot tee shirts, flags, and other patriotic paraphernalia. Some of them were walking alongside passing out literature, including copies of the US Constitution and Bill of Rights, provided, according to the imprint on the back, by the Heritage Foundation in Washington, DC, one of the richest conservative think tanks in the country. It turns out that Tea Party activities like these were supported by a Koch brothers–funded outfit called Freedom Works that provides webinars, funding, and other assistance to local Tea Party groups like the one I saw in North Carolina.[46]

All this further exacerbated gridlock in the country. Shortly after the ACA's introduction in 2010, as Figure 7.2 illustrates, the public was split, with 46 percent approving and 40 percent disapproving of the legislation. By 2016, things remained about the same, 49 percent approving and 38 percent disapproving. As was true of the public's opinion of financial crisis management and Dodd-Frank, the difference between Republicans and Democrats on the ACA was significantly larger. By 2016, according to one poll, 78 percent of Democrats but only 9 percent of Republicans approved of the program.[47] Furthermore, the Republican-led House voted more than fifty times to defund or repeal all or parts of the ACA after it became law.

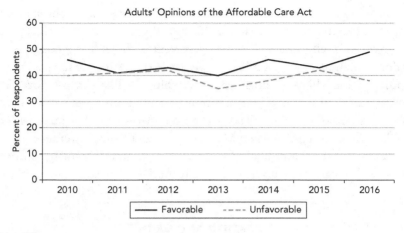

Figure 7.2:
The public's views on the Affordable Care Act, 2010–2016.
Source: Kaiser Health Tracking Poll 2017.

The Tea Party fueled a conservative takeover in the House in the 2010 midterm elections and pushed politics even deeper into gridlock. By some accounts the Tea Party Movement and its electoral victories also pushed the Republican Party to its most racially conservative and demographically exclusive point in fifty years.[48] Tea Party politicians formed the Freedom Caucus in the House, and were so extreme that they often beat moderate and sometimes even more conservative Republicans like Virginia's Eric Cantor in primary elections. Moreover, the Freedom Caucus became so stubbornly opposed to compromise—even within the Republican Party—that John Boehner, Republican Speaker of the House and a conservative guy in his own right, eventually quit politics in frustration.[49] California Republican Kevin McCarthy, Boehner's conservative heir apparent, suddenly turned down the speakership when the Freedom Caucus announced it would support someone else even more conservative than him. Paul Ryan, a neoliberal deficit hawk from Wisconsin, picked up the gavel. The Freedom Caucus fractured the House, making it virtually impossible for Democrats and Republicans there to agree on much of anything. In particular, it played a pivotal role in sparking the debt ceiling crises of 2011 and 2013. Things weren't much better in the Senate, over which the Republicans won control in 2015, again thanks in part to the Tea Party. But Tea Party victories in Senate elections merely added fuel to the fire, which was already being stoked by Mitch McConnell, who as Senate minority leader affirmed prior to the 2010 midterm elections that "The single most important thing we want to achieve is for President Obama to be a one-term president." In his mind, this took precedence over improving the economy, fixing health care, preventing another financial crisis, or doing much of anything else constructive to solve the country's problems.[50] It was the Republicans' number one objective and the reason for their gridlock strategy in the first place.

To recap briefly, during Obama's first term in the White House, polarization, which had been building slowly since the 1970s, finally passed the tipping point where gridlock seized Washington like never before. The epitome of it all was McConnell's unprecedented refusal in early 2016—nearly a year before Obama's second term ended—to either meet with or hold confirmation hearings on Merrick Garland, Obama's nominee for the Supreme Court. The public's disgust with government, which had been growing for years, crystalized accordingly. And Trump cashed in on it.

CAPITALIZING ON POLARIZATION AND GRIDLOCK

On the campaign trail Trump took full advantage of the public's loathing of polarization and gridlock, how the government had handled the financial crisis, and, of course, the ACA. First let's look at polarization and gridlock. Trump offered plenty of platitudes—but no specifics—about how he would overcome polarization and unify the country. He was adamant about this during the campaign. As he explained to CNN's Jake Tapper: "I'm going to unify. This country is totally divided. Barack Obama has divided this country unbelievably. And it's all, it's all hatred, what can I tell you. I've never seen anything like it. . . . I've gotten along with Democrats and I've gotten along with Republicans. . . . I will be a great unifier for our country."[51] He continued to harp on this theme after the election, tweeting in January 2017 that "For many years our country has been divided, angry and untrusting. Many say it will never change, the hatred is too deep. IT WILL CHANGE!!!!."[52] Over four million people disagreed when a day after his inauguration they protested his election in some six hundred cities and towns across the country. If there was any sign of unification during his first few months in office, it was the fact that by late March 2017, nearly 60 percent of all Americans agreed that he was doing a lousy job as president—an all-time low for presidents at that stage of their first term in office.[53]

When it came to gridlock, Trump blamed it on the general dysfunction of Washington politicians, often egged on, he said, by high-paid lobbyists and others, refusing to set aside their parochial interests and work together. This is one reason he pledged to "drain the swamp" in Washington. He put it this way in his announcement that he was running for president: "They [politicians] will never make America great again. They don't even have a chance. They're controlled fully—they're controlled fully by the lobbyists, by the donors, and by the special interests, fully."[54] And perhaps more to the point, as he told Iowa voters, he was immune from all that given his vast wealth: "You know the nice part about me? I don't need anybody's money. They [lobbyists, donors] have total control over Jeb [Bush] and Hillary [Clinton] and everybody else that takes that money. I will tell you this: Nobody's putting up millions of dollars for me. I'm putting up my own money."[55] The unfortunate irony, as it turned out, was that once in office, Trump appointed an unprecedented number of Wall Street bankers, millionaires, billionaires, and former lobbyists to important positions in his administration, including his daughter and son-in-law.[56] It seemed that rather than draining the swamp, he was restocking it.

Another way he promised to fix things was to copy Obama by circumventing Congress whenever necessary by issuing executive orders. This too was ironic because Obama was the man he so vehemently criticized, both during and after the campaign. The list of things he said he would fix by using this presidential power was extensive. By the end of his third month in office, he had issued no less than twenty-nine executive orders designed to "Make America Great Again" by, for example, reducing regulations, eliminating trade abuses, promoting oil and gas exploration, finishing the Keystone pipeline, and banning White House and congressional officials from lobbing for five years after leaving government service. But in most cases his orders were vague and in many cases merely symbolic.

Immigration was another issue he wanted to tackle with executive orders to cut the Gordian knot of gridlock and "Make America Great Again." After all, he claimed repeatedly during the campaign that he would crack down on immigration. In one interview Trump explained how in addition to building a wall along the Mexican border, he would use executive orders to take care of that problem: "The immigration laws of the United States give the president powers to suspend entry into the country of any class of persons. I will use this power to protect the American people."[57] In a stump speech in Phoenix, Arizona, he elaborated: "I am going to create a new special deportation task force, focused on identifying and removing quickly the most dangerous criminal and illegal immigrants in America.... Our enforcement priorities will include removing criminals, gang members, security threats, visa overstays, public charges—that is, those relying on public welfare or straining the safety net."[58] Incidentally, there it was again—dog whistle politics pointing the finger at immigrants, presumably members of minority groups, who were allegedly sponging off the welfare state at everyone else's expense. As it turned out, his first two attempts to use executive orders to keep immigrants out were stopped dead in their tracks by the courts, which ruled that they were unconstitutional. The Supreme Court temporarily reinstated a partial ban but only until it had a chance to hear the case and issue a final ruling.

Trump also exploited the public's discontent with how the government had handled the financial crisis. The big corporate bailouts were a thing of the past; nobody could un-ring those bells. But he was undoubtedly as aware as anyone else in the race that the public was frustrated and dissatisfied with the bank bailouts, and that many Americans viewed them as socialism for Wall Street while everyone else on Main Street had to suffer for the banks' foolishness, incompetence, and extravagance. So, when confronted with the fact that long before he decided to run for office he said that the TARP program may have been a good idea, his campaign tried to deny it. In an interview with Jake Tapper, Trump's spokesperson Kellyanne Conway claimed that "when you go back and look at TARP, which we got from a Republican president and continued by a Democratic president, Donald Trump would not be for that. And that benefits all these big banks who didn't need the help, [and] in some cases were forced to take the money."[59] He also waffled on the auto bailout, telling Fox News in 2008 when the idea was first floated that "I think the government should stand behind them one hundred percent. You cannot lose the auto companies. They're great. They make wonderful products." But later, when it had become clear that there was some public trepidation about it, he hedged, telling reporters on the campaign trail that "You could have let it go bankrupt, frankly, and rebuilt itself. . . . Or you could have done it the way it went. I could have done it either way. . . . I think you would have wound up in the same place."[60] Here was a veteran pitchman at work trying to make everybody happy.

The way he handled the Dodd-Frank legislation was particularly clever because he developed a pitch simultaneously appealing to both Wall Street and Main Street. In a May 2016 interview he said that one of his top priorities if elected would be to dismantle the Dodd-Frank legislation because "Dodd-Frank has made it impossible for bankers to function." That would certainly please Wall Street. But then he added that the problem for bankers spilled over to Main Street because Dodd-Frank "makes it very hard for bankers to loan money for people to create jobs, for people with businesses to create jobs. And that has to stop."[61] So his promise was geared to everybody on either side of the issue and tied back into his overarching narrative, "Make America Great Again," by creating jobs through old-time neoliberal deregulation.

When it came to the ACA, he was even more slippery, which made sense politically given that the country was so split over the issue. On the one hand, in a nod to those who hated the ACA, he promised again and again that he would get rid of it immediately. As he told a reporter on *60 Minutes* in September 2015, "Obamacare's going to be repealed and replaced. Obamacare is a disaster if you look at what's going on with premiums where they're up 40, 50, 55 percent." But then a few minutes later in the same interview he said that in its place he would put a new program that insures everybody and is, in effect, all things to all people: "The government's gonna pay for it. But we're going to save so much money on the other side. But for the most part it's going to be a private plan and people are going to be able to go out and negotiate great plans with lots of different competition with lots of competitors with great companies and they can have their doctors, they can have plans, they can have everything."[62] Never mind that a private plan paid for by the government sounded like a contradiction in terms or that it seemed similar to the ACA. In the end, when it came to repealing and replacing the ACA, he didn't have a plan after all, but simply left it up to Congress to figure out.

Overall, then, Trump capitalized on polarization and gridlock throughout his campaign. These were themes he milked for all they were worth. And he did so, again, with the expertise of a seasoned pitchman who had honed his skills in high-end real estate markets in New York City and around the world, and as a star on his own hit reality television show. As it turned out, millions of American voters loved him for it.

CONCLUSION

We have covered a lot of ground in this and the preceding chapters. And despite my effort to track the single red thread running through the argument, it remains a complicated story worth reviewing briefly to be sure that we have the full picture in view before we continue.

The story began with several simultaneously developing trends. First were the economic changes associated with the demise of the postwar Golden Age and the emergence of stagflation and global competition. This included the disappearance of good manufacturing jobs, wage stagnation, rising family debt, increased inequality, and reduced mobility that hit the working and middle classes hard. Second were changes in race and ethnic relations. Despite lagging in achieving the American Dream, African Americans, Hispanics, and Muslims were scapegoated for many of the country's economic and social ills. Scapegoating was made possible by deteriorating economic opportunities and America's long history of racism, but it was exacerbated by politicians as a ploy to win voters, and then by immigration and the 9/11 terrorist attacks. Third were ideological changes, notably the development of the neoliberal policy paradigm that also resulted from the country's economic problems, and that helped push many people's thinking in a more conservative direction. Neoliberalism plus long-standing public sentiments, such as beliefs in small government and traditional family values, provided politicians with raw materials for framing their increasingly conservative messages. Fourth, these three trends flowed together to help generate a rising tide of political polarization as both Republicans and Democrats shifted to the right but in different degrees so that the political distance between them expanded. Finally, when the financial crisis hit and the Obama administration came to power, polarization overflowed, drowning Washington in gridlock. Trump took advantage of all of this. He blamed lousy trade agreements, unfair foreign competition, minorities, immigration, and inept and corrupt politicians. He played on the public's suffering, anxieties, disgust, and discontent with politics-as-usual, often capitalizing on their misperceptions and misunderstandings, as well as their values and beliefs. He often distorted and misrepresented the facts. And he promised to fix everything and "Make America Great Again."

In sum, Donald Trump came along at just the right time to cash in politically on everything I have described. His candidacy was only the tip of a huge iceberg that had been developing for decades. On Election Day, November 8, 2016, that iceberg crashed into the political status quo, sending shock waves across America.

CHAPTER 8

The Election and American Politics in Perspective

Sometimes long shots win. In 1913, Donerail galloped out of the starting gate at the Kentucky Derby as a ninety-one–to–one long shot. A little more than two minutes later, he paid $184.90 on a $2.00 bet—the longest long-shot win in Derby history and a complete shock to everyone at Churchill Downs watching the race that day.

Election night 2016 was a shock to many people too. Almost all the public opinion polling predicted that Hillary Clinton would win the presidency. She led by only 2 or 3 percent in most polls, but most people believed that she had a safe lead in the Electoral College bolstered by a firewall of blue states in the upper Midwestern Rustbelt and a few others like Pennsylvania and Florida. Odds Shark, an online betting site, gave her a 75 percent chance of winning.[1] Trump seemed like a long shot. But by midnight it had become clear that he had breached the firewall and won several states the Democrats had assumed they would win. Clinton won nearly three million more votes than Trump, but he carried the Electoral College and grabbed the brass ring. I have tried to explain why. But the proof is in the pudding, and in this case the pudding is the presidential election exit poll data.

Exit polling shows that Trump's campaign resonated strongly with the fears and anxieties of the American public, which stemmed from the trends I have described. First, consider the economy as discussed in chapter 3. His major campaign theme "Make America Great Again" was in part a promise to revitalize the economy and create more jobs for Americans—a clear reference to the wage stagnation and overwork of recent decades, as well as people's concerns for the economic future of themselves and their kids. He also promised to foster an environment where more and more Americans could become richer, which would presumably help reduce household debt and income inequality and enable more Americans to achieve the American Dream. Table 8.1 reports CNN exit polling based on a sample of 24,537 respondents from 350 voting places across the country on Election Day, and 4,398 telephone interviews with early and absentee voters.[2] It shows that two-thirds of those people who worried that the economy was in poor shape flocked to Trump, while nearly three-quarters of those who thought the economy was in good shape went to Clinton. Trump had clearly seized on an issue of great concern to the public. Furthermore, although the differences were not as large in terms of which income groups tended to support Trump and Clinton, he won nearly two-thirds of the votes of people who felt that life for the next generation would be worse than today. Put differently, it was not class per se that mattered as much as people's perceptions about the prospects of moving to a different class—that is, intergenerational mobility.* Trump also won roughly two-thirds of the votes of people who believed that international trade takes away American jobs, another major campaign theme for him.

Let's take a closer look at the issue of class. Many people, including Bernie Sanders, have argued that Trump won because he had the support of working-class voters.[3] In fact, according to the CNN data, Trump had a bit more support from people with incomes over $50,000 per year than from people with incomes under that. That is, richer rather than poorer people tended to vote for Trump, but the difference wasn't great.[4] This does not mean, however, that economic issues didn't matter, which is the conclusion that some people seem to have drawn who, for example, argue that racial resentment rather than economic anxiety or class was the key factor delivering Trump his victory.[5] For one thing, as just noted, people who were pessimistic about the next generation's economic future supported Trump. For another thing, disentangling economic and racial effects is very tricky. There is a very long history of economically driven racism in the United States. This includes unions refusing to allow African Americans to join their ranks and segregating jobs for different ethnic groups. It also includes companies hiring black or ethnic minorities as strikebreakers in a divide-and-conquer strategy for breaking the back of working-class solidarity.[6] And as I showed in earlier chapters, since the 1970s, there has been lots

* Trump's support during the campaign covered a wide range of income and demographic types. However, those most likely to support his campaign were people with less than a high school education; reporting ancestry as simply "American"; living in a mobile home; working in "old economy" jobs like agriculture, construction, manufacturing, and trade; having a history of voting for segregationists; being unemployed; being born in the United States; being an evangelical Christian; having a history of voting for liberal Republicans; and being a white Anglo-Saxon Protestant (Irwin and Katz 2016).

Table 8.1 CNN PRESIDENTIAL EXIT POLL RESULTS

	Percent Support for Clinton	Percent Support for Trump
Condition of national economy:		
Good	77	18
Poor	31	63
Income:		
$50,000 or less per year	52	41
$50,000 or more per year	47	49
Life for the next generation of Americans will be:		
Better than today	59	38
Worse than today	31	63
About the same as today	54	39
Effect of international trade:		
Creates US jobs	59	35
Takes away US jobs	31	65
Does not affect jobs	63	30
Terrorism is a big problem for the country:	39	57
Race:		
White	37	58
White men	31	63
White women	43	53
Nonwhite	74	21
Black	88	8
Latino	65	29
Illegal immigrants working in the United States should be:		
Offered legal status	60	34
Deported to home country	14	84
Education:		
College graduate	52	43
Did not graduate from college	44	52
Age:		
18–29 years	55	37
30–44 years	50	42
45–64 years	44	53
65 and older	45	53
Ideology:		
Liberal	84	10
Moderate	52	41
Conservative	15	81

(*continued*)

Table 8.1 CONTINUED

	Percent Support for Clinton	Percent Support for Trump
Religion:		
White born-again/evangelical Christian	16	81
Protestant	37	60
Catholic	45	52
Other Christian	43	55
Jewish	71	24
Feelings about the federal government:		
Enthusiastic/satisfied	76	20
Dissatisfied/angry	36	58
Opinions of Obama as president:		
Approve	84	10
Disapprove	6	90
View of the Affordable Care Act:		
Did not go far enough	78	18
Was about right	82	10
Went too far	13	83
Financial situation compared to four years ago:		
Better today	72	24
Worse today	19	78
About the same	46	46

Source: CNN 2016.

of racial and ethnic scapegoating by people who believe they have lost out economically to people from racial and ethnic groups other than their own. Indeed, scapegoating like this is exactly what Trump did, particularly by accusing Mexicans of taking jobs from Americans.

Insofar as race and immigration, the subjects of chapter 4, are concerned Trump promised to crack down on immigration by preventing Muslims who posed a terrorist threat from entering the country, and to build a wall along the Mexican border to keep out immigrants who were criminals or intended to take American jobs. His pitch built on America's recent fears of terrorism, its longer history of racism, and people's misunderstanding of the real causes of unemployment and economic hardship for the middle and working classes. It all worked to his benefit. For instance, 57 percent of those who felt that terrorism was a big problem for the country voted for Trump, but only 39 percent of them voted for Clinton. Given Trump's pandering to issues of race, we shouldn't be surprised that he won 58 percent of the white vote, while Clinton won a whopping 74 percent of the nonwhite vote. This is consistent with other studies, which have shown that people who frowned on racial diversity in America were much more likely to vote for Trump than people who looked kindly upon it.[7] Additionally, analyses of data from the American National Election Survey found that people's perceptions of race were more highly correlated with who they voted for in 2016 than in any presidential election in nearly thirty years. For instance, people who believed that African Americans should not get any special favors to work their way up in society or who felt that if blacks only tried harder they would be just as well off as whites were far more likely to vote for Trump than Clinton.[8] Notably, nearly two-thirds of white men voted for him. But more than half of the white women did too, which might be surprising considering his sexist and misogynist remarks during the campaign—that is, until we remember that his attitudes toward gender issues resonated with conservative family values, something we will return to in a minute. Given all this, it is no wonder that Trump had the support of so many members of the Tea Party and a variety of right-wing extremists, including David Duke, a former Imperial Wizard of the Ku Klux Klan. Trump's disparaging comments about African Americans certainly contributed to his loss of the African American vote—Clinton won 88 percent, while Trump got only 8 percent.

We have seen that racial issues also intersected with slowly developing demographic trends. Trump's condemnation of Hispanic immigration as a growing threat to Americans undoubtedly explains why he won less than a third of the Hispanic vote to Clinton's two-thirds. Of course, the relationships between demographic change, race, and economic concerns are intertwined in complex ways, but they help account for the fact that 84 percent of those who felt that undocumented immigrants working in the United States should be deported voted for Trump, presumably because they thought immigrants were taking jobs away from Americans or threatening national security.

The CNN data in Table 8.1 also show that relatively less educated people tended to vote for Trump, which may signal that the fake news and alternative fact echo chamber worked to his advantage. In more detailed CNN data reported elsewhere, a formidable 67 percent of whites without a college degree went for Trump—fourteen points more than Mitt Romney won as the Republican candidate in the previous presidential election.[9] Some people believe that this was the critical swing vote that ultimately gave Trump his victory.[10] The age structure of the electorate mattered too. Older voters were more likely to vote for Trump; younger voters were more apt to support Clinton—perhaps an indication that people nearing retirement were concerned about their finances and the general state of the economy.

It's not surprising given the arguments presented in chapter 5 that ideas and ideology were also important. Trump appealed to the conservatives with considerable effect, winning 81 percent of the conservative vote. It is worth mentioning that 35 percent of those polled by CNN said they were conservative, while only 26 percent said they were liberal—a manifestation of the rightward shift in American politics described in chapter 6. Equally telling was Trump's appeal to Christians and especially white evangelicals, who supported him by an overwhelming margin, 81 percent to 16 percent. Despite the declining influence of the Moral Majority, the religious Right remains a powerful force in American politics that he exploited. Returning to my earlier point, this may help explain why so many white women voted for Trump—they accepted as part of the traditional family values frame not only that men might act boorishly toward women but also that it might be acceptable, or at least not something to get terribly upset about.

Chapter 7 showed that Trump, the self-professed antiestablishment outsider, promised to overcome political polarization and gridlock, and get government in Washington back on the right track because he knew how to drain the swamp. In a similar vein, by using his own fortune to finance his campaign, he claimed that he could not be bought by corporate or other interests that had corrupted the political system through exorbitant spending on political campaigns and lobbying. These arguments seemed to resonate with voters too. The public's dissatisfaction with gridlock in Washington was evident in the voting. Fifty-eight percent of those who felt dissatisfied or angry with the federal government went for Trump, while 76 percent of those who felt enthusiastic or satisfied with it supported Clinton.

I also argued in chapter 7 that Trump tried to capitalize on events during Obama's presidency that finally turned political polarization into gridlock. Exit polls support this too. Table 8.1 shows that an overwhelming 90 percent of those disapproving of Obama's presidency voted for Trump, while 84 percent of those who approved of his presidency voted for Clinton. And 83 percent of those who believed that the Affordable Care Act—the lightning rod that energized the Tea Party—had gone too far supported Trump, while 78 percent of those who believed it hadn't gone far enough supported Clinton. Lingering concerns about the financial crisis also came into play. Seventy-eight percent of those worried that the financial situation of the country was worse than it was four years ago voted for Trump.

One question will plague researchers, pundits, and political operatives for years to come about this election: why did the results come as such a surprise to so many presumably well-informed and astute observers? For one thing, we seem to have forgotten our own history. After all, this wasn't the first time that a populist politician mounted a serious challenge to the political establishment. The Democratic Party's William Jennings Bryan ran for president in 1896 on a platform that included several populist planks. Huey Long—the Kingfish from Louisiana—was poised to challenge Roosevelt for the presidency in 1936 on a populist platform before being assassinated. Alabama's George Wallace ran strong populist campaigns too in the 1960s and early 1970s. So did Pat Buchanan, who ran for the Republican nomination in 1992 and 1996, and Ross Perot, who ran as an independent in 1992. Of course, Bernie Sanders mounted a strong populist challenge to Hillary Clinton in 2016 for the Democratic nomination. Trump's campaign was populist too, especially on trade issues. Indeed, Perot, Sanders, and Trump all attacked the North American Free Trade Agreement (NAFTA) as a job killer for American workers.[11] We should have seen this coming.

For another thing, many observers and pundits lost touch with the average American voter. A few excellent books have been published lately based on in-depth conversations with working- and middle-class men and women around the country. They reveal that there were growing segments of the working and middle classes that were becoming increasingly disgruntled thanks particularly to the economic trials and tribulations they have endured since the 1970s. These books also show that people became fed up with the political status quo and were ready for change, even if it meant voting against their own economic interests.[12] J. D. Vance's *Hillbilly Elegy*, for instance, tells how working-class folks in Kentucky and Ohio felt trapped "in an economy that failed to deliver the most basic promise of the American Dream—a steady wage." But they also simply hated Barack Obama and were deeply skeptical of the most basic institutions in society, including the mainstream television news programs, universities, and government, not to mention politicians.[13] Research on other countries also shows that when people begin to distrust government institutions, the door swings open for populist upheaval, especially when economic times have been tough for a while.[14] I'll have more to say about this later. The point is that fine-grained studies like these show that intellectuals who study politics would do well to get out and talk to the electorate more often.

Several things are especially important about the election's outcome. First, even if Trump's success stemmed partly from the more proximate factors I reviewed in chapter 1, such as his media-savvy experience, FBI concerns about Clinton's private email server, or the brilliance or ineptitude of campaign strategies, there was far more to it than this. Trump's victory owed much to the deep-seated trends I have described. It benefited from and fed off the gradual confluence of economic, racial, ideological, and political changes spanning decades in the United States. This is why it is difficult to boil Trump's victory down to a single factor regardless of whether it is class, economic anxiety, race, or something else.

Second, Trump's victory was teeming with irony. Even though many mainstream Republicans opposed his candidacy, Trump's ascendance was partly the culmination of forces set in motion long ago by Republicans themselves. One was the Republicans' aggressive and heavily financed advocacy of neoliberalism, which contributed so much to policies during and after the Reagan years, including the easing of regulatory oversight of banking and financial services that led to the financial crisis that helped propel Trump to the White House. Another was the racism associated with the Republicans' Southern Strategy, which also benefited Trump's campaign. In fact, some Republicans, including both former Bush presidents and Mitt Romney, were so appalled during the campaign by his racist and xenophobic remarks that they repudiated him. And several big Republican donors, the Koch brothers among them, decided to spend their money on Republicans running for legislative offices instead of him. The ranks of the Republican Party were never so divided over a presidential candidate in the last half century.

Third, it does not appear that Trump's victory will lay polarization and gridlock to rest anytime soon. Despite his promises to unify the country, the prospects look grim. In addition to the deep divisions now within the Republican Party, the Democratic Party is split, although not as severely, between the liberal Sanders wing and the moderate Clinton wing. The public remains divided too, which is why after Trump's inauguration millions of people marched in cities and towns across the country protesting against him. I was in Montpelier, Vermont's state capital, that day where an estimated 17,250 people turned out—roughly two and a half times the city's population.[15] State troopers temporarily closed three exits on the interstate highway when it became obvious that the town couldn't hold more cars. Bernie Sanders made a surprise appearance speaking to the crowd from the steps of the golden-domed state house, urging people to continue the struggle after the march was over, and calling Trump "a fraud" in no uncertain terms. The implication of Sanders's remark was clear: millions of American voters had been duped—bamboozled—by Trump and his campaign. Another set of rallies occurred in April where scientists across the country protested Trump's denial of climate change and his general disregard of scientific facts, data, and truthfulness.

Finally, Trump's victory marked one of the most significant power shifts in Washington since World War II. The Republicans retained control of both houses of Congress. And Trump moved quickly to nominate a very conservative judge, Neil Gorsuch, to the Supreme Court. Gorsuch could very well push the court to the right just as his predecessor, Antonin Scalia, did.

But Democrats and even some Republicans worried that the American system of checks and balances might be on shaky ground given Trump's authoritarian tendencies. I was at a panel discussion at the Brookings Institution the day after the election. Everyone on the panel, Republicans and Democrats alike, agreed that the Trump administration would be a real test of the Constitution and the separation of powers. It soon turned out that they were right. Only six months into his presidency, the courts had blocked Trump's executive orders restricting immigration. They argued that his orders violated the Constitution. In addition, Congress planned to impose sanctions on Russia for meddling in the 2016 election—a direct challenge to Trump's presidential foreign policy prerogatives. And after listening to Trump complain for weeks about former FBI director Robert Mueller, who was now the special prosecutor investigating possible collusion between the Russians and the Trump campaign, Congress warned that there would be serious consequences if Trump tried to fire Mueller as he seemed to be threatening. Republican Senator Lindsey Graham said, "Any effort to go after Mueller could be the beginning of the end of the Trump presidency unless Mueller did something wrong." Democratic Senator Ed Markey concurred, adding, "Honestly, it'd be a full blown constitutional crisis." Graham went so far as to outline bipartisan legislation that would block Trump from firing Mueller without a judicial review first.[16] There was more, but the point is that politics in Washington had taken a strange and in many people's eyes a very dangerous turn.

In short, the 2016 presidential election was unique. Its ramifications for public policy and the American political system will be with us for years, even if it is not clear yet what they will be. What is clear, however, is that the election also crystalized a new form of American politics.

THE NEW AMERICAN POLITICS

At the risk of oversimplification, the fundamental battle lines of postwar US politics pitted the Left against the Right. The Left in varying degrees favored Keynesian government intervention, including welfare state expansion and higher taxes, while the Right favored the opposite. Many liberals, unions, African Americans, and other minorities supported the Left, while conservatives, business, and relatively affluent white people supported the Right. So, to a considerable extent, the politics of race were tied closely to the traditional left–right distinction.

One thing that was especially pronounced about the 2016 presidential election was the populist streak that ran through it. Trump's campaign was rooted in right-wing populist rhetoric about the evils of big government and

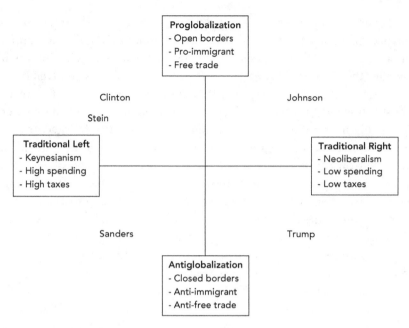

Figure 8.1:
The new American politics.

freeloaders taking advantage of government largesse. In contrast, Bernie Sanders offered a left-wing populist alternative during the Democratic primaries, condemning big banks, big corporations, and the richest 1 percent of Americans for the nation's troubles. But there was more to it than that.

Although populism has been around for a long time, traditional populist appeals focused typically on domestic villains. Now foreign ones were targeted too. Put differently, in addition to the traditional left–right dimension in American politics, we now have a pro- and antiglobalization dimension. The second is orthogonal to the first as Figure 8.1 illustrates with reference to several candidates involved in the 2016 election. Trump capitalized on an antiglobalization nationalist platform favoring trade protectionism, anti-immigration policies, and isolationism. By some accounts, Trump's victory in the all-important states of Ohio and Pennsylvania stemmed mainly from the defection of white working-class voters from the Democratic Party who lived in areas that were "the epicenter of the revolt against globalization" thanks to job flight to Mexico and elsewhere.[17] Bernie Sanders was also antiglobalization—he too believed that globalization had cost Americans thousands of jobs. The difference, of course, was that Trump was farther to the right, while Sanders was much farther to the left. And Sanders detested Trump's racism, nationalism, xenophobia, and sexism. Hillary Clinton did too but was proglobalization insofar as she was supportive of international trade agreements and less isolationist than Trump in foreign policy matters—she never suggested revisiting America's commitment to NAFTA and the North Atlantic Treaty Organization (NATO), whereas Trump did. She was also more to the left than Trump on many economic and social issues. Jill Stein, the Green Party candidate, was on the proglobalization left too, supporting international cooperation on environmental and climate change issues. Gary Johnson, the Libertarian Party candidate, was on the proglobalization right, favoring free trade and neoliberalism. Had a traditional Republican neoconservative like former president George W. Bush been in the race favoring aggressive US foreign policy, he or she would have shared the proglobalization right-wing space with Johnson. That right-wing libertarians oppose Trump's antiglobalization protectionism became clear after the election. The wealthy Koch brothers and a host of conservative organizations launched a furious campaign to stop Trump and the House Republicans from imposing border taxes on various goods coming into the United States.[18]

Whereas racism had been linked historically to the traditional left–right dimension in American politics, it has now been partly detached thanks to the emergence of the globalization issue. The anti-immigration view, at least as represented by Trump, focuses on Hispanic and Muslim immigrants. The proglobalization view is significantly more tolerant, refusing, for instance, to consider mass deportations of undocumented foreigners, which Trump promised. The proglobalization view also recognizes that the United States doesn't have enough home-grown workers in agriculture, information technology, biotechnology, and other sectors of the economy, and therefore needs immigrants to fill those jobs.

Both the Republican and Democratic Parties will have to sort out how they navigate this new and more complicated terrain of American politics. Insofar as the Republicans are concerned, the Trump wing of the Republican Party can expect resistance from the neoconservatives, who oppose antiglobal isolationism and favor an expansionist foreign policy. As noted, many Republicans also oppose trade protectionism, which flies in the face of neoliberalism. The renegade Tea Party faction in Congress is deeply committed to neoliberalism, especially the Freedom Caucus in the House, and not inclined to compromise on much of anything. Complicating matters further, minority groups continue to constitute an ever-larger proportion of the electorate, which means that sticking with anti-immigrant and racially charged policies will be increasingly risky for the Republicans if they want to continue winning elections. How all this gets resolved is anyone's guess. Maybe the Tea Party Movement will give rise to a real independent third party in American politics, something that might become institutionally more likely if states continue to shift to a proportional system of distributing Electoral College votes, as a few have done recently. Or maybe moderate Republicans will break away and form their own new party. But I doubt it. Another possibility is that the Tea Party Movement will eventually run out of steam, creating more opportunity for moderation within the party and in Congress. But for the moment, that doesn't seem likely either.

The Democrats have problems of their own. Given Clinton's defeat, the Democrats will have to reconcile demands from the moderate wing of their party with the Sanders wing in terms of how they want to handle the globalization issues and how far left they are willing to go on other issues. Regardless of how they do this, hope for the Democrats may come from the growing number of minority voters who typically favor the Democratic Party and from the fact that the millennial generation, which so far tends to vote Democrat, will replace the baby boom generation, many of whom have grown more conservative in their old age. Of course, both parties' fortunes will also depend on the ability of Trump and the rest of the Republicans to deliver on their campaign promises.

EUROPEAN SIMILARITIES AND DIFFERENCES

Europe has also undergone a Trump-like political metamorphosis with strong antiglobalization, populist colorings. France, Switzerland, Denmark, Germany, the Netherlands, Belgium, Poland, Hungary, and a few other countries have all recently experienced the emergence of nationalist, xenophobic, anti-immigrant political parties and movements. Greece, for instance, witnessed the rise of the neo-Nazi Golden Dawn Party on the far right. France has Marine Le Pen's National Front—a party that has mellowed a bit since she took it over from her father, Jean-Marie, but still one with xenophobic and occasionally racist tendencies. In the Netherlands, Geert Wilders's Party for Freedom, a Dutch nationalist and right-wing populist party founded in 2006, became the fifth-largest party in the House of Representatives that year, moved up to be the second largest in 2017, and came in third in the 2014 European Parliament election. In Austria, Norbert Hofer, a gun-toting, anti-immigrant leader of the right-wing nationalist Freedom Party, just barely lost a runoff election in 2016 for the presidency. The margin of victory for his opponent was razor thin—a mere 31,000 votes out of 4.6 million votes cast. Switzerland's nationalist People's Party, led by Christian Blocher and opposing immigrant rights of various sorts, won two of the seven seats on the Swiss Federal Council. The Danish People's Party has also campaigned with considerable success on an anti-immigration platform calling for tougher border controls, further restrictions on immigration, and limited social benefits for immigrants. Since

2000, the People's Party has been a crucial supporter of several Danish coalition governments. And in Germany, the nationalist anti-immigrant and anti-Europe Alternative for Germany (AfD) won a surprising 13 percent of the vote in elections in October 2017. With policy positions resembling Le Pen's National Front, the AfD entered Parliament for the first time ever as the third largest party in the legislature, next only to Angela Merkel's Christian Democratic Union and the Social Democratic Party.

Unlike the AfD, which was founded in 2013, some of these parties have been around for a while, like the Danish People's Party, which was born in 1995 as a spinoff of the Progress Party founded in 1973. France's National Front was founded in 1972. The longevity of these parties stems from the fact that European countries have multiparty proportional systems of representation where political parties can win seats in the legislature by securing only a small fraction of the vote. In the United States, it's a winner-take-all game. Typically, if your party doesn't get a clear majority of the vote, it wins nothing. This is one reason populist parties of the past in America have been so short lived. But another reason for the longevity of European populist parties is that many of them support generous welfare programs—if immigrants and asylum seekers aren't allowed to freeload off them. This distinguishes European populism from Trump's version. Examples include the Danish People's Party, the Norwegian Progress Party, France's National Front, and Austria's Freedom Party, which was once neoliberal in orientation but since the early 1990s much less so. In fact, some European populist parties emerged in the first place thanks in part to the demise of the Soviet Union and in turn the weakening of the Communist and Socialist Parties in their own countries, which created political openings for new left-wing parties—including nationalist and populist ones—to represent the working class.[19]

There is, however, one additional and very big difference between the European and American situations when it comes to issues of globalization and populism: sovereignty, the capacity for countries to govern themselves. In Europe, antiglobalization populism is very much a reaction against the European Union and the European Monetary Union, often called Euroscepticism. The concern is that Europeanization threatens national sovereignty. EU members relinquish much control over the movement of people, goods, services, and capital across borders from their national capitals to the European Union in Brussels. For instance, the anti-immigration movement in Europe is tied to the broader issue of Europeanization because rising immigration stems to a significant degree from EU rules permitting the free movement of people among member countries. This is one reason the recent Syrian refugee crisis has wrought such political havoc in Europe—once accepted into the European Union, refugees can move around more or less as they wish.

But there are also plenty of other examples of how sovereignty, populism, and Euroscepticism are intertwined. Greece's left-leaning populist Syriza Party came to power in 2015 due to concerns about sovereignty and its membership in the European Monetary Union. Greece had been hammered by austerity policies forced down its throat by the Troika—the European Central Bank, European Commission, and International Monetary Fund (IMF)—when Greece ran into serious debt and deficit problems after the 2008 financial crisis. Greeks were incensed that membership in the Eurozone had led to this.[20] Similarly, in Spain, the leftist Podemos Party railed against European-imposed austerity policies that drove unemployment rates above 20 percent by 2015. In both countries, there was talk of leaving the Eurozone and going it alone. The United States faces nothing like this in terms of having its sovereignty compromised. As sociologist Patrick Le Galès has argued, "Election after election, those [populist] parties are gaining ground at the local, regional, EU and national level by attacking immigration, the EU and singing the praise of sovereign nations."[21]

Britain's decision to leave the European Union, known as Brexit, in a national referendum held in June 2016 illustrates Le Galès's point especially well. Slightly more than 51 percent of voters opted to leave the European Union, while 48 percent wanted to remain. The UK Independence Party (UKIP), a right-wing populist party founded in 1993 and headed eventually by Nigel Farage, led the "Leave" campaign stressing an anti-immigrant platform. The UKIP was a reformed version of the Anti-Federalist League, established in 1991 shortly after the Maastricht Treaty paved the way for Europe's adoption of the euro as its common currency. Britain, of course, chose not to enter the Eurozone. Nevertheless, the Brexit vote turned largely on issues of ethic nationalism, economic protectionism, and sovereignty more generally. Many in favor of Brexit wondered why they should obey laws they didn't make or politicians they didn't elect. Prime Minister Theresa May captured much of this sentiment in her disparaging remark about EU membership when she said, "If you believe you are a citizen of the world, you are a citizen of nowhere."

Sovereignty was not an issue in the Trump campaign, but there were still similarities with Brexit. Both Brexit and Trump supporters were prone to xenophobic and economic nationalism, disdain for conventional political elites, and distrust of traditional forms of professional political expertise. Moreover, supporters of both campaigns often hailed from either semirural areas or those in industrial decline, feared for their kids' futures, and worried about the loss of national cultural traditions.[22] Furthermore, people supporting the Leave position tended to be less educated, older, retired, Christian, and either manual workers or unemployed, much like many of

Trump's supporters. This profile resembles many Eurosceptics in other countries too.[23] Like Trump's supporters, those backing the Leave campaign were also likely to see multiculturalism, feminism, the green movement, globalization, and, as noted, immigration as forces for ill. Indeed, Brexit seems to have unleashed particularly nasty racist sentiment in Britain judging from the rise in hate crimes following the vote.[24] As in the United States, much of this is also associated with the decline of unions, which goes hand in hand with the loss of good manufacturing jobs and the collapse of large-scale factory employment. Today only about 15 percent of private sector workers in Britain belong to a union. The demise of coal mining is another similarity between the two countries insofar as displaced miners supported Brexit and Trump.[25] So is rising economic inequality, driven in part by the forces of globalization, as well as neoliberal cuts in welfare expenditures, which added fuel to the Leave and Trump campaigns.[26]

Anti-intellectualism also played an important role in the Brexit referendum. The intellectual elite failed to make themselves heard above the cantankerous noise of both the Leave and Remain sides in the campaign. The result was that the public was vulnerable to lots of misinformation and lies about the need for and possible consequences of either leaving or staying in the European Union. As we have seen, disdain for intellectuals and the rise of alternative facts were hallmarks of the Trump campaign too.[27]

The possibility for Britain to leave the European Union emerged in the first place when Prime Minister David Cameron called for the referendum. His plan was to use it to constrain the right wing of his Conservative Party and stem the rising UKIP tide. His bet that the referendum would be voted down and the UKIP would fade away failed in spectacular fashion and he resigned soon thereafter in ignominious defeat. Here too there are similarities between Britain and the United States. After all, whereas Cameron tried to appease the Far Right, Trump appealed to the Tea Party and the rest of the so-called alt-Right in America. Moreover, dog whistle politics were on display in Britain just as they had been historically in the United States. The UKIP created an infamous poster depicting immigrants on the march—a condensed visualization of anti-immigrant nationalism that had been a political issue for years in Britain. The issue was receiving heightened attention because of rising immigration whereby many British workers were having to compete with workers from poorer EU countries at the deteriorating bottom of the labor market. The Leave campaign also frequently referred to an imaginary Polish plumber who slipped into Britain, sapped the welfare state, and deprived British plumbers of work by getting paid under the table—a framing tactic reminiscent of US politicians' references to the fictitious welfare queen who created problems for the working class. So, as in America, economic and demographic trends mixed with issues of race and ethnicity to create a toxic populist brew that grew worse following the 2008 financial crisis. Brexit may have been a political accident, but it was an accident waiting to happen—much like Trump's rise to power in America was the result of the long-developing trends that he happened to exploit.[28]

That much of what is happening in Europe stems from the tension between pro- and antiglobalization sentiments with an emphasis on sovereignty and the European Union was also evident in the 2017 national elections in France. The National Front's Marine Le Pen finished second in the first round of voting with a little over 21 percent of the vote in a field of eleven, forcing a second-round runoff election. Her speeches were filled with rhetoric about the need to regain France's sovereignty. She wanted to impose protectionist trade barriers; cut immigration from sixty-five thousand to ten thousand per year; tax firms that hire foreigners; and hold a referendum on withdrawal from the European Union, just like the British did. She said she would close mosques suspected of radicalism and deport foreigners suspected of jihadist connections. Le Pen was also a great admirer of Vladimir Putin, much like Trump, and wanted to strengthen ties between France and Russia. She regularly derided the first-round winner and her opponent in the second round, Emmanuel Macron, who won 24 percent of the first-round vote. Le Pen portrayed him as the candidate of the banks operating against the interests of the French people—rhetoric eerily reminiscent of American populism in the late nineteenth and early twentieth centuries, not to mention in Sanders's recent anti–Wall Street crusade. Indeed, Le Pen's campaign slogan, "In the Name of the People," was pure populism. Macron, a pro-EU investment banker, had come out of nowhere as a political novice when the leading candidate, François Fillon, was brought down by a corruption scandal.[29] In fact, neither the traditional left-wing nor right-wing parties, the Socialists and Republicans, made the second round of voting. This was the first time this had happened since the founding of the Fifth Republic in 1958. Macron had formed his own eclectic party blending traditional left and right policy positions.

According to Bruno Cautrès, a political analyst, the fact that both Le Pen and Macron were from outside the traditional left–right party structure meant that "France is going through deep political tensions: clashes over the global economy, the integration of France into the global economy and into Europe." Globalization with the EU focus has now become a second dimension of French politics cross-cutting the old left–right axis.[30] According to both Le Pen and Macron, what matters in French politics these days is not whether you are on the left or right, but whether you are a nationalist or globalist.[31]

Ultimately, Le Pen lost to Macron in the second round by a formidable two-to-one margin. But she still won 34 percent of the vote, suggesting that the people's xenophobic and Eurosceptic concerns are not going away anytime soon. This is reinforced by the fact that since 2005, the number of votes the National Front has won has been rising in regional, legislative, presidential, and European elections.[32]

As in the Trump and Brexit cases, Le Pen's strong showing also reflected tough underlying economic realities, as well as racial and other social tensions between those for and against globalization. Unemployment in France had been above 10 percent since 2012, and twice that for young people. Economic growth was slow, which meant that tax revenue was not sufficient to pay for all the public services to which voters were accustomed. In the first round, she won the traditionally conservative southern strongholds, as well as much of the French rustbelt in the north and east. She also did well among voters in the rural and semirural areas that had lost jobs, shops, and services, and among less educated voters. Anti-immigrant, racial, and religious tensions, already running high in France, which has the second largest Muslim population in Europe, were exacerbated by recent jihadist attacks in Paris and Nice and gave her further political ammunition for attacking her opponents and blasting the European Union. By some accounts, anti-EU sentiment in the run-up to the French election was even stronger than it was in Britain prior to their referendum. Moreover, her performance was so strong that, according to an analysis by *The Economist*, if France had a winner-take-all Electoral College like America's, she would have won the presidency.[33]

In France and Britain, the events just described threw conventional politics into chaos. Traditional parties on the left and right are scrambling to make sense of what happened and, in some cases, overhaul themselves to restore their competitive edge. As I suggested previously, something similar is happening to the Republican and Democratic Parties in the United States. I am confident that the new globalization dimension in American politics is here to stay. It took a while to emerge compared to the European variant, which has been around in one form or another for decades. This is because ever since World War II, the European economies have been more open and exposed to globalization than the US economy. But the American economy has become more open and exposed since the 1970s. So, if Europe is any indication, we can expect similar longevity for this new form of politics in America.

The similarities between Europe and the United States underscore a core part of my argument about the rise of Donald Trump. Just as Trump's victory cannot be boiled down to his talent as a pitchman, the populist antiglobalization insurgencies in Europe were not fundamentally the result of charismatic politicians. Instead, long-developing trends set the stage for these leaders to work their political magic. Neither Trump nor his European counterparts could have succeeded otherwise.

A big part of my argument has been that Trump benefited from a tipping point in American politics. Now that he is in office, we may face another one. As I mentioned briefly at the beginning of chapter 1, one reason his victory is so important is that it might undermine American hegemony.

In fact, even before Trump's election, several things—including some of those discussed in previous chapters—had been pushing the United States toward a tipping point beyond which its hegemony could be permanently compromised. One is increasing global competition from Western Europe and Japan during the 1970s and 1980s, and since then from a host of other countries, notably the BRICS (Brazil, Russia, India, China, and South Africa). Although still strong, America is no longer quite the overwhelming economic powerhouse in world markets it was during the Golden Age.

Another factor driving US hegemony toward a tipping point is America's ballooning national debt, which increased since the 1980s from 30 percent to about 100 percent of gross domestic product (GDP). But it isn't just debt per se that matters. At least as important are the political fights over raising the debt ceiling—fights that have been fueled by rising polarization and partisanship in Washington. As we have seen, this has already resulted in a downgrading of America's credit rating.[34] These things have started to undermine the dollar's preeminence as the world's reserve currency, one of the cornerstones of US economic and political hegemony.[35] If this continues, it could become more expensive for the United States to borrow. It could also erode America's influence abroad. Indeed, some countries have already made agreements to move away from using the dollar in international trade. In 2011, China and Japan agreed to direct currency convertibility, where their firms would no longer have to use the dollar as the medium of exchange when they did business with each other. That same year the BRICS announced an agreement where they would no longer require that members use dollars to facilitate trade within the group; they could use their own currencies instead. China and Russia have also forged a bilateral agreement permitting the use of their own currencies when trading with each other. Finally, the IMF added the Australian and Canadian dollars to its list of the world's safest currencies, which in addition to the US dollar already included the euro, British pound, Japanese yen, and Swiss franc. The idea was to guard against volatility in international markets that economic problems in the United States might trigger.[36]

US ideological hegemony has also been shaken. The 2008 world financial crisis stemmed in large part from neoliberal deregulation in American financial markets. Until the crisis, neoliberalism had become accepted to varying degrees in many countries as the appropriate approach for managing national economies. In the same vein, free trade agreements like NAFTA, the European Union, Mercosur in South America, and others were based on this doctrine. Few questioned any of this. But the financial crisis cast a shadow over neoliberalism, at least for a while, and led to tougher regulations governing banking and the financial services industries in many countries. It also led to tougher international regulatory norms—the Basel Accords—that specified, for example, how much capital banks should keep on hand to hedge against risk.

There are signs that American hegemony has been slipping in other areas too. America's ill-fated invasions of Iraq and Afghanistan, justified by faulty intelligence and the Bush administration's misrepresentation of facts to the international community, undermined US political legitimacy as a world power. The Obama administration did a lot to restore that legitimacy. Nevertheless, the United States has been at war in the Middle East for nearly fifteen years without accomplishing its nation-building goals, defeating the Islamic State in Iraq and Syria (ISIS), or bringing peace and stability to the region. The fact that the United States remains bogged down in that quagmire casts doubt on how effective American military might really is.

I am not suggesting that economic globalization, rising debt, continued political polarization, the weakening status of the dollar, the financial crisis, or prolonged fighting in the Middle East will inevitably destroy US hegemony. The sky is not falling. The US economy is still the biggest in terms of GDP and the most innovative in the world. The dollar is still strong. America continues to be a powerful player in international politics. And US military power remains unsurpassed.[37] However, it looks like the United States has been gravitating toward a tipping point where its hegemony can no longer be taken for granted.

Whether the Trump administration can maintain the country's hegemony is anyone's guess. It is not off to a good start. First, even before taking office, Trump stunned the Mexican government by promising not only that he would build a wall along the southern border to keep Mexicans from sneaking illegally into the United States but also that the Mexicans would pay for it. They were furious. Once elected, he quickly managed to say and do things that also alienated the Chinese, Russians, Australians, British, Germans, and Canadians, among others. He also inflamed tensions with North Korea by belittling its leader, Kim Jong Un, calling him "rocket man," and by threatening that if the North Korean government did not abandon its quest for nuclear weapons, the United States would unleash the full "fire and fury" of its military and "totally destroy" that rogue nation—threats that North Korea branded as tantamount to a declaration of war. Many observers took Trump's remarks to be a serious breach of diplomatic protocol and a sign that the United States was no longer acting rationally as a world leader. This does little to bolster America's hegemonic position in the world.

Second, Trump's promise to renegotiate NAFTA has upset its trading partners. So has its threat to deal with European countries not as an EU bloc but on an individual bilateral basis in matters of trade. None of this bodes well for the international free trade regime or America's leading role in it. Nor does the administration's threat to impose stiff import tariffs on its trading partners, such as China and Mexico, who do not in Trump's terms "deal fairly" with the United States. Indeed, the possibility that behavior like this could trigger a tit-for-tat trade war is all too reminiscent of the early part of the twentieth century where protectionism led to economic, political, and military disaster for much of the world. Christopher Hemmer and Peter Katzenstein, two highly regarded political scientists, have argued that effective multilateralism, and I would add bilateralism, requires respect for the identities of the partners involved.[38] In other words, racism and prejudice can undermine it. However, we saw plenty of both from the Trump campaign and even some from the White House since he took office. Despite Trump's frequent claims to be a fabulous dealmaker, this does not look promising for America's continued leadership on the world stage or its hegemony. This is especially true when it comes to "soft power," the ability to influence other governments and international organizations with persuasion, and leading by example rather than intimidation. As Jonathan Kirshner, an international relations expert, observes, "a little statesmanship and political functionality might go a long way."[39] So far, given Trump's knack for insulting foreign leaders, not to mention the level of polarization and gridlock in Washington, the Trump administration has demonstrated neither. The fact that he wants to cut funding and staff at the State Department is another indication that American soft power may be in jeopardy.[40]

Third, one cornerstone of Trump's campaign was the promise of deep supply-side tax cuts. Within months of taking office, he announced plans for an enormous reduction in the corporate income tax rate from 35 percent to 15 percent with promises that it would generate so much economic growth and additional revenue that it would not increase the size of the deficit. As noted, prominent economists on the left and right immediately warned that the growth rates he predicted were sheer fantasy and that implementation of his plan would add trillions of dollars to the national debt over the next decade.[41] If this happens, it will be not only another blow to America's economic hegemony but also another example of neoliberalism gone awry and, therefore, a blow to American ideological hegemony too.

Fourth, Trump's trip to Europe in May 2017—his first as president—hurt US political hegemony. At a NATO summit in Brussels and then a G-7 meeting in Italy, Trump alienated America's European allies in several ways.

One was lecturing NATO members on the need for them to meet their formal financial commitments to the alliance. Another was his refusal to publicly endorse NATO's Article 5, in which members agreed to come to each other's defense if attacked. The Trump administration's position on NATO is worrisome. If the United States pulls back on its commitment to the alliance, particularly in the face of Russia's incursion into the Crimea and escalating saber rattling elsewhere, it will forfeit much goodwill and leadership both politically and militarily on the European continent. America is, after all, the primary source of finance and military muscle for NATO. American isolationism could also embolden countries like Russia, North Korea, and Iran if they perceive that the United States is abdicating its role as the world's foremost policeman. Another point of alienation on his European trip was Trump's repeated warnings that the European Union needs to deal more fairly with the United States in trade. And a final point was Trump's refusal to endorse the Paris agreement on climate change, which included a pledge by the United States to limit greenhouse gas emissions—an agreement to which 195 countries had pledged their support. Once back at the White House, Trump formally announced that the United States would withdraw from that agreement. Considering all this, Germany's Chancellor Angela Merkel acknowledged the shift in US policy, intimating that it was the end of an era when the United States could be counted on for world leadership. As she put it, "I can only say that we Europeans must really take our fate into our own hands." The Trump administration denied it was stepping back from its leadership role, but a former US envoy to NATO disagreed, explaining:

> The president's failure to endorse Article 5 in a speech at NATO headquarters, his continued lambasting of Germany and other allies on trade, his apparent decision to walk away from the Paris climate agreement—all suggest that the United States is less interested in leading globally than has been the case for the last 70 years.[42]

This impression was borne out two months later by the United States' somewhat aloof behavior at a meeting of the G-20 countries.[43]

Trump's presidency is still only about six months old as I finish writing this book. But given what we have seen so far from the administration, US hegemony appears to be on shakier ground than it has been in a long time.

BAMBOOZLED OR NOT?

With all the talk of how prevalent alternative facts and fake news are nowadays, and how much of an impact they may have had on the election, one question still hangs in the air over everything I have argued. Were Trump's supporters bamboozled or not? That is, did they vote for him because they were suckered into believing the falsehoods, distortions, and fabrications that he uttered during the campaign? That's what Bernie Sanders suggested in Montpelier when he showed up at the women's march after Trump's inauguration. Or did people vote for him because they were hurting so much economically and so fed up with the political status quo that even though they saw through the deceit, they simply wanted an outsider promising fundamental change?

The answer is certainly both—some were duped while others were clear-eyed and placed their bets pragmatically. That's often the way of politics regardless of who wins the election. The Tea Party provides a clear window into this. On the one hand, we know, thanks to careful research by sociologists Theda Skocpol and Vanessa Williamson, that members of the Tea Party are often ill informed about specific policy issues that they care about, including the Affordable Care Act that they despise.[44] Many of them believed, for instance, that there would be "death panels" as Sarah Palin claimed incorrectly. This suggests that many people probably voted for Trump because they believed his erroneous statements. On the other hand, we also know that Tea Party activists were initially opposed to Trump because they didn't think he was a real conservative. In their view, he was a RINO—Republican in Name Only. But they eventually supported him once he won the Republican nomination because they hated Hillary Clinton, viewed the Democratic Party as a wedge for creeping socialism, and were disenchanted with the Republican establishment.[45] This implies that many people voted for him even though they may not have believed everything he said because he was a political renegade and because his election might provide them with an inroad to government that could prove useful later. There is evidence, for example, that activists opposed to immigration supported Trump hoping that his election would provide such inroads and were pleased initially at how many high-level government positions he filled with people who shared their views, such as Attorney General Jeff Sessions and several of Sessions's former Senate staff members.[46]

Regardless of whether people voted for Trump out of ignorance, desperation, pragmatism, wishful thinking, or something else, one thing is certain. He did not end up in the White House simply because he ran a better campaign than Clinton or caught a few breaks as the campaign unfolded. Nor did he win simply because he was Donald Trump. There was a lot more to it than that. Trump was the lucky beneficiary of sweeping trends and rising discontent decades in the making in American society. Until that discontent subsides, we will continue to experience plenty of political turbulence upon which Trump and others like him can capitalize.

Polarization and the Rightward Drift

There are several views on how and why polarization in America has shifted since World War II. Insofar as the public is concerned, a few people argue that there has not been much polarization at all.[1] Others disagree for various reasons. Some researchers maintain that conservatives moved farther to the right, while the liberals stayed more or less in the same place, so polarization increased.[2] Other researchers say that polarization increased because both groups moved in opposite directions, although some believe that the conservatives moved farther than the liberals, while others believe that the liberals moved farther than the conservatives.[3] What about the Republican and Democratic Parties—that is, the elites? Some scholars find that both parties moved to the right, with the Democrats moving farthest, thereby reducing polarization.[4] Some believe that they moved in opposite directions, increasing polarization.[5] This debate has been going on for years and is still not yet settled.

My view is this. Both liberals and conservatives in the electorate and both parties moved to the right on key issues, but the conservatives and Republican Party moved farther than the liberals and Democratic Party, thus increasing polarization overall.[6] Polarization was more pronounced between the two parties than within the public.

Much of the debate revolves around the quantitative analysis of public opinion polling data, congressional roll-call votes, and party platforms to determine how liberal or conservative voters and the Republican and Democratic Parties are; how they have changed both ideologically and with respect to specific issues; and how much party unity there is for and against various pieces of legislation. There is much to be said for this research, and on balance most researchers find that the two parties, if not always the public, have become more polarized. But why the lack of consistency across studies?

Sometimes it's like comparing apples and oranges. For instance, one person may examine trends in political party platforms, while another looks at roll-call votes. Somebody might examine how voters describe their general ideological orientation, while somebody else might look at their views on specific policy issues. Making matters worse, James Campbell points out that there are many tricky methodological problems with these data and their analysis.[7] I don't want to get into all of them here, but I do want to raise two important points to defend my position, particularly insofar as the quantitative evidence is so mixed and points in several directions.

First, what constitutes "liberal" or "moderate" or "conservative" views is not static; these views have shifted to the right since the 1960s, at least on most economic issues, the main focus of this book, for reasons laid out in chapter 5.[8] Put differently, neoliberalism tended to grip more and more people's imaginations. Indeed, as James Campbell acknowledges, the meaning attributed to ideological labels and policy issues evolves over time and may be quite different in different historical contexts. He and others have noted, for example, that the median voter, which I presume would call him- or herself a "moderate" regardless of when he or she was surveyed, has shifted significantly to the right since the 1960s.[9] On a more personal note, if given the choice of labeling myself a liberal, moderate, or conservative, my answer would be the same today as it was when I was in college in the early 1970s. I would describe myself as a liberal. But my opinions today, while still liberal, are more conservative than they were then. I suspect I am not alone. As noted in chapter 6, most people become more conservative as they get older. This would include that huge demographic bulge we call the baby boom generation, many of whom grew up in the 1960s like me but have mellowed a bit politically since then, and have become more materialistic and self-centered. Despite having a slight Democratic bias, they have grown more conservative in their voting habits, especially the white baby boomers.[10] Furthermore, even today not all liberals (or conservatives) are the same. My brand of liberalism is more social democratic in European terms than fiscally conservative, which puts me to the left of many other self-professed liberals in the Democratic Party. Indeed, most elections have races where there are a range of ideological positions on both the liberal and conservative sides. Ohio Governor John Kasich, for example, was less conservative than many others seeking the Republican nomination in 2016. Bernie Sanders was more liberal than Hillary Clinton that year in the Democratic primary.

Second, Democrats remain liberal on social issues but have become more conservative on fiscal and other economic issues since the mid-1970s. Consider the recent Democratic presidents. Lyndon Johnson had no qualms about running up deficits to pay for the Vietnam War. Compare that liberalism to Jimmy Carter's 1978 tax reform, a clear example of fiscal conservatism, or his moves to deregulate the airline industry and begin to deregulate trucking and telecommunications.[11] Bill Clinton and his "New Democrat" disciples were also to the right of Johnson, and even more so compared to George McGovern. After all, Johnson's Great Society initiative expanded social welfare programs, while Clinton, another Democratic president, cut them back, all the while proclaiming that he was "ending welfare as we know it." Indeed, Clinton and other centrists in the Democratic Party emphasized personal responsibility more than their predecessors as they reinvented the party along the lines of Tony Blair's New Labour Movement in Britain, which sought a "Third Way" between his party's traditional social democratic view and the neoliberalism of Margaret Thatcher's Conservative Party.[12] The rightward shift in the Democratic Party is also clear from Clinton's kowtowing to Wall Street interests in his pursuit of financial deregulation, including putting important parts of the financial services industry off limits to regulators, thereby helping to light the fuse that led to the financial crisis. Much of this was Clinton's reaction to the Republicans' big 1994 win recapturing the House with the promise of Newt Gingrich's "Contract with America"—an aggressive and starkly conservative ten-point action plan.[13] And Obama, a moderate to begin with, was pushed to the right by pressure from the Tea Party Movement.[14]

In Congress, Tip O'Neill, an old-school New Deal liberal who served as Speaker of the House in the 1970s and 1980s, was more to the left than Nancy Pelosi, another Democrat who held the post in the 2000s. Once she became Speaker, a fellow congressman remarked, "There isn't one shred of evidence that she's veered off to the left with the Democratic caucus. In fact, some of us on the left wish she would tilt a little more our way from time to time."[15]

There is additional evidence supporting my view that both Democrats and Republicans shifted to the right. Larry Bartels's research shows that public opinion generally shifted to the right on Obama's watch for two reasons: the recovery from the Great Recession was slower than most people wanted, and they felt that the administration had gone too far and too fast in its initiatives.[16] Insofar as the two parties are concerned, Stephanie Mudge has shown through an exhaustive analysis of political party platforms between 1945 and 2004 that both the Republican and Democratic Parties shifted in neoliberal directions beginning in the 1970s, as did most center-left and center-right parties in other advanced capitalist countries.[17] Similarly, Edward Ashbee reports that the Democratic Party bought into neoliberal austerity much like the Republicans in terms of macroeconomic policy, even though Republican intransigence prevented much compromise between the parties, especially during the Obama administration.[18]

Finally, evidence of a general rightward shift by the two parties is clear from the budget fights in Washington. The 2011 budget, for instance, pitted House Republicans against the Democratic Obama administration but with each side offering its own plan for performing major surgery on federal spending—both agreed that cuts were in order; the question was where and how deep to cut.[19] In the end, the general rightward shift should not be surprising. Observers conclude that Reagan's presidency and its shadow were so formidable "that all of his successors—including Obama—have been forced to conform more closely to Reagan's general economic vision than Reagan ever had to himself."[20]

NOTES

PREFACE

1. RealClear Politics 2017.
2. Rucker 2015.
3. Dann 2017; Gallup Polling 2017e.
4. Shear 2017.
5. Baker 2017.
6. https://twitter.com/trump_regrets

A NOTE ON SOURCES, ALTERNATIVE FACTS, AND FAKE NEWS

1. Pete Townsend. 1971. "Won't Get Fooled Again." From the record album *Who's Next* by The Who.
2. Yee 2016.
3. "Combating Fake News: An Agenda for Research and Action," Harvard Law School, February 17, 2017, sponsored by the Shorenstein Center on Media, Politics and Public Policy and the Ash Center for Democratic Governance and Innovation, both at the Harvard Kennedy School, and the NU Lab for Texts, Maps and Networks and the Network Science Institute, both at Northeastern University.
4. Loveless 2017.
5. Temin 2017, chap. 10.
6. Hofstadter 1962, chap. 2; Kozol 1967.
7. Hochschild 2016, pp. 122–128.
8. Hofstadter 1962, part 2.
9. Packer 2013, pp. 299–304.
10. Cadwalladr 2017; Mayer 2017.
11. Cadwalladr 2017; Mayer 2017.
12. Osnos et al. 2017.

CHAPTER 1

1. O'Rourke 2017, chap. 29; Judis 2016, p. 18; Stone 2017.
2. Lakoff 2004. See also Alexander 2010; Bauerlein and Bellow 2015, part 3; and Block 1996. An obvious Democratic exception was Bill Clinton's phrase, "It's the economy, stupid!"
3. Nussbaum 2017, p. 22.
4. Hochschild 2016, pp. 14–16, 225–227.
5. VanDerWerff 2015.
6. Chozick 2016b; Nance 2016.
7. US Office of the Director of National Intelligence 2017, p. 7.

8. Chozick 2016a.
9. Clinton 2017, p. 75. See also pp. 403–406.
10. Clinton 2017, pp. 289–323.
11. Allen and Parnes 2017; Ashbee 2017a; Smith 2016.
12. Dovere 2016.
13. Bartels 2016, pp. 3, 310; Skocpol 2000.
14. Stone 2017.
15. Green 2017.
16. Judis 2016.
17. Brennan 2016; O'Rourke 2017, chap. 30.
18. Bartels 2016, pp. 113–124, 128–131.
19. PolitiFact 2017.
20. Valverde 2016.
21. Farley 2016; Public Policy Polling 2016; Wines 2016.
22. Foran 2016.
23. Allen and Parnes 2017.
24. Wilhelm 2016.
25. Taibbi 2017.
26. Herrman 2016.
27. Cadwalladr 2017; Mayer 2017.
28. Swift 2016.
29. Rutenberg and Poniewozik 2016; Taibbi 2017.
30. Kennedy 2016.
31. Pew Research Center 2014b.
32. Benkler et al. 2017.
33. Clinton 2017.
34. Dionne, Ornstein, and Mann 2017, p. 4 and chap. 6.
35. Campbell and Pedersen 2001; Crouch 2011; Mudge 2008. See also Block and Somers 2014; and Heilbroner and Milberg 1995.
36. Edsall 2012; Hacker and Pierson 2010.
37. Brock et al. 2012; Cook 2005.
38. Taibbi 2017, chap. 9. For more general discussions of dumbing down, see Alexander 2010, Bai 2007, Campbell 1998, Lakoff 2004, and Lim 2008.
39. Ashbee 2017a.
40. Fukuyama 2014.
41. Waldman 2016.
42. Bai 2007; Mayer 2016.
43. Skocpol and Hertel-Fernandez 2016.
44. McAdam and Kloos 2014.
45. Edsall and Edsall 1992; Hacker and Pierson 2010; Putnam 2015; Stiglitz 2012.
46. McAdam and Kloos 2014.
47. Edsall 2012; Hacker and Pierson 2010.
48. Kingdon 1995.
49. Hofstadter 1962.
50. Mills 1959.
51. Judis 2016, chap. 1; Lipset and Raab 1970.
52. Lipset 1996.
53. Prokop 2016.
54. *Washington Post* 2015.
55. Frank 2016, pp. 260–261.

56. Frank 2004, p. 6. Frank (2016) later modified his tune, arguing that the Democrats' miserable showing lately in many elections was because they favored the interests of the liberal professional elites and ignored the economic interests of the working and middle classes.
57. Bartels 2006; Bartels 2016, chap. 3.
58. Center for Responsive Politics 2017a, 2017b.
59. Cramer 2016. See also Dionne, Ornstein, and Mann 2017.

CHAPTER 2
1. Sanger and Haberman 2016.
2. Thomas 2016.
3. Maddison 2001, pp. 184, 185, 351.
4. Rosenfeld 2014.
5. Keohane 1984, chaps. 3 and 8.
6. US Bureau of Labor Statistics 2017a.
7. Mishel et al. 2015.
8. US Census Bureau 2017a.
9. US Department of Transportation 2017.
10. Weiss 2014.
11. US Department of Veterans Affairs 2017.
12. Ruff 2007.
13. Piven and Cloward 1993, chap. 6.
14. US Arms Control and Disarmament Agency 1970, pp. 9–11, 14–15.
15. North Atlantic Treaty Organization 1970.
16. Vine 2015.
17. Keohane 1984, chap. 8.
18. Alpert 2013; Campbell and Hall 2015, chap. 6.
19. Hall 1989; Yonay 1998.
20. Babb 2001; Dezalay and Garth 2002; Fourcade 2006, 2009; Fourcade-Gourinchas and Babb 2002.
21. Gill and Law 1988, pp. 13, 31; Keohane 1984, chap. 3.
22. US Census Bureau 2017c, Table F-7.
23. US Census Bureau 2017b, Table 2.
24. Mills 1951.
25. Rosenfeld 2014, p. 15; Western 1997, p. 23.
26. Freeman and Medoff 1984, p. 53.
27. Dixon 2016; Rosenfeld 2014; US National Labor Relations Board 2017.
28. Petras and Morley 1975.
29. Zinn 2003, p. 431.
30. John Birch Society 2017.
31. Equal Justice Initiative 2015, p. 6.
32. Skrentny 1996.
33. Pew Research Center 2015a.
34. Piven and Cloward 1993.

CHAPTER 3
1. Miller 2016.
2. Cutcher-Gershenfeld et al. 2015, Figure B.
3. Chandler 1977.
4. Cutcher-Gershenfeld et al. 2015, Figure B.
5. Dertouzos et al. 1989, p. 18, appendix A.
6. Dertouzos et al. 1989, p. 186.

7. Wojdyla 2011.
8. Huffman 2010.
9. Dertouzos et al. 1989, pp. 19–20; Scherrer 1991.
10. Piore and Sabel 1984.
11. Cutcher-Gershenfeld et al. 2015; Dertouzos et al. 1989, appendix A.
12. Cutcher-Gershenfeld et al. 2015; Harrison and Bluestone 1988, p. 30.
13. Cutcher-Gershenfeld et al. 2015.
14. Dertouzos et al. 1989.
15. Baily and Bosworth 2014.
16. Harrison and Bluestone 1988, p. 8.
17. Cappelli et al. 1997, chap. 2.
18. Danziger and Gottschalk 1995, chap. 7; Harrison and Bluestone 1988, pp. 28–35.
19. Cappelli et al. 1997, chap. 1; Danziger and Gottschalk 1995, chap. 7; Freeman and Katz 1994, p. 46.
20. Sherk 2010.
21. Griswold 2016.
22. Krugman 2015.
23. Lin and Tomaskovic-Devey 2013; Schwartz 2016.
24. Leicht and Fitzgerald 2014, pp. 108–109, 177; Mishel et al. 2015; US Department of Health and Human Services 2017.
25. Leicht and Fitzgerald 2014, pp. 108–109, 177; Temin 2017, p. 34; US Social Security Administration 2009.
26. Wilmers 2017.
27. Cappelli et al. 1997, chap. 1; Davis 2009, chap. 3.
28. Harrison 1994.
29. Helyar 2003.
30. Pearlstein 2012.
31. Danziger and Gottschalk 1995, chap. 7.
32. Scott 2015.
33. Rosenfeld 2014, chap. 5.
34. Kristensen and Zeitlin 2005; Thelen 2004. Similar things have happened recently in the United States not because unions are strong but because state governments have encouraged it (Whitford 2005).
35. Freeman and Katz 1994.
36. Rosenfeld 2014, p. 15.
37. Desilver 2015.
38. McKinley and Arches 1985; Thompson and Salmon 2006, 2014.
39. Fantasia and Voss 2004; Ganz 2000.
40. Edsall 1984, p. 152; Goldfield 1989, pp. 110, 196.
41. Rosenfeld 2014, p. 24. See also Freeman 2007, p. 77.
42. Rosenfeld 2014, p. 29.
43. Edsall 1984, p. 161.
44. Harrison and Bluestone 1988, chap. 2; Rosenfeld 2014, p. 21.
45. Cramer 2016.
46. National Right to Work Committee 2017.
47. Danziger and Gottschalk 1995, chap. 6; Freeman and Katz 1994, pp. 51–54; Western 1997.
48. Economic Policy Institute 2017. See also Mishel et al. 2012, p. 179.
49. Temin 2017, p. 3.
50. Mishel et al. 2012, pp. 380–81.
51. OECD 2016, Tables 1 and 5.
52. Danziger and Gottschalk 1995, chaps. 1 and 7.

53. Leicht and Fitzgerald 2014, p. 47.
54. McLanahan and Sandefur 1994.
55. Rhee 2013.
56. Federal Reserve Bank of San Francisco 2009. See also Federal Reserve Bank of St. Louis 2009.
57. Mishel et al. 2012, p. 405.
58. Seamster and Charron-Chénier 2017, p. 3. See also Mishel et al. 2012, p. 403.
59. Campbell 2010.
60. Domhoff 2013, p. 227.
61. Leicht and Fitzgerald 2007, p. 185.
62. Danziger and Gottschalk 1995, chap. 2. The EITC is a means-tested program only for people who work. If they earn less than a certain income threshold, then they receive a tax return, which is in effect an income subsidy from the government.
63. US Department of Labor 2017.
64. Kenworthy 2014, p. 53.
65. Kenworthy 2014, pp. 166–167.
66. Grusky et al. 2016, pp. 5–6. See also Brady 2009 and Kenworthy 2011, 2014, 2016.
67. Pew Research Center 2015f. Middle class is defined here as the middle quartile of the income distribution. See also Temin 2017.
68. Leicht and Fitzgerald 2014; Skocpol 2000; Temin 2017.
69. Hoxie 2016; Newport 2015.
70. Gallup Polling 2017f.
71. Pew Research Center 2016e.
72. Ryssdal 2016.
73. Gallup Polling 2016b.
74. Fingerhut 2016.
75. Pew Research Center 2016e.
76. US Bureau of Labor Statistics 2017b.
77. Brookings Institution 2013; Corak 2016; Wilkinson and Pickett 2009, chap. 12. Some researchers argue that this is associated with rising income inequality. Others disagree. Lane Kenworth (2016) has an excellent review of this issue with statistical analysis.
78. Danziger and Gottschalk 1995, chap. 6.
79. Hacker and Pierson 2010, p. 28; Mishel et al. 2012, chap. 3; Wilkinson and Pickett 2009, p. 161.
80. Mishel et al. 2012, pp. 142–143.
81. Williams 2016. See also Vance 2016.
82. Rubin 1994.
83. Hochschild 2016, chap. 9. See also *The Economist, Special Report* 2017 and Vance 2016.
84. Cramer 2016. See also Anderson 2017.
85. Krauss and Corkery 2016.
86. Sanati 2016.
87. *The Washington Post* 2015.
88. Gillespie 2016.
89. Luhby 2015.
90. Reeves 2016.
91. Bartels 2016, pp. 106–110; Vance 2016; Williams 2016. The belief that the rich have earned their wealth is misguided to the extent that much of it is often inherited (Allen 1988; Keister 2005).
92. Duina 2017.
93. Reeves 2016.

94. Vance 2016, p. 194.
95. Skocpol 2000.
96. Piore 1995.

CHAPTER 4

1. Lopéz 2014.
2. Lee 2015. I use the term "Hispanic" rather than "Latino" because it seems to be the convention in US government documents like the census and other sources that I rely on here.
3. Davis and Preston 2016.
4. Park 2016.
5. Diamond 2016.
6. CNN 2016.
7. Flitter and Kahn 2016.
8. Kiely et al. 2017.
9. McAdam and Kloos 2014, chap. 3; Temin 2017, p. 27.
10. Lopéz 2014, chap. 1.
11. Frank 2004, chap. 9; Vance 2016. Demography was also involved. As the generations of the Great Depression and World War II died off and younger generations took their place, beginning with the baby boomers, memories began to fade about why liberal Democratic social policies had been established in the first place—to provide a social safety net for those in need and to prevent political turmoil (Gibney 2017, chap. 1; Judt 2010). This generational amnesia was another reason people became less willing to pay taxes for social programs. State-level tax revolts emerged in California, Massachusetts, and elsewhere during the 1970s and eventually became a national issue led by Americans for Tax Reform, an organization that pressed anybody running for office to sign a pledge not to raise any taxes (Edsall and Edsall 1992; Martin 2008).
12. Hochschild 2016, pp. 92, 149; Vance 2016, pp. 140–144.
13. Aistrup 1996; Edsall 2012, p. 41; Edsall and Edsall 1991.
14. McAdam and Kloos 2014, chap. 3.
15. McAdam and Kloos 2014, p. 119.
16. McAdam and Kloos 2014, pp. 104–119.
17. Pew Research Center 2015e.
18. *Time Magazine* 1990.
19. Alba 2015. This estimate is riddled with confusion largely due to how racial and ethnic categories are defined, the prevalence of mixed-race marriages, and other methodological issues.
20. Zengerle 2017.
21. Anderson 2017; Waldman 2016.
22. O'Keefe and Johnson 2016.
23. Sherman and Shepard 2016.
24. Corbett-Davies et al. 2016.
25. House and Dennis 2017.
26. Waldman 2016.
27. Anderson 2017, p. 169.
28. Pew Research Center 2016a.
29. Rosenfeld 2014.
30. US Census Bureau 2017d, Table A-2.
31. US Census Bureau 2017c, Table F-4.
32. Pattillo-McCoy 1999.
33. O'Flaherty 2015, pp. 144–145; Wilson 1987, 1990.
34. Bump 2016a.

35. US Census Bureau 2016, Table 3.
36. Pew Research Center 2016a.
37. Wilson 2009, pp. 44–45.
38. Pew Research Center 2016a.
39. Barry-Jester 2015; Bonilla-Silva 2006.
40. Ryan 1971.
41. Wilson 1987, 1997, 2009. See also Edin and Kefalas 2005.
42. Fausset et al. 2016.
43. Edsall and Edsall 1992; Temin 2017, pp. 104–105.
44. Temin 2017, chap. 9; Sentencing Project 2017.
45. Baum 2016.
46. O'Flaherty 2015, p. 360.
47. Ghandnoosh 2014.
48. Carson 2015, Tables 10, 11, and 12.
49. Harrell et al. 2014, Tables 6 and 8. These figures are for poor urban populations. There was little difference between urban and rural areas.
50. Ghandnoosh and Rovner 2017.
51. Landgrave and Nowrasteh 2017.
52. O'Flaherty 2015, p. 337.
53. Sampson and Lauritsen 1997, p. 311.
54. Alexander 2012, pp. 125–126; Manza and Uggen 2008.
55. O'Flaherty 2015, pp. 346–347. See also American Civil Liberties Union 2017.
56. Temin 2017, pp. 106–107.
57. Ghandnoosh 2014; O'Flaherty 2015, p. 340.
58. O'Flaherty 2015, pp. 346–347. See also American Civil Liberties Union 2017.
59. Massey 2015.
60. Trump 2016a. See also Desjardins 2016.
61. Abrajano and Hajnal 2015.
62. Doherty 2016.
63. Krogstad et al. 2016; O'Flaherty 2015, chap. 6.
64. Gonzalez-Barrera 2015; Appelbaum 2017; Massey 2015; Massey and Gentsch 2014.
65. Massey 2015; Massey and Gentsch 2014; O'Flaherty 2015, pp. 158–166; Preston 2016; US Chamber of Commerce 2017.
66. Pedraza and Zhu 2015.
67. Santana 2014.
68. US Chamber of Commerce 2017.
69. Gee et al. 2016.
70. US Social Security Administration 2013.
71. Pedraza and Zhu 2015.
72. Badger 2017.
73. Lieberson 1980. See also Emirbayer and Desmond 2015.
74. Doherty 2016.
75. Kurzman 2017.
76. Fox News 2014; Martel 2014.
77. Kohn 2016.
78. Jones et al. 2011. Republicans who say they most trust Fox News are much more likely to believe that American Muslims are trying to establish Shari 'a law in the United States than Republicans who say they most trust other news sources.
79. Potok 2017; US Federal Bureau of Investigation 2017.
80. Quigley 2017. Much of this was contingent on funding.

CHAPTER 5

1. https://www.hillaryclinton.com/issues/
2. https://www.donaldjtrump.com/policies
3. Frank 2016, p. 261.
4. Campbell 1998.
5. Skidelsky 2009.
6. Hall 1989.
7. Heilbroner and Milberg 1995.
8. Alt and Chrystal 1983, pp. 62–66; Friedman 1962, chap. 3; Klamer 1983, chap. 1.
9. Lucas 1972.
10. Klamer 1983, chap. 1.
11. Amacher et al. 1976.
12. Mirowski and Plehwe 2009.
13. Campbell and Pedersen 2014, chap. 2.
14. Campbell and Pedersen 2014, chap. 2; Temin 2017, pp. 17–19. The Koch brothers also focused on state-level politics, founding and funding the conservative and highly secretive American Legislative Exchange Council (ALEC) in 1973. ALEC drafts neoliberal legislation and distributes it to state legislators, who then work to have it enacted (Jackman 2013).
15. Teles 2008.
16. Cohen 2008; MacLean 2017.
17. Domhoff 2013, chaps. 9–11; Domhoff 2014, pp. 15–20; Temin 2017, p. 18.
18. Drutman 2015.
19. Bartels 2016, p. 76.
20. Cillizza 2014; Clawson 1998; Mayer 2016; Temin 2017, pp. 79–80.
21. Campbell 1998.
22. Murray 1984.
23. Fahri 2009. Estimates vary widely, but this is a conservative one.
24. *Talkers* 2017.
25. Brock et al. 2012.
26. Soergel 2016.
27. Bowles et al. 1983, chap. 3; Martin 1991, chap. 7; Roberts 1984; Steinmo 1993, p. 165.
28. Bowles et al. 1983, chap. 3; Edsall 2012. Much empirical evidence questions this argument, including some presented in chapter 4.
29. Bawden and Palmer 1984, p. 178.
30. Black and Sprague 2016.
31. Cato Institute 2017 and author's calculations.
32. Fox News 2016.
33. Fox News 2016; Gleckman 2016.
34. Fox News 2016. Advocating for these entitlement programs was an ideological inconsistency faced by many conservatives in the neoliberal camp. Although the public often favors lower taxes and spending, they also support Social Security and Medicare, to which they contribute through payroll taxes and upon which they depend in retirement (Pierson 1994; Skocpol 2000). Politicians view these programs as a third rail in politics—touch it with a budget axe and your political career is dead! Trump understood this and embraced the inconsistency just like many neoliberal politicians.
35. Fox News 2016.
36. Gleckman 2016.
37. Bakija et al. 2016. See also Kenworthy 2004 and Pontusson 2005.
38. Blyth 2013.

39. Begg et al. 1992. Several panelists at a 2017 conference at the Harvard Law School on fake news found much the same thing about repetition. For details, see my "Note on Sources, Alternative Facts, and Fake News" at the beginning of this book.
40. Brock et al. 2012, pp. 13–14.
41. Feldman 2016.
42. Allen and Parnes 2017, p. 323; Stone 2017, pp. 28–29, 265.
43. https://www.hillaryclinton.com/issues/
44. Ackerman 1982, chap. 2.
45. Duina 2017.
46. Gilder 1981, chaps. 1 and 2.
47. Jamieson 1996, pp. 396–399.
48. Graham 1992, p. 158.
49. Gallup Polling 2015.
50. Gallup Polling 2017c.
51. Pew Research Center 2015b.
52. Pew Research Center 2015b.
53. Trump 2011, pp. 62–63.
54. Tanner 2016.
55. Collinson 2016.
56. Trump 2016b.
57. Bykowicz 2016.
58. Hochschild 2016, p. 6.
59. Roff 2014.
60. Judis 2016, chap. 3
61. The Economist 2016.
62. Irwin 2016.
63. Hochschild 2016, pp. 225–227.
64. https://www.hillaryclinton.com/issues/
65. Ashbee 2017a; Judis 2016.
66. Bauerlein and Bellow 2015; Frank 2004, chap. 10; Goodwyn 1978; Hofstadter 1962, pp. 6–7.
67. Frank 2004, pp. 191–195. See also Raphael 2016.
68. Judis 2016.
69. O'Rourke 2017, p. 188.
70. Fischer 2016.
71. Ashbee 2017a.
72. New York Times 2016a.
73. CNN 2016.
74. CNN 2016.
75. Bump 2016b.
76. Waldman 2016, pp. 185–186.
77. Gallup Polling 2017a.
78. Guttmacher Institute 2017.
79. Lakoff 2004.
80. Planned Parenthood 2017.
81. Williams 2016.
82. The Economist, Special Report 2017, p. 10.
83. Pressman and Chenoweth 2017.
84. Cadwalladr 2017.
85. Mayer 2017.

CHAPTER 6

1. Pew Research Center 2012b.
2. Abramowitz 2013, pp. 42–43.
3. Pew Research Center 2016d.
4. James Campbell 2016 (see especially chaps. 1 and 4). See also Dionne 2016 and Edsall 1985.
5. Pew Research Center 2014a.
6. Abramowitz 2013.
7. Pew Research Center 2014.
8. Abramowitz 2013.
9. James Campbell 2016, p. 140, chaps. 1 and 5.
10. Edsall 2012, pp. 140–141.
11. Pew Research Center 2015b.
12. Bunch 2009.
13. Frank 2016, p. 53.
14. Franken 2017, p. 246.
15. Skocpol and Hertel-Fernandez 2016.
16. Waldman 2016, pp. 185–186.
17. McCammon 2016.
18. Edsall 2012; McAdam and Kloos 2014.
19. McAdam and Kloos 2014, p. 66.
20. Edsall 1984.
21. Frank 2004, p. 243; Frank 2016, pp. 54–56.
22. Frank 2016, pp. 28–30, 56–60.
23. Edsall 1984, pp. 149–150; Frank 2016, p. 54.
24. Judis 2016, p. 44.
25. Edsall 1984.
26. Edsall 1984; Rosenfeld 2014, chap. 7. See also Fantasia and Voss 2004 and Western 1997.
27. Shabecoff 1972.
28. Frank 2016, p. 51; Sanders 2017.
29. Edsall 2012, pp. 69–72; 1985; Ferguson and Rogers 1986; Judis 2016, p. 43. This shift may be reversing to a degree insofar as new technology firms supported Obama (Bai 2007).
30. Useem 1984.
31. Mizruchi 2013, pp. 8–9.
32. Gibney 2017.
33. College Board 2015a, 2015b; Kingkade 2012.
34. Pew Research Center 2016c.
35. Manza and Brooks 1998; Tyson and Maniam 2016.
36. Jones 2012.
37. Edsall 2012, p. 41; Edsall and Edsall 1992; James Campbell 2016, p. 158; Judis 2016, pp. 36–37.
38. Johnson 2017, p. 173; Pew Research Center 2016a.
39. McAdam and Kloos 2014, pp. 104, 254–255.
40. Edsall 2012, pp. 68–72.
41. Agiesta and Ross 2012. Religious intolerance increased too. The United States experienced a rise in social hostilities involving religion between 2007 and 2013. Although moderate during that time compared to all countries in the world, the Pew Research Center's Social Hostilities Index for the United States rose from 1.9 to 3.1, the third highest of the thirty-five countries in the Americas (Pew Research Center 2015d, p. 58).
42. Abrajano and Hajnal 2015; Abramowitz 2013, chap 2.
43. McAdam and Kloos 2014.

44. Mudge and Chen 2014, p. 314.
45. McAdam and Kloos 2014, p. 169.
46. James Campbell 2016, p. 176.
47. Abramowitz 2013, pp. 97–99.
48. Temin 2017, pp. 95–96.
49. Waldman 2016, pp. 225–229, 238.
50. Associated Press 2017.
51. Associated Press 2017.
52. Zengerle 2017.
53. Evans 2011.
54. McAdam and Kloos 2014.
55. Frank 2016, p. 52.
56. Troy 2017.

CHAPTER 7

1. Binder 2014.
2. McAdam and Kloos 2014, chap. 7.
3. Shear 2013.
4. Wheeler 2016.
5. Franken 2017, pp. 229–230.
6. Mann and Ornstein 2012, pp. 88–90.
7. McAdam and Kloos 2014, chap. 7.
8. Gallup Polling 2016a.
9. Gallup Polling 2017d.
10. Campbell 2011.
11. Campbell 2011; Lewis 2011.
12. Edsall 2012, pp. 140–141
13. Megerian 2016.
14. Tesler and Sears 2010, p. 9.
15. Tesler and Sears 2010, p. 92.
16. Johnson 2017. See also Tesler and Sears 2010, pp. 92–93.
17. López 2014, p. 160.
18. Pew Research Center 2015e.
19. Edsall 2012, chap. 4.
20. James Campbell 2016, pp. 234–235.
21. Kessler 2012.
22. Franken 2017, pp. 235–236, 246.
23. Capehart 2012. See also Hacker and Pierson 2010, pp. 262–263.
24. Edsall 2012, pp. 56, 73.
25. James Campbell 2016, pp. 236–237.
26. Hulse 2017.
27. Amadeo 2017c.
28. Stiglitz 2009.
29. Rasmussen Reports 2013.
30. Bowman 2015; Drake 2013.
31. Pew Research Center 2012a.
32. Pew Research Center 2015c.
33. Bartels 2016, p. 294.
34. Panagopoulos 2011.
35. Pew Research Center 2014a.

36. Abramowitz 2013, pp. 9–12.
37. Edsall 2012, pp. 28–30.
38. Holan 2009.
39. Media Matters for America 2011; YouTube 2012.
40. Skocpol and Williamson 2012, chap. 2.
41. Abramowitz 2013, p. 120.
42. Edsall 2012, chap. 5.
43. Tesler and Sears 2010, pp. 155–158. See also López 2014, pp. 205–207.
44. López 2014, pp. 152–153.
45. Skocpol and Williamson 2012, chap. 3.
46. Skocpol and Williamson 2012, chap. 3.
47. Pew Research Center 2016b.
48. McAdam and Kloos 2014, p. 273.
49. James Campbell 2016, p. 194.
50. Kessler 2012.
51. Diamond 2015.
52. Goldberg 2017.
53. Gallup Polling 2017e.
54. *Washington Post* 2015.
55. *Investor's Business Daily* 2015. Trump did eventually succumb to the need for outside financing to run his campaign.
56. Harrington 2017.
57. Bender 2016.
58. Desjardins 2016.
59. Stein 2016.
60. Weigel 2015. See also Howard 2016.
61. *Fortune Magazine* 2016.
62. Roy 2015.

CHAPTER 8

1. http://www.oddsshark.com/entertainment/us-presidential-odds-2016-futures
2. CNN 2016. The data were collected by Edison Research for the National Election Pool, a consortium of CNN, ABC News, the Associated Press, CBS News, Fox News, and NBC News.
3. Frank 2016, pp. 259–284; Sanders 2017.
4. For further analysis supporting this argument, see Carnes et al. 2017.
5. McElwee and McDaniel 2017.
6. Lieberson 1980.
7. McElwee and McDaniel 2017.
8. Wood 2017.
9. *New York Times* 2016b.
10. Ashbee 2017a.
11. Judis 2016.
12. Duina 2017; Hochschild 2016; Packer 2013.
13. Vance 2016, pp. 188, 190–194.
14. Kriesi 2016.
15. Pressman and Chenoweth 2017.
16. Samuelsohn 2017.
17. Davis 2017, p. 6.
18. Confessore and Rappeport 2017.
19. Judis 2016, chap. 4.

20. Campbell and Hall 2017, chap. 5.
21. Le Galès 2016.
22. Ascherson 2016; Barnes 2017; Finlayson 2017.
23. Fligstein 2008.
24. O'Reilly 2016.
25. Froud et al. 2016.
26. Boyer 2016, p. 837; Le Galès 2016.
27. Grey 2016; Wood and Wright 2016.
28. Frerichs and Sankari 2016; Le Galès 2016; Warhurst 2016.
29. *The Economist* 2017b, 2017c; Nossiter 2017.
30. Rubin 2017.
31. *The Economist* 2017e.
32. *The Economist* 2017a.
33. *The Economist* 2017c, 2017d, 2017f.
34. US Federal Reserve 2013.
35. Acharya 2014, pp. 20, 29.
36. International Monetary Fund 2013; Kirshner 2014, pp. 14, 162.
37. Brooks and Wohlforth 2016.
38. Hemmer and Katzenstein 2002, p. 588.
39. Kirshner 2014, p. 166.
40. Cohen 2017.
41. Davis et al. 2017.
42. Smale and Erlanger 2017.
43. Erlanger and Davis 2017.
44. Skocpol and Williamson 2012.
45. Yates 2016.
46. Kulish 2017.

APPENDIX

1. DiMaggio et al. 1996; Fiorina 2005; McAdam and Kloos 2014.
2. Mann and Ornstein 2012.
3. Abramowitz 2013, chap. 3; James Campbell 2016; Edsall 2012, p. 139; Pew Research Center 2014.
4. Mudge 2011.
5. James Campbell 2016; Edsall 2012; McAdam and Kloos 2014.
6. See also Dionne 2016, Edsall 1984, Frank 2016, and Hacker and Pierson 2010, pp. 264, 266.
7. James Campbell 2016.
8. See also Edsall 2012.
9. James Campbell 2016, pp. 106–108, 181, 191. See also Pew Research Center 2014.
10. Gibney 2017, pp. 128–129, 387 fn. 21.
11. Derthick and Quirk 1985, chap. 5.
12. Somers and Block 2005.
13. McAdam and Kloos 2014, p. 225.
14. Judis 2016, pp. 54–56.
15. Darman 2006.
16. Bartels 2016, pp. 271, 282–291, 337–340.
17. Mudge 2011. See also Fourcade-Gourinchas and Babb 2002 and Prasad 2006.
18. Ashbee 2017b, p. 148.
19. Edsall 2012, p. 181.
20. McAdam and Kloos 2014, p. 229.

REFERENCES

Abrajano, Marisa, and Zoltan Hajnal. 2015. *White Backlash: Immigration, Race and American Politics*. Princeton, NJ: Princeton University Press.

Abramowitz, Alan. 2013. *The Polarized Public?* New York: Pearson.

Acharya, Amitav. 2014. *The End of American World Order*. New York: Polity.

Ackerman, Frank. 1982. *Reaganomics: Rhetoric vs. Reality*. Boston: South End Press.

Agiesta, Jennifer, and Sonya Ross. 2012. "AP Poll: Majority Harbor Prejudice Against Blacks." http://bigstory.ap.org/article/ap-poll-majority-harbor-prejudice-against-blacks (accessed December 2016).

Aistrup, Joseph. 1996. *The Southern Strategy Revisited*. Lexington: University of Kentucky Press.

Alba, Richard. 2015. "The Myth of a White Minority." *New York Times*, June 11. https://www.nytimes.com/2015/06/11/opinion/the-myth-of-a-white-minority.html (accessed June 2017).

Alexander, Jeffrey. 2010. *The Performance of Politics*. New York: Oxford University Press.

Alexander, Michelle. 2012. *The New Jim Crow: Mass Incarceration in the Age of Colorblindness*. New York: New Press.

Allen, Jonathan, and Amie Parnes. 2017. *Shattered: Inside Hillary Clinton's Doomed Campaign*. New York: Crown.

Allen, Michael Patrick. 1988. *Founding Fortunes*. New York: Dutton.

Alpert, Daniel. 2013. *The Age of Oversupply*. New York: Penguin.

Alt, James, and K. Alec Chrystal. 1983. *Political Economics*. Berkeley: University of California Press.

Amacher, Ryan, Robert Tollison, and Thomas Willett, editors. 1976. *The Economic Approach to Public Policy*. Ithaca, NY: Cornell University Press.

Amadeo, Kimberley. 2017a. "Bush Administration: Economic Policies." *The Balance*, January 17. https://www.thebalance.com/bush-administration-economic-policies-3305556 (accessed February 2017).

———. 2017b. "What Has Obama Done? 11 Major Accomplishments." *The Balance*, February 21. https://www.thebalance.com/what-has-obama-done-11-major-accomplishments-3306158 (accessed February 2017).

———. 2017c. "What Is the Dodd-Frank Wall Street Reform Act?" *The Balance*, February 7. https://www.thebalance.com/dodd-frank-wall-street-reform-act-3305688 (accessed February 2017).

American Civil Liberties Union. 2017. "The War on Drugs." https://www.aclu.org/issues/mass-incarceration/war-drugs (accessed January 2017).

American National Election Studies. 2017. "Liberal-Conservative Self-Identification, 1972-2012." http://www.electionstudies.org/nesguide/toptable/tab3_1.htm (accessed March 2017).

Anderson, Carol. 2017. *White Rage*. New York: Bloomsbury Press.

Appelbaum, Binyamin. 2017. "Few Immigrants Mean More Jobs? Not So, Economists Say." *New York Times*, August 4. https://www.nytimes.com/2017/08/03/us/politics/legal-immigration-jobs-economy.html (accessed August 2017).

Ascherson, Neal. 2016. "England Prepared to Leave the World." *London Review of Books* 38(22): 7–10.

Ashbee, Edward. 2017a. *The Trump Phenomenon*. Manchester, England: Manchester University Press.

———. 2017b. "Macroeconomic Policy and Processes of Neoliberalization During the Obama Years." In *The Obama Presidency and the Politics of Change*, edited by Edward Ashbee and John Dunbrell, pp. 123–160. New York: Palgrave Macmillan.

Associated Press. 2017. "Analysis Indicates Partisan Gerrymandering Has Benefited GOP." *New York Times*, June 25. https://www.nytimes.com/aponline/2017/06/25/us/ap-us-redrawing-america-imbalance-of-power.html?mcubz=0 (accessed June 2017).

Babb, Sarah. 2001. *Managing Mexico*. Princeton, NJ: Princeton University Press.

Bager, Emily. 2017. "Immigrant Shock: Can California Predict the Nation's Future?" *New York Times*, February 2. https://www.nytimes.com/2017/02/01/upshot/strife-over-immigrants-can-california-foretell-nations-future.html?&moduleDetail=section-news-5&action=click&contentCollection=The%20Upshot&region=Footer&module=MoreInSection&version=WhatsNext&contentID=WhatsNext&pgtype=article (accessed February 2017).

Bai, Matt. 2007. *The Argument: Billionaires, Bloggers and the Battle to Remake Democratic Politics*. New York: Penguin.

Baily, Martin Neil, and Barry Bosworth. 2014. "U.S. Manufacturing: Understanding Its Past and Its Potential Future." *Journal of Economic Perspectives* 28(1): 3–26.

Baker, Peter. 2017. "Trump Tries to Regroup as the West Wing Battles Itself." *New York Times*, July 29. https://www.nytimes.com/2017/07/29/us/politics/trump-presidency-setbacks.html?mcubz=0 (accessed July 2017).

Bakija, Jon, Lane Kenworthy, Peter Lindert, and Jeff Madrick. 2016. *How Big Should Our Government Be?* Berkeley: University of California Press.

Barnes, Julian. 2017. "Diary: People Will Hate Us Again." *London Review of Books* 39(8): 41–43.

Barry-Jester, Anna Maria. 2015. "Attitudes Toward Racism and Inequality Are Shifting." *Five Thirty Eight*, June 23. https://fivethirtyeight.com/datalab/attitudes-toward-racism-and-inequality-are-shifting/ (accessed May 2017).

Bartels, Larry. 2016. *Unequal Democracy*: Princeton, NJ: Princeton University Press.

———. 2006. "What's the Matter with *What's the Matter with Kansas?*" *Quarterly Journal of Political Science* 1: 201–226.

Bauerlein, Mark, and Adam Bellow, editors. 2015. *The State of the American Mind*. New York: Templeton Press.

Baum, Dan. 2016. "Legalize It All: How to Win the War on Drugs." *Harper's Magazine*, April. http://harpers.org/archive/2016/04/legalize-it-all/ (accessed January 2017).

Bawden, D. Lee, and John Palmer. 1984. "Social Policy: Challenging the Welfare State." In *The Reagan Record*, edited by John Palmer and Isabel Sawhill, pp. 177–216. Cambridge, MA: Ballinger.

Begg, Ian Maynard, Ann Anas, and Suzanne Farinacci. 1992. "Dissociation of Processes in Belief: Source Recollection, Statement Familiarity, and the Illusion of Truth." *Journal of Experimental Psychology* 121(4): 446–458.

Bender, Michael. 2016. "Trump Embraces Executive Orders to Avoid Congressional Gridlock." *Bloomberg Politics*, June 27. https://www.bloomberg.com/politics/articles/2016-06-27/trump-eyes-executive-orders-to-sidestep-congressional-gridlock (accessed February 2017).

Benkler, Yochai, Robert Faris, Hal Roberts, and Ethan Zuckerman. 2017. "Study: Brietbart-Led Right-Wing Media Ecosystem Altered Broader Media Agenda." *Columbia Journalism Review*, March 3. https://www.cjr.org/analysis/breitbart-media-trump-harvard-study.php (accessed May 2017).

Binder, Sarah. 2014. "Polarized We Govern?" Washington, DC: Brookings Institution, Center for Effective Public Management.

Black, Rachel, and Aleta Sprague. 2016. "The 'Welfare Queen' Is a Lie." *The Atlantic*, September 28. https://www.theatlantic.com/business/archive/2016/09/welfare-queen-myth/501470/ (accessed February 2017).

Block, Fred. 1996. *The Vampire State: And Other Myths and Fallacies About the U.S. Economy.* New York: New Press.

Block, Fred, and Margaret Somers. 2014. *The Power of Market Fundamentalism.* Cambridge, MA: Harvard University Press.

Bowles, Samuel, David Gordon, and Thomas Weisskopf. 1983. *Beyond the Waste Land.* New York: Anchor Press/Doubleday.

Blyth, Mark. 2013. *Austerity.* New York: Oxford University Press.

Bonilla-Silva, Eduardo. 2006. *Racism Without Racists.* New York: Rowman & Littlefield.

Bowman, Karlyn. 2015. "Public Opinion Five Years After Dodd-Frank." *Forbes*, July 21. https://www.forbes.com/sites/bowmanmarsico/2015/07/21/public-opinion-five-years-after-dodd-frank/#206482727477 (accessed March 2017).

Boyer, Robert. 2016. "Brexit: The Day of Reckoning for the Neo-Functionalist Paradigm of European Union." *Socio-Economic Review* 14(4): 836–840.

Brady, David. 2009. *Rich Democracies, Poor People.* New York: Oxford University Press.

Brennan, Jason. 2016. "Trump Won Because Voters Are Ignorant, Literally." *Foreign Policy*, November 10. http://foreignpolicy.com/2016/11/10/the-dance-of-the-dunces-trump-clinton-election-republican-democrat/ (accessed January 2017).

Brock, David, Ari Rabin-Havt, and Media Matters. 2012. *The Fox Effect.* New York: Anchor.

Brookings Institution. 2013. "The Relationship between Income Inequality and Social Mobility." Hamilton Project, July 18. http://www.hamiltonproject.org/charts/the_relationship_between_income_inequality_and_social_mobility (accessed January 2017).

Brooks, Stephen G., and William C. Wohlforth. 2016. *America Abroad: The United States' Global Role in the 21st Century.* New York: Oxford University Press.

Bump, Philip. 2016a. "It's Hard to Imagine a Much Worse Pitch Donald Trump Could Have Made for the Black Vote." *Washington Post*, August 20. https://www.washingtonpost.com/news/the-fix/wp/2016/08/20/its-hard-to-imagine-a-much-worse-pitch-donald-trump-could-have-made-for-the-black-vote/?utm_term=.044d5a62c371 (accessed February 2017).

———. 2016b. "Donald Trump Took 5 Different Positions on Abortion in 3 Days." *Washington Post*, April 3. https://www.washingtonpost.com/news/the-fix/wp/2016/04/03/donald-trumps-ever-shifting-positions-on-abortion/?utm_term=.1cc8f8a18a10 (accessed February 2017).

Bunch, Will. 2009. *Tear Down This Myth.* New York: Free Press.

Business Week Team. 1982. *The Reindustrialization of America.* New York: McGraw Hill.

Bykowicz, Julie. 2016. "Trump Says Newt Gingrich 'Incorrectly States' That He Was Dropping 'Drain the Swamp' Mantra." *PBS News Hour.* http://www.pbs.org/newshour/rundown/trump-ditching-drain-swamp-rally-cry-adviser-says/ (accessed February 2017).

Cadwalladr, Carole. 2017. "Robert Mercer, the Big Data Billionaire Waging War on Mainstream Media." *The Guardian*, February 26. https://www.theguardian.com/politics/2017/feb/26/robert-mercer-breitbart-war-on-media-steve-bannon-donald-trump-nigel-farage (accessed March 2017).

Campbell, James E. 2016. *Polarized.* Princeton, NJ: Princeton University Press.

Campbell, John L. 1998. "Institutional Analysis and the Role of Ideas in Political Economy." *Theory and Society* 27: 377–409.

———. 2010. "Neoliberalism's Penal and Debtor States." *Theoretical Criminology* 14(1): 59–73.

———. 2011. "The U.S. Financial Crisis: Lessons for Theories of Institutional Complementarity." *Socio-Economic Review* 9: 211–234.

Campbell, John L., and John A. Hall. 2015. *The World of States.* New York: Bloomsbury Press.

———. 2017. *The Paradox of Vulnerability: States, Nationalism and the Financial Crisis.* Princeton, NJ: Princeton University Press.

Campbell, John L., and Ove K. Pedersen. 2001. "The Rise of Neoliberalism and Institutional Analysis." In *The Rise of Neoliberalism and Institutional Analysis*, edited by John L. Campbell and Ove K. Pedersen, pp. 1–24. Princeton, NJ: Princeton University Press.

———. 2014. *The National Origins of Policy Ideas: Knowledge Regimes in the United States, France, Germany and Denmark.* Princeton, NJ: Princeton University Press.

Capehart, Jonathan. 2012. "Republicans Had It in for Obama Before Day 1." *Washington Post*, August 10. https://www.washingtonpost.com/blogs/post-partisan/post/republicans-had-it-in-for-obama-before-day-1/2012/08/10/0c96c7c8-e31f-11e1-ae7f-d2a13e249eb2_blog.html?utm_term=.6fd86a311738 (accessed March 2017).

Cappelli, Peter, Laurie Basi, Harry Katz, David Knoke, Paul Osterman, and Michael Useem. 1997. *Change at Work.* New York: Oxford University Press.

Carnes, Nicholas, and Noam Lupu. 2017. "It's Time to Bust the Myth: Most Trump Voters Were Not Working Class." *Washington Post*, June 5. https://www.washingtonpost.com/news/monkey-cage/wp/2017/06/05/its-time-to-bust-the-myth-most-trump-voters-were-not-working-class/?utm_term=.50a3b1a7be11 (accessed June 2017).

Carson, E. Ann. 2015. "Prisoners in 2014." US Department of Justice, Office of Justice Programs, Bureau of Justice Statistics NCJ 248955. Washington, DC: US Department of Justice. https://www.bjs.gov/content/pub/pdf/p14.pdf (accessed January 2017).

Cato Institute. 2017. "Downsizing the Federal Government." https://www.downsizinggovernment.org/charts/ (accessed February 2017).

Center for Responsive Politics. 2017a. OpenSecrets.org. http://www.opensecrets.org/outsidespending/summ.php?cycle=2006&chrt=V&disp=O&type=A (accessed February 2017).

———. 2017b. "2016 Presidential Race: Summary." OpenSecrets.org. https://www.opensecrets.org/pres16 (accessed June 2017).

Chandler, Alfred D., Jr. 1977. *The Visible Hand.* Cambridge, MA: Harvard/Belknap Press.

Chozick, Amy. 2016a. "Hillary Clinton Blames F.B.I. Director for Election Loss." *New York Times*, November 12. https://www.nytimes.com/2016/11/13/us/politics/hillary-clinton-james-comey.html?_r=0 (accessed January 2017).

———. 2016b. "Clinton Says 'Personal Beef' by Putin Led to Hacking Attacks." *New York Times*, December 16. https://www.nytimes.com/2016/12/16/us/politics/hillary-clinton-russia-fbi-comey.html?emc=edit_na_20161216&nlid=59075373&ref=headline&_r=0 (accessed January 2017).

Cillizza, Chris. 2014. "How Citizens United Changed Politics, in 7 Charts." *Washington Post*, January 22. https://www.washingtonpost.com/news/the-fix/wp/2014/01/21/how-citizens-united-changed-politics-in-6-charts/?utm_term=.5ee609bb9463 (accessed February 2017).

Clawson, Dan, Alan Neustadtl, and Mark Weller. 1998. *Dollars and Votes.* Philadelphia, PA: Temple University Press.

Clinton, Hillary Rodham. 2017. *What Happened.* New York: Simon and Schuster.

CNN. 2016. *CNN Politics: Exit Polls.* http://www.cnn.com/election/results/exit-polls (accessed February 2017).

Cohen, Patricia. 2008. "Conservatives Try New Tack on Campuses." *New York Times*, September 22. http://www.nytimes.com/2008/09/22/education/22conservative.html (accessed February 2017).

Cohen, Roger. 2017. "The Desperation of Our Diplomats." *New York Times*, July 28. https://www.nytimes.com/2017/07/28/opinion/sunday/trump-tillerson-state-department-diplomats.html?mcubz=0 (accessed July 2017).

College Board. 2015a. *Trends in Student Aid 2015*. Princeton, NJ: College Board. http://trends.collegeboard.org/sites/default/files/trends-student-aid-web-final-508-2.pdf (accessed April 2016).

———. 2015b. *Trends in College Pricing 2015*. Princeton, NJ: College Board. http://trends.collegeboard.org/sites/default/files/trends-college-pricing-web-final-508-2.pdf (accessed April 2016).

Collinson, Stephen. 2016. "Why Trump's Talk of a Rigged Vote Is so Dangerous." CNN, October 19. http://www.cnn.com/2016/10/18/politics/donald-trump-rigged-election/ (accessed February 2017).

Confessore, Nicholas, and Alan Rappeport. 2017. "Conservative Split over Import Tax Imperils Trump's Overhaul." *New York Times*, April 1. https://www.nytimes.com/2017/04/01/us/politics/trump-border-tax-import-koch.html?ref=todayspaper&_r=0 (accessed April 2017).

Cook, Timothy. 2005. *Governing the News*. Chicago: University of Chicago Press.

Corak, Miles. 2016. "Economic Mobility." In *Pathways* (Special Issue), pp. 51–57. Stanford, CA: Stanford Center on Poverty and Inequality.

Corbett-Davies, Sam, Tobias Konitzer, and David Rothschild. 2016. "Poll: 60% of Republicans Believe Illegal Immigrants Vote; 43% Believe People Vote Using Dead People's Names." *Washington Post*, October 24. https://www.washingtonpost.com/news/monkey-cage/wp/2016/10/24/poll-60-of-republicans-believe-illegal-immigrants-vote-43-believe-people-vote-using-dead-peoples-names/?utm_term=.f2215d9e5d99 (accessed February 2017).

Cramer, Katherine. 2016. *The Politics of Resentment*. Chicago: University of Chicago Press.

Crouch, Colin. 2011. *The Strange Non-Death of Neoliberalism*. London: Polity Press.

Cutcher-Gerschenfeld, Joel, Dan Brooks, and Martin Mulloy. 2015. "The Decline and Resurgence of the U.S. Auto Industry." Economic Policy Institute, Briefing Paper #399, May 6. Washington, DC: Economic Policy Institute. http://www.epi.org/publication/the-decline-and-resurgence-of-the-u-s-auto-industry/ (accessed January 2017).

Dann, Carrie. 2017. "Trump's Job Approval Stands at Just 44 Percent as Partisan Splits Reign." *NBC News*, February 26. http://www.nbcnews.com/politics/first-read/trump-s-job-approval-stands-just-44-percent-partisan-splits-n725621 (accessed March 2017).

Danziger, Sheldon, and Peter Gottschalk. 1995. *America Unequal*. Cambridge, MA: Harvard University Press.

Darman, Jonathan. 2006. "Behind Their Smiles." *Newsweek*, November 19. http://www.newsweek.com/behind-their-smiles-106787 (accessed February 2017).

Davis, Gerald. 2009. *Managed by the Markets*. New York: Oxford University Press.

Davis, Julie Hirschfeld, and Julia Preston. 2016. "What Donald Trump's Vow to Deport up to 3 Million Immigrants Would Mean." *New York Times*, November 14. https://www.nytimes.com/2016/11/15/us/politics/donald-trump-deport-immigrants.html (accessed January 2017).

Davis, Julie Hirschfeld, Alan Rappeport, Kate Kelly, and Rachel Abrams. 2017. "Trump's Tax Plan: Low Rate for Corporations, and for Companies Like His." *New York Times*, April 25. https://www.nytimes.com/2017/04/25/us/politics/tax-plan-trump.html?_r=0 (accessed April 2017).

Davis, Mike. 2017. "Election 2016." *New Left Review* 103 (January/February): 5–8.

Derthick, Martha, and Paul Quirk. 1985. *The Politics of Deregulation*. Washington, DC: Brookings Institution.

Dertouzos, Michael, Richard Lester, and Robert Solow. 1989. *Made in America*. Cambridge, MA: MIT Press.

Desilver, Drew. 2015. "Job Categories Where Union Membership Has Fallen Most." Pew Research Center, April 27. http://www.pewresearch.org/fact-tank/2015/04/27/union-membership/ (accessed April 2017).

Desjardins, Lisa. 2016. "The 6 New, Significant Things Donald Trump Said on Immigration." *PBS News Hour*, September 1. http://www.pbs.org/newshour/updates/six-new-significant-things-donald-trump-said-immigration/ (accessed April 2017).

Dezalay, Yves, and Bryant Garth. 2002. *The Internationalization of Palace Wars*. Chicago: University of Chicago Press.

Diamond, Jeremy. 2015. "Trump: 'I Will Be a Great Unifier.'" CNN Politics, October 26. http://www.cnn.com/2015/10/25/politics/donald-trump-democrats-republicans-bipartisanship-great-unifier/ (accessed March 2017).

———. 2016. "Trump Refers to 'Ghettos' in Discussing African-American Issues." CNN Politics, October 17. http://www.cnn.com/2016/10/27/politics/donald-trump-ghettos-african-americans/ (accessed January 2017).

DiMaggio, Paul, John Evans, and Bethany Bryson. 1996. "Have Americans' Social Attitudes Become More Polarized?" *American Journal of Sociology* 102: 690–755.

Dionne, E. J. 2016. *Why the Right Went Wrong: Conservatism from Goldwater to the Tea Party and Beyond*. New York: Simon and Schuster.

Dionne, E. J., Norman J. Ornstein, and Thomas E. Mann. 2017. *One Nation After Trump*. New York: St. Martin's Press.

Dixon, Marc. 2016. "Labor Rights in the Midwest." Unpublished manuscript, Department of Sociology, Dartmouth College.

Doherty, Carroll. 2016. "5 Facts About Trump Supporters' Views on Immigration." Pew Research Center, August 25. http://www.pewresearch.org/fact-tank/2016/08/25/5-facts-about-trump-supporters-views-of-immigration/ (accessed March 2017).

Domhoff, G. William. 2013. *The Myth of Liberal Ascendency*. Boulder, CO: Paradigm Publishers.

———. 2014. "Is the Corporate Elite Fractured, or Is There Continuing Corporate Dominance? Two Contrasting Views." *Class, Race and Corporate Power* 3(1): 1–42.

Dovere, Edward-Isaac. 2016. "How Clinton Lost Michigan—and Blew the Election." *Politico*, December 14. http://www.politico.com/story/2016/12/michigan-hillary-clinton-trump-232547 (accessed January 2017).

Drake, Bruce. 2013. "Public Has Mixed Views About Government Regulation of Banks." Pew Research Center, November 20. http://www.pewresearch.org/fact-tank/2013/11/20/public-has-mixed-views-about-government-regulation-of-banks/ (accessed March 2017).

Drutman, Lee. 2015. "How Corporate Lobbyists Conquered American Democracy." *The Atlantic*, April 20. https://www.theatlantic.com/business/archive/2015/04/how-corporate-lobbyists-conquered-american-democracy/390822/ (accessed June 2017).

Duina, Francesco. 2017. *Broke and Patriotic: Why Poor Americans Love Their Country*. Stanford, CA: Stanford University Press.

Economic Policy Institute. 2017. "State of Working America Data Library." http://www.epi.org/data/#?subject=wage-avg (accessed May 2017).

The Economist. 2016. "How Donald Trump Thinks About Trade." November 9. http://www.economist.com/news/united-states/21709921-americas-next-president-wants-pull-out-existing-trade-deals-and-put-future-ones (accessed February 2017).

———. 2017a. "The Rage Against Macron." May 6, p. 47.

———. 2017b. "Don't Discount Marine Le Pen: France's Election." May 6, pp. 10–11.

———. 2017c. "The Happy Gambler: France's Presidential Election." April 29, p. 37.

———. 2017d. "Time to Decide: The French Election." April 22, p. 10.

———. 2017e. "Beyond the Hexagon: Foreign Policy in France's Election." April 1, p. 45.

———. 2017f. "France's Next Revolution." March 4, p. 7.

The Economist, Special Report. 2017. "Trump's America." July 1, pp. 1–10.

Edin, Kathryn, and Maria Kefalas. 2005. *Promises I Can Keep: Why Poor Women Put Motherhood Before Marriage.* Berkeley: University of California Press.

Edsall, Thomas Byrne. 1984. *The New Politics of Inequality.* New York: Norton.

———. 2012. *The Age of Austerity: How Scarcity Will Remake American Politics.* New York: Doubleday.

Edsall, Mary, and Thomas Byrne Edsall. 1991. *Chain Reaction: The Impact of Race, Rights, and Taxes on American Politics.* New York: Norton.

Emirbayer, Mustafa, and Matthew Desmond. 2015. *The Racial Order.* Chicago: University of Chicago Press.

Equal Justice Initiative. 2015. *Lynching in America.* 2nd ed. Montgomery, AL: Equal Justice Initiative.

Erlanger, Steven, and Julie Hirschfeld Davis. 2017. "Once Dominant, the United States Finds Itself Isolated at G-20." *New York Times,* July 7. https://www.nytimes.com/2017/07/07/world/europe/trump-g-20-trade-climate.html?mcubz=0 (accessed July 2017).

Evans, C. Lawrence. 2011. "Growing the Vote: Majority Party Whipping in the U.S. House, 1955-2002." Paper presented at the 10th Annual Congress and History Conference, Brown University, June 9–10. http://www.vanderbilt.edu/csdi/events/Evans_Growing-the-vote.pdf (accessed February 2017).

Fahri, Paul. 2009. "Limbaugh's Audience Size? It's Largely Up in the Air." *Washington Post,* March 7. http://www.washingtonpost.com/wp-dyn/content/article/2009/03/06/AR2009030603435.html (accessed February 2007).

Fantasia, Rick, and Kim Voss. 2004. *Hard Work: Remaking the American Labor Movement.* Berkeley, CA: University of California Press.

Farley, Robert. 2016. "Trump's Bogus Voter Fraud Claims." FactCheck.org, October 19. http://www.factcheck.org/2016/10/trumps-bogus-voter-fraud-claims/ (accessed January 2017).

Fausset, Richard, Alan Blinder, and John Eligon. 2016. "Donald Trump's Description of Black America is Offending Those Living in It." *New York Times,* August 24. https://www.nytimes.com/2016/08/25/us/politics/donald-trump-black-voters.html?_r=0 (accessed February 2017).

Federal Reserve Bank of San Francisco. 2009. "U.S. Household Deleveraging and Future Consumption Growth." FRBSF Economic Letter, May 15. San Francisco, CA: US Federal Reserve Bank. http://www.frbsf.org/economic-research/publications/economic-letter/2009/may/us-household-deleveraging-consumption-growth/#1 (accessed January 2017).

Federal Reserve Bank of St. Louis. 2013. *Federal Debt: Total Public Debt as Percent of Gross Domestic Product.* St. Louis, MO: US Federal Reserve Bank. http://research.stlouisfed.org/fred2/series/GFDEGDQ188S (accessed November 2013).

Feldman, Brian. 2016. "The Fake Donald Trump Quote That Just Won't Die." *New York Magazine,* November 4. http://nymag.com/selectall/2016/11/the-fake-donald-trump-quote-that-just-wont-die.html (accessed February 2017).

Ferguson, Thomas, and Joel Rogers. 1986. *Right Turn.* New York: Hill and Wang.

Fingerhut, Hannah. 2016. "Most Americans Say U.S. Economic System Is Unfair, but High-Income Republicans Disagree." Pew Research Center, February 10. http://www.pewresearch.org/fact-tank/2016/02/10/most-americans-say-u-s-economic-system-is-unfair-but-high-income-republicans-disagree/ (accessed May 2017).

Finlayson, Alan. 2017. "Brexitism." *London Review of Books* 39(10): 22–23.

Fiorina, Morris. 2005. *Culture War? The Myth of a Polarized America.* New York: Pearson.

Fischer, Marc. 2016. "Donald Trump Doesn't Read Much. Being President Probably Wouldn't Change That." *Washington Post,* July 17. https://www.washingtonpost.com/politics/donald-trump-doesnt-read-much-being-president-probably-wouldnt-change-that/2016/07/17/d2ddf2bc-4932-11e6-90a8-fb84201e0645_story.html?utm_term=.c4755bb9eff6 (accessed March 2017).

Fligstein, Neil. 2008. *Euro-Clash.* New York: Oxford University Press.

Flitter, Emily, and Chris Kahn. 2016. "Exclusive: Trump Supporters More Likely to View Blacks Negatively—Reuters/Ipsos Poll." Reuters, June 28. http://www.reuters.com/article/us-usa-election-race-idUSKCN0ZE2SW (accessed January 2017).

Foran, Clare. 2016. "The Curse of Hillary Clinton's Ambition." *The Atlantic,* September 17. http://www.theatlantic.com/politics/archive/2016/09/clinton-trust-sexism/500489/ (accessed January 2017).

Fortune Magazine. 2016. "Donald Trump Says He Would Dismantle Dodd-Frank Wall Street Regulation." May 18. http://fortune.com/2016/05/18/trump-dodd-frank-wall-street/ (accessed February 2017).

Fourcade, Marion. 2006. "The Construction of a Global Profession: The Transnationalization of Economics." *American Journal of Sociology* 112: 145–94.

———. 2009. *Economists and Societies.* Princeton, NJ: Princeton University Press.

Fourcade-Gourinchas, Marion, and Sarah Babb. 2002. "The Rebirth of the Liberal Creed: Paths to Neoliberalism in Four Countries." *American Journal of Sociology* 108: 533–79.

Fox News. 2014. "FBI National Domestic Threat Assessment Omits Islamist Terrorism." August 29. http://www.foxnews.com/politics/2014/08/29/fbi-national-domestic-threat-assessment-omits-islamist-terrorism.html (accessed January 2017).

———. 2016. "Trump Outlines Vision for Economy, Promising Large Tax Cuts." September 15. http://www.foxnews.com/politics/2016/09/15/trump-outlines-vision-for-economy-promising-large-tax-cuts.html (accessed February 2017).

Frank, Thomas. 2004. *What's the Matter with Kansas?* New York: Picador.

———. 2016. *Listen, Liberals.* New York: Picador.

Franken, Al. 2017. *Al Franken, Giant of the Senate.* New York: Twelve.

Freeman, Richard B. 2007. *America Works.* New York: Russell Sage Foundation.

Freeman, Richard B., and Lawrence Katz. 1994. "Rising Wage Inequality: The United States vs. Other Advanced Countries." In *Working Under Different Rules,* edited by Richard Freeman, pp. 29–62. New York: Russell Sage Foundation.

Freeman, Richard B., and James L. Medoff. 1984. *What Do Unions Do?* New York: Basic Books.

Frerichs, Sabine, and Suvi Sankari. 2016. "Workers No Longer Welcome? Europeanization of Solidarity in the Wake of Brexit." *Socio-Economic Review* 14(4): 840–844.

Froud, Julie, Sukhdev Johal, and Karel Williams. 2016. "Multiple Economies: Before and After Brexit." *Socio-Economic Review* 14(4): 814–819.

Fukuyama, Francis. 2014. *Political Order and Political Decay.* New York: Farrar, Straus and Giroux.

Gallup Polling. 2015. "Big Government Still Named as Biggest Threat to U.S." December 22. http://www.gallup.com/poll/187919/big-government-named-biggest-threat.aspx (accessed May 2017).

———. 2016a. "U.S. Congress Approval Remains Low." http://www.gallup.com/poll/190598/congress-approval-remains-low.aspx (accessed February 2017).

———. 2016b. "Economy Continues to Rank as Top U.S. Problem." http://www.gallup.com/poll/191513/economy-continues-rank-top-problem.aspx (accessed April 2017).

———. 2017a. "Abortion." http://www.gallup.com/poll/1576/abortion.aspx (accessed January 2017).

———. 2017b. "Trust in Government." http://www.gallup.com/poll/5392/trust-government. aspx (accessed February 2017).

———. 2017c. "Taxes." http://www.gallup.com/poll/1714/taxes.aspx (accessed February 2017).

———. 2017d. "Presidential Approval Ratings—Gallup Historical Statistics and Trends." http://www.gallup.com/poll/116677/presidential-approval-ratings-gallup-historical-statistics-trends.aspx (accessed February 2017).

———. 2017e. "Gallup Daily: Trump Job Approval." http://www.gallup.com/poll/201617/gallup-daily-trump-job-approval.aspx (accessed July 2017).

———. 2017f. "Economy." http://www.gallup.com/poll/1609/consumer-views-economy. aspx (accessed April 2017).

Ganz, Marshall. 2000. "Resources and Resourcefulness: Strategic Capacity in the Unionization of California Agriculture, 1959-1966." *American Journal of Sociology* 103: 1003–62.

Gee, Lisa Christensen, Matthew Gardner, and Meg Wiehe. 2016. "Undocumented Immigrants' State and Local Tax Contributions." Washington, DC: Institute on Taxation and Economic Policy.

Ghandnoosh, Nazgol. 2014. "Race and Punishment: Racial Perceptions of Crime and Support for Punitive Policies." Washington, DC: Sentencing Project. http://www.sentencingproject. org/wp-content/uploads/2015/11/Race-and-Punishment.pdf (accessed January 2017).

Ghandnoosh, Nazgol, and Josh Rovner. 2017. "Immigration and Public Safety." Washington, DC: Sentencing Project. http://www.sentencingproject.org/wp-content/uploads/2017/03/Immigration-and-Public-Safety.pdf (accessed June 2017).

Gibney, Bruce. 2017. *A Generation of Sociopaths.* New York: Hachette Books

Gilder, George. 1981. *Wealth and Poverty.* New York: Bantam.

Gill, Stephen, and David Law. 1988. *The Global Political Economy.* Baltimore, MD: Johns Hopkins University Press.

Gillespie, Patrick. 2016. "Donald Trump Check: Has NAFTA 'Destroyed Our Country'?" *CNN Money,* September 16. http://money.cnn.com/2016/09/16/news/economy/donald-trump-nafta-mexico-china-tariff/ (accessed February 2017).

Gleckman, Howard. 2016. "Do Deficits Matter? Trump Says No; Clinton Says Yes." *Forbes Magazine,* October 20. http://www.forbes.com/sites/beltway/2016/10/20/do-deficits-matter-trump-says-no-clinton-says-yes-but/#3eb65bcb6c11 (accessed February 2017).

Goldberg, Jonah. 2017. "Trump Says He'll Unite the Country. Yeah, Right." *Los Angeles Times,* January 16. http://www.latimes.com/opinion/op-ed/la-oe-goldberg-trump-john-lewis-20170117-story.html (accessed February 2017).

Goldfield, Michael. 1989. *The Decline of Organized labor in the United States.* Chicago, IL: University of Chicago Press.

Gonzalez-Barrera, Ana. 2015. "More Mexicans Leaving Than Coming to the U.S." Pew Research Center, Hispanic Trends, November 19. http://www.pewhispanic.org/2015/11/19/more-mexicans-leaving-than-coming-to-the-u-s/ (accessed January 2017).

Goodwyn, Lawrence. 1978. *The Populist Movement.* New York: Oxford University Press.

Graham, Otis L., Jr. 1992. *Losing Time: The Industrial Policy Debate.* Cambridge, MA: Harvard University Press.

Green, Joshua. 2017. *Devil's Bargain: Steve Bannon, Donald Trump, and the Storming of the Presidency.* New York: Penguin Press.

Grey, Christopher. 2016. "The New Politics of Cosmopolitans and Locals." *Socio-Economic Review* 14(4): 829–832.

Griswold, Daniel. 2016. "Globalization Isn't Killing Factory Jobs. Trade Is Actually Why Manufacturing Is Up 40%." *Los Angeles Times,* August 1. http://www.latimes.com/opinion/op-ed/la-oe-griswold-globalization-and-trade-help-manufacturing-20160801-snap-story. html (accessed January 2017).

Grusky, David, Marybeth Mattingly, and Charles Varner. 2016. "The Poverty and Inequality Report." In *Pathways* (Special Issue), pp. 3–9. Stanford, CA: Stanford Center on Poverty and Inequality.

Guttmacher Institute. 2017. "An Overview of Abortion Laws." January 1. Guttmacher Center for Population Research Innovation and Dissemination. https://www.guttmacher.org/state-policy/explore/overview-abortion-laws (accessed January 2017).

Hacker, Jacob, and Paul Pierson. 2010. *Winner-Take-All Politics*. New York: Simon and Schuster.

Hall, Peter, editor. 1989. *The Political Power of Economic Ideas: Keynesianism Across Nations*. Princeton, NJ: Princeton University Press.

Harrell, Erika, Lynn Langton, Lance Couzens, and Hope Smiley-McDonald. 2014. "Household Poverty and Nonfatal Violent Victimization, 2008-2012." Washington, DC: US Department of Justice. https://www.bjs.gov/content/pub/pdf/hpnvv0812.pdf (accessed January 2017).

Harrington, Brooke. 2017. "Yes, Trump's Cabinet Is Super Rich. That's Not Why We Should Be Worried." *The Atlantic*, January 19. https://www.washingtonpost.com/posteverything/wp/2017/01/19/trump-rich-cabinet/?utm_term=.d06b77fee66f (accessed April 2017).

Harrison, Bennett. 1994. *Lean and Mean*. New York: Basic Books.

Harrison, Bennett, and Barry Bluestone. 1988. *The Great U-Turn*. New York: Basic Books.

Heilbroner, Robert, and William Milberg. 1995. *The Crisis of Vision in Modern Economic Thought*. New York: Cambridge University Press.

Helyar, John. 2003. "RJR Goes from Ashes to Ashes: How a 15-Year-Old LBO Still Haunts a Once-Mighty Brand." *Fortune Magazine*, October 13. http://archive.fortune.com/magazines/fortune/fortune_archive/2003/10/13/350888/index.htm (accessed January 2017).

Hemmer, Christopher, and Peter J. Katzenstein. 2002. "Why Is There No NATO in Asia? Collective Identity, Regionalism, and the Origins of Multilateralism." *International Organization* 56: 575–607.

Herrman, John. 2016. "What We've Learned About the Media Industry During This Election." *New York Times*, November 8. https://www.nytimes.com/2016/11/09/business/media/what-weve-learned-about-the-media-industry-during-this-election.html (accessed January 2017).

Hirsch, Barry, and David Macpherson. 2016. "U.S. Historical Tables: Union Membership, Coverage, Density and Employment, 1973-2015." Unionstats.com, Union Membership and Coverage Database from the CPS. http://www.unionstats.com/ (accessed January 2017).

Hochschild, Arlie. 2016. *Strangers in Their Own Land*. New York: New Press.

Hofstadter, Richard. 1962. *Anti-Intellectualism in American Life*. New York: Vintage.

Holan, Angie Drobnic. 2009. "Sarah Palin Falsely Claims Barack Obama Runs a 'Death Panel.'" *PolitiFact*, August 10. http://www.politifact.com/truth-o-meter/statements/2009/aug/10/sarah-palin/sarah-palin-barack-obama-death-panel/ (accessed February 2017).

House, Billy, and Steven Dennis. 2017. "Trump Says Undocumented Immigrants Cost Him Popular Vote." *Bloomberg Politics*, January 24. https://www.bloomberg.com/politics/articles/2017-01-24/trump-again-claims-undocumented-immigrants-cost-him-popular-vote (accessed February 2017).

Howard, Adam. 2016. "Trump's Auto Bailout Inconsistency Could Leave Michigan Cold." *NBC News*, August 8. http://www.nbcnews.com/news/us-news/trump-s-auto-bailout-inconsistency-could-leave-michigan-cold-n625226 (accessed February 2017).

Hoxie, Josh. 2016. "Americans Want to Be More Equal." *U.S. News and World Report*, August 31. https://www.usnews.com/opinion/articles/2016-08-31/we-arent-as-divided-on-inequality-as-data-on-donald-trump-voters-suggest (accessed May 2017).

Huffman, John Pearley. 2010. "How the Chevy Vega Nearly Destroyed GM." *Popular Mechanics*, October 19. http://www.popularmechanics.com/cars/a6424/how-the-chevy-vega-almost-destroyed-gm/ (accessed January2017).

Hulse, Carl. 2017. "The Republicans in Power: From 'We Got This' to 'What Now?'" *New York Times*, March 27. https://www.nytimes.com/2017/03/27/us/politics/republicans-congress-failure-health-care-law.html (accessed March 2017).

International Monetary Fund. 2013. "IMF Releases Data on the Currency Composition of Foreign Exchange Reserves with Additional Data on Australian and Canadian Dollar Reserves." IMF Press Releases, June 28. http://www.imf.org/external/np/sec/pr/2013/pr13236.htm (accessed November 2013).

Investor's Business Daily. 2015. "Can't-Be-Bought Trump Just Got Bought." October 19. http://www.investors.com/politics/editorials/can-not-be-bought-donald-trump-got-bought/ (accessed March 2017).

Irwin, Neil. 2016. "Donald Trump Trashes NAFTA. But Unwinding It Would Come at a Huge Cost." *New York Times*, October 3. https://www.nytimes.com/2016/10/04/upshot/donald-trump-trashes-nafta-but-unwinding-it-would-come-at-a-huge-cost.html?_r=0 (accessed February 2017).

Irwin, Neil, and Josh Katz. 2016. "The Geography of Trumpism." *New York Times*, March 12. http://www.nytimes.com/2016/03/13/upshot/the-geography-of-trumpism.html?_r=0 (accessed April 2016).

Jackman, Molly. 2013. "ALEC's Influence over Lawmaking in State Legislatures." Brookings Institution, December 6. https://www.brookings.edu/articles/alecs-influence-over-lawmaking-in-state-legislatures/ (accessed June 2017).

Jamieson, Kathleen Hall. 1996. *Packaging the Presidency.* New York: Oxford University Press.

John Birch Society. 2017. "History." http://www.jbs.org/about-jbs/history (accessed January 2017).

Johnson, Richard. 2017. "Racially Polarized Partisanship and the Obama Presidency." In *The Obama Presidency and the Politics of Change*, edited by Edward Ashbee and John Dumbrell, pp. 161–180. New York: Palgrave Macmillan.

Jones, Jeffrey M. 2012. "Gender Gap in 2012 Vote is Largest in Gallup's History." *Gallup News*, November 9. http://news.gallup.com/poll/158588/gender-gap-2012-vote-largest-gallup-history.aspx (accessed April 2017).

Jones, Robert P., Daniel Cox, E. J. Dionne Jr., and William A. Galston. 2011. "What It Means to Be American: Attitudes in an Increasingly Diverse America Ten Years after 9/11." Public Religion Research Institute. http://www.prri.org/research/what-it-means-to-be-american/ (accessed January 2017).

Judis, John. 2016. *The Populist Explosion.* New York: Columbia Global Reports.

Judt, Tony. 2010. *Ill Fares the Land.* New York: Penguin.

Kaiser Health Tracking Poll. 2017. "The Public's Views on the ACA." February 24. http://kff.org/interactive/kaiser-health-tracking-poll-the-publics-views-on-the-aca/#?response=Favorable--Unfavorable&label&rMax=1464672214588.2354&rMin=1401513814588.2354 (accessed March 2017).

Keister, Lisa. 2005. *Getting Rich: America's New Rich and How They Got That Way.* New York: Cambridge University Press.

Kennedy, Dan. 2016. "How the Media Blew the 2016 Campaign." *U.S. News and World Report*, November 6. http://www.usnews.com/news/politics/articles/2016-11-06/how-the-media-blew-the-2016-campaign (accessed January 2017).

Kenworthy, Lane. 2011. *Progress for the Poor*. New York: Oxford University Press.

———. 2014. *Social Democratic America*. New York: Oxford University Press.

———. 2016. "Is Income Inequality Harmful?" https://lanekenworthy.net/is-income-inequality-harmful/#equality-of-opportunity (accessed May 2017).

Keohane, Robert O. 1984. *After Hegemony*. Princeton, NJ: Princeton University Press.

Kessler, Glenn. 2012. "When Did McConnell Say He Wanted to Make Obama a One-Term President?" *Washington Post*, September 25. https://www.washingtonpost.com/blogs/fact-checker/post/when-did-mcconnell-say-he-wanted-to-make-obama-a-one-term-president/2012/09/24/79fd5cd8-0696-11e2-afff-d6c7f20a83bf_blog.html?utm_term=.87fbf9ce7fdf (accessed February 2017).

Kieley, Eugene, Lori Robertson, and Robert Farley. 2017. "President Trump's Inaugural Address." FactCheck.org, January 20. http://www.factcheck.org/2017/01/president-trumps-inaugural-address/ (accessed January 2017).

Kingdon, John. 1995. *Agendas, Alternatives, and Public Policies*. 2nd ed. New York: Harper Collins.

Kingkade, Tyler. 2012. "State Budget Cuts Drive Up Tuition at Public Universities: New York Federal Reserve Report." *Huffington Post*, September 25. http://www.huffingtonpost.com/2012/09/25/state-budget-cuts-drive-tuition-hikes_n_1911044.html (accessed April 2016).

Kirshner, Jonathan. 2014. *American Power After the Financial Crisis*. Ithaca, NY: Cornell University Press.

Klamer, Arjo. 1983. *Conversations with Economists*. Totowa, NJ: Roman and Allenhald.

Kohn, Sally. 2016. "Trump Doesn't Understand What Sharia Is." CNN Opinion, August 25. http://www.cnn.com/2016/08/25/opinions/trump-doesnt-understand-sharia-kohn/ (accessed January 2017).

Kozol, Jonathan. 1967. *Death at an Early Age*. Boston: Houghton Mifflin.

Krauss, Clifford, and Michael Corkery. 2016. "A Bleak Outlook for Trump's Promise to Coal Miners." *New York Times*, November 19. https://www.nytimes.com/2016/11/20/business/energy-environment/a-bleak-outlook-for-trumps-promises-to-coal-miners.html?_r=0 (accessed February 2017).

Kriesi, Hanspeter. 2016. "The Implications of the Euro-Crisis for Democracy." Paper presented at the IPP World Forum, Order and Governance in the Contemporary World, Institute for Public Policy, South China University of Technology, Guangzhou, August 20–21, 2016.

Kristensen, Peer Hull, and Jonathan Zeitlin. 2005. *Local Players in Global Games*. New York: Oxford University Press.

Krogstad, Jens Manuel, Jeffrey Passel, and D'Vera Cohn. 2016. "5 Facts About Illegal Immigration in the U.S." Pew Research Center, November 3. http://www.pewresearch.org/fact-tank/2016/11/03/5-facts-about-illegal-immigration-in-the-u-s/ (accessed January 2017).

Krugman, Paul. 2015. "Trade and the Decline of U.S. Manufacturing Employment." *New York Times*, May 19. http://krugman.blogs.nytimes.com/2015/05/19/trade-and-the-decline-of-us-manufacturing-employment/ (accessed January 2017).

Kulish, Nicholas. 2017. "With Ally in Oval Office, Immigration Hard-Liners Ascend to Power." *New York Times*, April 25. https://www.nytimes.com/2017/04/24/us/with-ally-in-oval-office-immigration-hard-liners-ascend-to-power.html?_r=0 (accessed April 2017).

Kurzman, Charles. 2017. "Muslim-American Involvement with Violent Extremism, 2016." Triangle Center on Terrorism and Homeland Security, Department of Sociology, University of North Carolina-Chapel Hill. https://sites.duke.edu/tcths/files/2017/01/Kurzman_Muslim-American_Involvement_in_Violent_Extremism_2016.pdf (accessed January 2017).

Lakoff, George. 2004. *Don't Think of an Elephant! Know Your Values and Frame the Debate*. White River Junction, VT: Chelsea Green.

Landgrave, Michelangelo, and Alex Nowrasteh. 2017. "Criminal Immigrants: Their Numbers, Demographics, and Countries of Origin." Immigration Research and Policy Brief. Washington, DC: Cato Institute. https://object.cato.org/sites/cato.org/files/pubs/pdf/immigration_brief-1.pdf (accessed June 2017).

Le Galès, Patrick. 2016. "Brexit: UK as an Exception or the Banal Avant Garde of the Disintegration of the EU?" *Socio-Economic Review* 14(4): 848–854.

Lee, Michelle Ye Hee. 2015. "Donald Trump's False Comments Connecting Mexican Immigrants and Crime." *Washington Post*, July 2015. https://www.washingtonpost.com/news/fact-checker/wp/2015/07/08/donald-trumps-false-comments-connecting-mexican-immigrants-and-crime/?utm_term=.9ba93ee0cf3e (accessed January 2017).

Leicht, Kevin, and Scott Fitzgerald. 2007. *Postindustrial Peasants*. New York: Worth.

———. 2014. *Middle Class Meltdown in America*. New York: Routledge.

Lieberson, Stanley. 1980. *A Piece of the Pie*. Berkeley, CA: University of California Press.

Lim, Elvin. 2008. *The Anti-Intellectual Presidency*. New York: Oxford University Press.

Lin, Ken-Hu, and Donald Tomaskovic-Devey. 2013. "Financialization and U.S. Income Inequality, 1970-2008." *American Journal of Sociology* 118: 1284–1329.

Lipset, Seymour Martin. 1996. *American Exceptionalism*. New York: W. W. Norton.

Lipset, Seymour Martin, and Earl Raab. 1970. *The Politics of Unreason: Extremism in America, 1790-1977*. New York: Harper Collins.

Lopéz, Ian Haney. 2014. *Dog Whistle Politics*. New York: Oxford University Press.

Loveless, Tom. 2017. "How Well Are American Students Learning?" The 2017 Brown Center Report on American Education, March. Washington, DC: Brookings Institution, Brown Center on Education. https://www.brookings.edu/wp-content/uploads/2017/03/2017-brown-center-report-on-american-education.pdf (accessed April 2017).

Lucas, Robert. 1972. "Expectations and the Neutrality of Money." *Journal of Economic Theory* 4(2): 315–335.

Luhby, Tami. 2015. "Trump Says Wages Are Too Low." *CNN Money*, December 28. http://money.cnn.com/2015/12/28/news/economy/trump-wages/ (accessed February 2017).

MacLean, Nancy. 2017. Democracy in Chains: The Deep History of the Radical Right's Stealth Plan for America. New York: Viking.

Maddison, Angus. 2001. *The World Economy: A Millennial Perspective*. Paris: OECD.

Mann, Michael, and Norman Ornstein. 2012. *It's Even Worse Than It Looks*. New York: Basic Books.

Manza, Jeff, and Clem Brooks. 1998. "The Gender Gap in US Presidential Elections: When? Why? Implications?" *American Journal of Sociology* 103:1235–1266.

———. 2016. "Why Aren't Americans Angrier About Rising Inequality?" In *Pathways* (Winter), pp. 22–26. Stanford, CA: Stanford Center on Poverty and Inequality.

Manza, Jeff, and Christopher Uggen. 2008. *Locked Out: Felon Disenfranchisement and American Democracy*. New York: Oxford University Press.

Martel, Frances. 2014. "Report: Islamist Terrorism Absent from FBI Lists of Domestic Terror Threats." *Breitbart*, September 1. http://www.breitbart.com/national-security/2014/09/01/report-islamist-terrorism-absent-from-fbi-list-of-domestic-terror-threats/ (accessed January 2017).

Martin, Cathie Jo. 1991. *Shifting the Burden: The Struggle over Growth and Corporate Taxation*. Chicago, IL: University of Chicago Press.

Martin, Isaac. 2008. *The Permanent Tax Revolt*. Stanford, CA: Stanford University Press.

Massey, Doug. 2015. "The Real Hispanic Challenge." In *Pathways* (Spring), pp. 3–7. Stanford, CA: Stanford Center on Poverty and Inequality.

Massey, Doug, and Kerstin Gentsch. 2014. "Undocumented Migration and the Wages of Mexican Immigrants." *International Migration Review* 48(2): 482–499.

Mayer, Jane. 2016. *Dark Money: The Hidden History of the Billionaires Behind the Rise of the Radical Right*. New York: Doubleday.

———. 2017. "Trump's Money Man." *New Yorker*, March 27, pp. 34–45.

McAdam, Doug, and Karina Kloos. 2014. *Deeply Divided*. New York: Oxford University Press.

McCammon, Sarah. 2016. "Conservative Christians Grapple with Whether 'Religious Freedom' Includes Muslims." *National Public Radio*, June 29. http://www.npr.org/2016/06/29/483901761/conservative-christians-grapple-with-what-religious-freedom-means-for-muslims (accessed February 2017).

McElwee, Sean, and Jason McDaniel. 2017. "Fear of Diversity Made People More Likely to Vote Trump." *The Nation*, March 14. https://www.thenation.com/article/fear-of-diversity-made-people-more-likely-to-vote-trump/ (accessed June 2017).

McKinley, John, and Joan Arches. 1985. "Towards the Proletarianization of Physicians." *International Journal of Health Services* 15: 161–195.

McLanahan, Sara, and Gary Sandefur. 1994. *Growing Up with a Single Parent*. Cambridge, MA: Harvard University Press.

Media Matters for America. 2011. "Fox's Five Agree with Limbaugh that 'Comrade Obama' Is Indeed a Socialist." December 22. http://mediamatters.org/video/2011/12/22/foxs-five-agree-with-limbaugh-that-comrade-obam/185706 (accessed February 2017).

Megerian, Chris. 2016. "What Donald Trump Has Said Through the Years About Where President Obama Was Born." *Los Angeles Times*, September 16. http://www.latimes.com/politics/la-na-pol-trump-birther-timeline-20160916-snap-htmlstory.html (accessed February 2017).

Miller, S. A. 2016. "Donald Trump: I'll Be the Greatest President for Jobs That God Ever Created." *Washington Post*, September 28. http://www.washingtontimes.com/news/2016/sep/28/donald-trump-ill-be-greatest-president-jobs-god-ev/ (accessed January 2017).

Mills, C. Wright. 1951. *White Collar: The American Middle Classes*. New York: Oxford University Press.

———. 1959. *The Sociological Imagination*. New York: Oxford University Press.

Mirowski, Philip, and Dieter Plehwe, editors. 2009. *The Road from Mont Pelerin: The Making of the Neoliberal Thought Collective*. Cambridge, MA: Harvard University Press.

Mishel, Lawrence, Elise Gould, and Josh Bivens. 2015. "Wage Stagnation in Nine Charts." Economic Policy Institute Report, January 6. http://www.epi.org/publication/charting-wage-stagnation/ (accessed January 2017).

Mishel, Lawrence, Josh Bivens, Elise Gould, and Heidi Shierholz. 2012. *The State of Working America*. 12th ed. Ithaca, NY: Cornell University Press.

Mizruchi, Mark. 2013. *The Fracturing of the American Corporate Elite*. Cambridge, MA: Harvard University Press.

Mudge, Stephanie. 2008. "What Is Neoliberalism?" *Socio-Economic Review* 6(4): 703–731.

———. 2011. "What's Left of Leftism? Neoliberal Politics in Western Party Systems, 1945-2008." *Social Science History* 35: 337–380.

Mudge, Stephanie, and Anthony Chen. 2014. "Political Parties and the Sociological Imagination: Past, Present and Future." *Annual Review of Sociology* 40: 305–330.

Murray, Charles. 1984. *Losing Ground*. New York: Basic Books.

Nance, Malcolm. 2016. *The Plot to Hack America*. New York: Skyhorse Publishing.

National Right to Work Committee. 2017. "State Right to Work Timeline." https://nrtwc.org/facts-issues/state-right-to-work-timeline-2016/ (accessed January 2017).

New York Times. 2016a. "Transcript: Donald Trump's Taped Comments About Women." October 8. https://www.nytimes.com/2016/10/08/us/donald-trump-tape-transcript.html?_r=0 (accessed February 2017).

———. 2016b. "Election 2016: Exit Polls." November 8. http://www.nytimmes.com/interative/2016/11/08/US/politics/election-exit-polls.html?_r=0 (accessed April 2017).

Newport, Frank. 2015. "Americans Continue to Say That U.S. Wealth Distribution Is Unfair." Gallup Polling, May 4. http://www.gallup.com/poll/182987/americans-continue-say-wealth-distribution-unfair.aspx (accessed May 2017).

North Atlantic Treaty Organization. 1970. "Defense Expenditures of NATO Countries." Press release M2(70)1/17, December 2. http://www.nato.int/nato_static_fl2014/assets/pdf/pdf_1970_12/20100830_1970-001.pdf (accessed January 2017).

Nossiter, Adam. 2017. "French Parties Unify Against Le Pen: 'This Is Deadly Serious Now.'" *New York Times*, April 23. https://www.nytimes.com/2017/04/23/world/europe/france-election-parties-unify-against-marine-le-pen.html (accessed April 2017).

Nussbaum, Emily. 2017. "Guilty Pleasure: How TV Created Donald Trump." *New Yorker*, July 31, pp. 22–26.

O'Flaherty, Brendan. 2015. *The Economics of Race in the United States.* Cambridge, MA: Harvard University Press.

O'Keefe, Ed, and Jenna Johnson. 2016. "Trump Suggests That Illegal Immigrants Will Vote as Parties Clash over Voter Access." *Washington Post*, October 7. https://www.washingtonpost.com/politics/trump-suggests-illegal-immigrants-will-vote-as-parties-clash-over-voter-access/2016/10/07/fdca9404-8ca2-11e6-875e-2c1bfe943b66_story.html?utm_term=.a2fac43a8b69 (accessed February 2017).

O'Reily, Jacqueline. 2016. "The Fault Lines Unveiled by Brexit." *Socio-Economic Review* 14(4): 808–814.

Organization for Economic Cooperation and Development. 2016. "Income Inequality Remains High in the Face of Weak Recovery." November. Centre for Opportunity and Equality. Paris: OECD. http://www.oecd.org/social/OECD2016-Income-Inequality-Update.pdf (accessed January 2017).

O'Rourke, P. J. 2017. *How the Hell Did This Happen?* New York: Atlantic Monthly Press.

Osnos, Evan, David Remnick, and Joshua Yaffa. 2017. "Active Measures: What Lay Behind Russian's Interference in the 2016 Election—and What Lies Ahead?" *New Yorker*, March 6, pp. 40–55.

Packer, George. 2013. *The Unwinding.* New York: Farrar, Straus and Giroux.

Panagopoulos, Costas. 2011. "Occupy Wall Street Survey Results, October 2011." Department of Political Science, Fordham University. https://www.fordham.edu/download/downloads/id/2538/occupy_wall_street_survey.pdf (accessed February 2017).

Park, Haeyoun. 2016. "Millions Could Be Blocked from Entering the U.S. Depending on How Trump Would Enforce a Ban on Muslim Immigration." *New York Times*, December 22. https://www.nytimes.com/interactive/2016/07/22/us/politics/trump-immigration-ban-how-could-it-work.html (accessed January 2017).

Pattillo-McCoy, Mary. 1999. *Black Picket Fences.* Chicago: University of Chicago Press.

Pearlstein, Steven. 2012. "Outsourcing: What's the True Impact? Counting Jobs Is Only Part of the Answer." *Washington Post*, July 1. https://www.washingtonpost.com/business/economy/outsourcings-net-effect-on-us-jobs-still-an-open-ended-question/2012/07/01/gJQAs1szGW_story.html?utm_term=.bc1b4c7c153e (accessed January 2017).

Pedraza, Francisco, and Ling Zhu. 2015. "The 'Chilling Effect' of America's New Immigration Enforcement Regime." In *Pathways* (Spring), pp. 13–17. Stanford, CA: Stanford Center on Poverty and Inequality.

Petras, James, and Morris Morley. 1975. *The United States and Chile.* New York: Monthly Review Press.

Pew Research Center. 2012a. "Auto Bailout Now Backed, Stimulus Divisive." Pew Research Center, February 23. http://www.people-press.org/2012/02/23/auto-bailout-now-backed-stimulus-divisive/ (accessed March 2017).

———. 2012b. "Partisan Polarization Surges in Bush and Obama Years." Pew Research Center, June 4. http://www.people-press.org/2012/06/04/partisan-polarization-surges-in-bush-obama-years/ (accessed May 2017).

————. 2014a. "Political Polarization in the American Public." Pew Research Center, US Politics and Policy, June 12. http://www.people-press.org/2014/06/12/political-polarization-in-the-american-public/ (accessed April 2016).

————. 2014b. "Media Sources: Distinct Favorites Emerge on the Left and Right." Pew Research Center, Journalism and Media, October 21. http://www.journalism.org/2014/10/21/section-1-media-sources-distinct-favorites-emerge-on-the-left-and-right/ (accessed May 2017).

————. 2015a. "Parenting in America." Pew Research Center Social and Demographic Trends, December 17. http://www.pewsocialtrends.org/2015/12/17/1-the-american-family-today/ (accessed January 2017).

————. 2015b. "General Opinions About the Federal Government." Pew Research Center, US Politics & Policy, November 23. http://www.people-press.org/2015/11/23/2-general-opinions-about-the-federal-government/ (accessed February 2017).

————. 2015c. "Most Say Government Policies Since Recession Have Done Little to Help Middle Class, Poor." Pew Research Center, March 4. http://www.people-press.org/2015/03/04/most-say-government-policies-since-recession-have-done-little-to-help-middle-class-poor/ (accessed February 2017).

————. 2015d. "Latest Trends in Religious Restrictions and Hostilities." Pew Research Center. http://www.pewforum.org/files/2015/02/Restrictions2015_fullReport.pdf (accessed December 2016).

————. 2015e. "Across Racial Lines, More Say Nation Needs to Make Changes to Achieve Racial Equality." Pew Research Center, August 5. http://www.people-press.org/2015/08/05/across-racial-lines-more-say-nation-needs-to-make-changes-to-achieve-racial-equality/ (accessed May 2017).

————. 2015f. "The American Middle Class Is Losing Ground." Pew Research Center, December 9. http://www.pewsocialtrends.org/2015/12/09/the-american-middle-class-is-losing-ground/ (accessed May 2017).

————. 2016a. "On Views of Race and Inequality, Blacks and Whites Are Worlds Apart." Pew Research Center Social and Demographic Trends, June 2016. http://www.pew-socialtrends.org/2016/06/27/3-discrimination-and-racial-inequality/ (accessed January 2017).

————. 2016b. "More Americans Disapprove Than Approve of Health Care law." Pew Research Center, April 27. http://www.people-press.org/2016/04/27/more-americans-disapprove-than-approve-of-health-care-law/ (accessed February 2017).

————. 2016c. "Party Affiliation Among Voters: 1992-2016." Pew Research Center, September 13. http://www.people-press.org/2016/09/13/2-party-affiliation-among-voters-1992-2016/ (accessed May 2017).

————. 2016d. "Partisanship and Political Animosity in 2016." Pew Research Center, June 22. http://www.people-press.org/2016/06/22/partisanship-and-political-animosity-in-2016/ (accessed May 2017).

————. 2016e. "The State of American Jobs." Pew Research Center Social and Demographic Trends, October 6. http://www.pewsocialtrends.org/2016/10/06/the-state-of-american-jobs/ (accessed May 2017).

Pierson, Paul. 1994. *Dismantling the Welfare State?* New York: Cambridge University Press.

Piore, Michael. 1995. *Beyond Individualism.* Cambridge, MA: Harvard University Press.

Piore, Michael, and Charles Sabel. 1984. *The Second Industrial Divide.* New York: Basic Books.

Piven, Frances Fox, and Richard Cloward. 1993. *Regulating the Poor.* New York: Vintage.

Planned Parenthood. 2017. "Planned Parenthood at a Glance." https://www.plannedparenthood.org/about-us/who-we-are/planned-parenthood-at-a-glance (accessed February 2017).

PolitiFact. 2017. http://www.politifact.com/ (accessed January 2017).

Pontusson, Jonas. 2005. *Inequality and Prosperity.* Ithaca, NY: Cornell University Press.

Potok, Mark. 2017. "The Trump Effect." Intelligence Report, Southern Poverty Law Center, February 15. https://www.splcenter.org/fighting-hate/intelligence-report/2017/trump-effect (accessed May 2017).

Prasad, Monica. 2006. *The Politics of Free Markets*. Chicago, IL: University of Chicago Press.

Pressman, Jeremy, and Erica Chenoweth. 2017. "Crowd Estimates." January 21. https://docs.google.com/spreadsheets/u/1/d/1xa0iLqYKz8x9Yc_rfhtmSOJQ2EGgeUVjvV4A8L-sIaxY/htmlview?sle=true (accessed February 2017).

Preston, Julia. 2016. "Immigrants Aren't Taking American's Jobs, New Study Finds." *New York Times*, September 21. https://www.nytimes.com/2016/09/22/us/immigrants-arent-taking-americans-jobs-new-study-finds.html?_r=0 (accessed January 2017).

Prokop, Andrew. 2016. "Why the Electoral College Is the Absolute Worst, Explained." *Vox*, December 19. http://www.vox.com/policy-and-politics/2016/11/7/12315574/electoral-college-explained-presidential-elections-2016 (accessed January 2017).

Public Policy Polling. 2016. "Trump Remains Unpopular; Voters Prefer Obama on SCOTUS Pick." Press release, December 9. Raleigh, NC: Public Policy Polling. http://www.publicpolicy-polling.com/pdf/2015/PPP_Release_National_120916.pdf (accessed January 2017).

Putnam, Robert. 2015. *Our Kids: The American Dream in Crisis*. New York: Simon and Schuster.

Quigley, Aiden. 2017. "All of Trump's Executive Actions So Far." *Politico*, January 25. http://www.politico.com/agenda/story/2017/01/all-trump-executive-actions-000288 (accessed January 2017).

Raphael, T. J. 2016. "A Policy Expert Explains How Anti-Intellectualism Gave Rise to Donald Trump." Public Radio International, August 2. https://www.pri.org/stories/2016-08-02/policy-expert-explains-how-anti-intellectualism-gave-rise-donald-trump (accessed March 2016).

Rasmussen Reports. 2013. "48% See Government as More Concerned with Making Wall Street Firms Profitable." April 4. http://www.rasmussenreports.com/public_content/business/general_business/april_2013/48_see_government_as_more_concerned_with_making_wall_street_firms_profitable (accessed March 2017).

RealClear Politics. 2017. "General Election: Trump vs. Clinton." *RCP Poll Average*, November 6. http://www.realclearpolitics.com/epolls/2016/president/us/general_election_trump_vs_clinton-5491.html (accessed January 2017).

Reeves, Richard. 2016. "Inequality Built the Trump Coalition, Even if He Won't Solve It." Brookings Institution, September 26. https://www.brookings.edu/blog/fixgov/2016/09/26/inequality-built-the-trump-coalition-even-if-he-wont-solve-it/ (accessed February 2017).

Rhee, Nari. 2013. "The Retirement Savings Crisis: Is It Worse Than We Think?" Washington, DC: National Institute on Retirement Security. http://www.nirsonline.org/storage/nirs/documents/Retirement%20Savings%20Crisis/retirementsavingscrisis_final.pdf (accessed January 2017).

Roberts, Paul Craig. 1984. *The Supply-Side Revolution*. Cambridge, MA: Harvard University Press.

Roff, Peter. 2014. "Americans Still Think Government Is the Problem." *U.S. News and World Report*, January 16. http://www.usnews.com/opinion/blogs/peter-roff/2014/01/16/gallup-poll-shows-americans-still-think-government-is-the-problem (accessed February 2017).

Rosenfeld, Jake. 2014. *What Unions No Longer Do*. Cambridge, MA: Harvard University Press.

Roy, Avik. 2015. "Donald Trump on Obamacare on '60 Minutes': 'Everybody's Got to Be Covered' and 'The Government's Gonna Pay for It.'" *Forbes*, September 28. https://www.forbes.com/sites/theapothecary/2015/09/28/donald-trump-on-obamacare-on-60-minutes-everybodys-got-to-be-covered-and-the-governments-gonna-pay-for-it/#615fbc2e540e (accessed March 2017).

Rubin, Alissa. 2017. "Emmanuel Macron and Marine Le Pen Advance in French Election." *New York Times*, April 24. https://www.nytimes.com/2017/04/23/world/europe/emmanuel-macron-marine-le-pen-france-election.html (accessed April 2017).

Rubin, Lillian 1994. *Families on the Fault Line*. New York: Harper Collins.

Rucker, Philip. 2015. "Trump Slams McCain for Being 'Captured' in Vietnam; Other Republicans Quickly Condemn Him." *Washington Post*, July 18. https://www.washingtonpost.com/news/post-politics/wp/2015/07/18/trump-slams-mccain-for-being-captured-in-vietnam/?utm_term=.c24e524fd38c (accessed April 2017).

Ruff, Joshua. 2007. "Levittown: The Archetype for Suburban Development." *HistoryNet*, October 4. http://www.historynet.com/levittown-the-archetype-for-suburban-development.htm (accessed January 2017).

Rutenberg, Jim, and James Poniewozik. 2016. "Can the Media Recover from This Election?" *New York Times*, November 8. https://www.nytimes.com/2016/11/09/arts/television/after-this-election-can-the-media-recover.html (accessed January 2017).

Ryan, William. 1971. *Blaming the Victim*. New York: Pantheon.

Ryssdal, Kai. 2016. "Poll Finds American's Economic Anxiety Reaches New High." *Marketplace*, October 13. https://www.marketplace.org/2016/10/13/economy/americans-economic-anxiety-has-reached-new-high (accessed May 2017).

Sabol, William J., and Heather C. West. 2008. *Bureau of Justice Statistics, Prisoners in 2007*. NCJ224280. Washington, DC: US Department of Justice.

Sampson, Robert, and Janet Lauritsen. 1997. "Racial and Ethnic Disparities in Crime and Criminal Justice in the United States." *Crime and Justice* 21: 311–374. https://dash.harvard.edu/bitstream/handle/1/3226952/sampson_racialethnicdisparities.pdf?sequence=2 (accessed June 1997).

Samuelsohn, Darren. 2017. "Want to See Bipartisanship in Washington? Fire Mueller." *Politico*, July 27. http://www.politico.com/story/2017/07/27/mueller-firing-bipartisan-unity-241052 (accessed July 2017).

Sanati, Cyrus. 2016. "Why Donald Trump Won't Bring Coal Jobs Back to West Virginia." *Fortune Magazine*, July 20. http://fortune.com/2016/07/20/why-donald-trump-wont-bring-coal-jobs-back-to-west-virginia/ (accessed February 2017).

Sanders, Bernie. 2017. "Bernie Sanders: How Democrats Can Stop Losing Elections." Opinion Pages, *New York Times*, June 13. https://www.nytimes.com/2017/06/13/opinion/bernie-sanders-how-democrats-can-stop-losing-elections.html (accessed June 2017).

Sanger, David, and Maggie Haberman. 2016. "In Donald Trump's Worldview, America Comes First, and Everybody Else Pays." *New York Times*, March 26. https://www.nytimes.com/2016/03/27/us/politics/donald-trump-foreign-policy.html?action=Click&contentCollection=BreakingNews&contentID=61307450&pgtype=Homepage&_r=0&mtrref=www.cnn.com&gwh=8CFEB077041D2FBE935717F787CCEED4&gwt=pay (accessed January 2017).

Santana, Maria. 2014. "5 Immigration Myths Debunked." CNN Money, November 20. http://money.cnn.com/2014/11/20/news/economy/immigration-myths/ (accessed January 2017).

Scherrer, Christophe. 1991. "Governance of the Automobile Industry: The Transformation of Labor and Supplier Relations." In *Governance of the American Economy*, edited by John L. Campbell, J. Rogers Hollingsworth, and Leon N. Lindberg, pp. 209–235. New York: Cambridge University Press.

Schwartz, Herman Mark. 2016. "Wealth and Secular Stagnation: The Role of Industrial Organization and Intellectual Property Rights." *Russell Sage Foundation Journal of the Social Sciences* 2(6): 226–249.

Scott, Robert. 2015. "The Manufacturing Footprint and the Importance of U.S. Manufacturing Jobs." Economic Policy Institute, Briefing Paper #388, January 22. Washington,

DC: Economic Policy Institute. http://www.epi.org/publication/the-manufacturing-footprint-and-the-importance-of-u-s-manufacturing-jobs/ (accessed January 2017).

Seamster, Louise, and Raphaël Charron-Chénier. 2017. "Predatory Inclusion and Education Debt: Rethinking the Racial Wealth Gap." *Social Currents*. Prepublication version. DOI:10.1177/2329496516686620. http://www.journals.sagepub.com/home/scu (accessed January 2017).

Sentencing Project. 2017. "Fact Sheet: Trends in U.S. Corrections." Washington, DC: Sentencing Project. http://sentencingproject.org/wp-content/uploads/2016/01/Trends-in-US-Corrections.pdf (accessed June 2017).

Shabecoff, Philip. 1972. "The 1972 Campaign." *New York Times*, July 30. http://www.nytimes.com/1972/07/30/archives/most-unions-found-supporting-mcgovern-despite-meany-stand.html (accessed February 2017).

Shear, Michael. 2013. "Politics and Vetting Leave Key U.S. Posts Long Unfulfilled." *New York Times*, May 2. http://www.nytimes.com/2013/05/03/us/politics/top-posts-remain-vacant-throughout-obama-administration.html (accessed May 2017).

———. 2017. "Trump's Biggest Obstacle to Policy Goals? His Own Missteps." *New York Times*, March 25. https://www.nytimes.com/2017/03/25/us/politics/trump-policy-goals-missteps.html?_r=0 (accessed March 2017).

Sherk, James. 2010. "Technology Explains Drop in Manufacturing Jobs." Backgrounder No. 2476, October 12. Washington, DC: Heritage Foundation. http://www.heritage.org/research/reports/2010/10/technology-explains-drop-in-manufacturing-jobs (accessed January 2017).

Sherman, Jake, and Steven Shepard. 2016. "Poll: 41 Percent of Voters Say Election Could be 'Stolen' from Trump." *Politico*, October 17. http://www.politico.com/story/2016/10/poll-41-percent-of-voters-say-the-election-could-be-stolen-from-trump-229871 (accessed February 2017).

Skidelsky, Robert. 2009. *Keynes: The Return of the Master*. New York: Public Affairs.

Skocpol, Theda. 2000. *The Missing Middle*. New York: Norton.

Skocpol, Theda, and Alexander Hertel-Fernandez. 2016. "The Koch Network and Republican Party Extremism." *Perspectives on Politics* 14(3): 681–699.

Skocpol, Theda, and Vanessa Williamson. 2012. *The Tea Party and the Remaking of Republican Conservatism*. New York: Oxford University Press.

Skrentny, John. 1996. *The Ironies of Affirmative Action*. Chicago, IL: University of Chicago Press.

Smale, Alison, and Steven Erlanger. 2017. "Merkel, After Discordant G-7 Meeting, Is Looking Past Trump." *New York Times*, May 28. https://www.nytimes.com/2017/05/28/world/europe/angela-merkel-trump-alliances-g7-leaders.html?_r=0 (accessed June 2017).

Smith, Adam. 2016. "How Donald Trump Blew Up the Electoral Map." *Business Insider*, November 13. http://www.businessinsider.com/how-hillary-clinton-lost-election-to-trump-2016-11 (accessed January 2017).

Soergel, Andrew. 2016. "Cable News Enjoys Banner Year as Fox News Takes Ratings Crown." *U.S. News and World Report*, December 29. http://www.usnews.com/news/national-news/articles/2016-12-29/fox-news-takes-ratings-crown-for-2016 (accessed February 2017).

Somers, Margaret, and Fred Block. 2005. "From Poverty to Perversity: Ideas, Markets, and Institutions over 200 Years of Debate." *American Sociological Review* 70: 260–287.

Stein, Sam. 2016. "Despite What His Campaign Says, Donald Trump Supported the Bank Bailout." *Huffington Post*, November 6. http://www.huffingtonpost.com/entry/donald-trump-bank-bailout_us_581f5893e4b0e80b02caa415 (accessed February 2017).

Steinmo, Sven. 1993. *Taxation and Democracy*. New Haven, CT: Yale University Press.

Stiglitz, Joseph. 2009. "America's Socialism for the Rich." *The Guardian*, June 12. https://www.theguardian.com/commentisfree/2009/jun/12/america-corporate-banking-welfare (accessed February 2017).

————. 2012. *The Price of Inequality*. New York: Norton.

Stone, Roger. 2017. *The Making of the President 2016*. New York: Skyhorse.

Swift, Art. 2016. "Americans' Trust in Mass Media Sinks to New Low." Gallup Polling, September 14, http://www.gallup.com/poll/195542/americans-trust-mass-media-sinks-new-low.aspx (accessed January 2017).

Taibbi, Matt. 2017. *Insane Clown President*. New York: Spiegel & Grau.

Talkers. 2017. "2016 Talkers Heavy Hundred." http://www.talkers.com/heavy-hundred/ (accessed February 2017).

Tanner, Michael. 2016. "Trump on 'Waste, Fraud, and Abuse.'" *National Review*, February 17. http://www.nationalreview.com/article/431446/trump-waste-fraud-and-abuse (accessed February 2017).

Teles, Steven. 2008. *The Rise of the Conservative Legal Movement*. Princeton, NJ: Princeton University Press.

Temin, Peter. 2017. *The Vanishing Middle Class*. Cambridge, MA: Massachusetts Institute of Technology Press.

Tesler, Michael, and David Sears. 2010. *Obama's Race*. Chicago, IL: University of Chicago Press.

Thelen, Kathleen. 2004. *How Institutions Evolve: The Political Economy of Skills in Germany, the United States and Japan*. New York: Cambridge University Press.

Thomas, Louisa. 2016. "America First, for Charles Lindbergh and Donald Trump." *New Yorker*, July 24. http://www.newyorker.com/news/news-desk/america-first-for-charles-lindbergh-and-donald-trump (accessed March 2017).

Thompson, S. L., and J. W. Salmon. 2006. "Strikes by Physicians: A Historical Perspective Toward an Ethical Evaluation." *International Journal of Health Services* 36(2): 331–354.

————. 2014. "Physician Strikes." *Chest* 146(5): 1369–1374.

Time Magazine. 1990. "America's Changing Colors: What Will the U.S. Be Like When Whites Are No Longer the Majority?" April 9, Vol. 135, No. 15. http://content.time.com/time/covers/0,16641,19900409,00.html (accessed July 2017).

Troy, Tevi. 2017. "Can Conservatives Find Their Way?" *New York Times*, Sunday Review Section, July 8. https://www.nytimes.com/2017/07/08/opinion/sunday/can-conservatives-find-their-way.html?mcubz=0 (accessed July 2017).

Trump, Donald J. 2011. *Time to Get Tough: Making America #1 Again*. Washington, DC: Regnery.

————. 2016a. "Donald J. Trump: Address on Immigration." Press release: Phoenix, Arizona. August 31. https://www.donaldjtrump.com/press-releases/donald-j.-trump-address-on-immigration (accessed January 2017).

————. 2016b. "Trump Pledges to Drain the Swamp and Impose Congressional Term Limits." Press release. https://www.donaldjtrump.com/press-releases/trump-pledges-to-drain-the-swamp (accessed February 2017).

Tyson, Alec, and Shiva Maniam. 2016. "Behind Trump's Victory: Divisions by Race, Gender, Education." Pew Research Center, November 9. http://www.pewresearch.org/fact-tank/2016/11/09/behind-trumps-victory-divisions-by-race-gender-education/ (accessed February 2017).

US Arms Control and Disarmament Agency. 1970. *World Military Expenditures*. Washington, DC: Bureau of Economic Affairs, US Arms Control and Disarmament Agency. https://www.state.gov/documents/organization/185677.pdf (accessed January 2017).

US Bureau of Economic Analysis. 2016. "Gross Domestic Product (GDP) by Industry Data. Value Added by Industry as a Percentage of GDP, 1947-2015." Washington, DC: US Department of Commerce. https://www.bea.gov/industry/gdpbyind_data.htm (accessed January 2017).

US Bureau of Labor Statistics. 2017a. "Data Bases, Tables and Calculators by Subject." Washington, DC: US Bureau of Labor Statistics. https://data.bls.gov/pdq/Survey OutputServlet (accessed January 2017).

———. 2017b. "Labor Force Statistics from the Current Population Survey." Washington, DC: US Bureau of Labor Statistics. https://www.bls.gov/cps/tables.htm#charunem_m (accessed May 2017).

US Census Bureau. 2016. "Income and Poverty in the United States: 2015." *Current Population Reports*, September P60-256(RV). Washington, DC: US Census Bureau. https://www.census.gov/content/dam/Census/library/publications/2016/demo/p60-256.pdf (accessed February 2017).

———. 2017a. "Historical Census of Housing Tables." Washington, DC: US Census Bureau. https://www.census.gov/hhes/www/housing/census/historic/owner.html (accessed January 2017).

———. 2017b. "Historical Poverty Tables: People and Families—1959–2015." Washington, DC: US Census Bureau. http://www.census.gov/data/tables/time-series/demo/income-poverty/historical-poverty-people.html (accessed January 2017).

———. 2017c. "Historical Income Tables: Families." Washington, DC: US Census Bureau. http://www.census.gov/data/tables/time-series/demo/income-poverty/historical-income-families.html (accessed January 2017).

———. 2017d. "Educational Attainment. CPS Historical Time Series Tables." Washington, DC: US Census Bureau. https://www.census.gov/hhes/socdemo/education/data/cps/historical/ (accessed January 2017).

US Chamber of Commerce. 2017. "Immigration: Myths and the Facts Behind the Fallacies." Washington, DC: US Chamber of Commerce, Labor, Immigration and Employee Benefits Division. https://www.uschamber.com/sites/default/files/legacy/issues/immigration/files/14484immigrationmythfacts.pdf (accessed January 2017).

US Department of Health and Human Services. 2017. "Medical Expenditure Panel Survey." Washington, DC: US Department of Health and Human Services. https://meps.ahrq.gov/mepsweb/data_stats/MEPSnetIC/mainsel.action (accessed May 2017).

US Department of Justice. 2003. *Sourcebook of Criminal Justice Statistics*. Washington, DC: US Department of Justice.

US Department of Labor. 2017. "Minimum Wage—U.S. Department of Labor—Chart 1." Washington, DC: US Department of Labor. https://www.dol.gov/featured/minimum-wage/chart1 (accessed January 2017).

US Department of Transportation. 2017. "Federal Highway Administration. Highway History: The Great Decade 1956-1966." Washington, DC: US Department of Transportation. https://www.fhwa.dot.gov/infrastructure/50interstate.cfm (accessed January 2017).

US Department of Veterans Affairs. 2017. "Education and Training: History Timeline." Washington, DC: US Department of Veterans Affairs. http://www.benefits.va.gov/gibill/history.asp (accessed January 2017).

US Federal Bureau of Investigation. 2017. "Uniform Crime Reports: Hate Crime Statistics." Washington, DC: US Department of Justice. https://ucr.fbi.gov/ucr-publications#Hate (accessed May 2017).

US National Labor Relations Board. 2017. "1959 Landrum-Griffin Act." Washington, DC: US National Labor Relations Board. https://www.nlrb.gov/who-we-are/our-history/1959-landrum-griffin-act (accessed January 2017).

US Office of the Director of National Intelligence. 2017. "Assess Russian Activities and Intentions in Recent U.S. Elections." ICA 2017-01D, January 6. Washington, DC: US Office of the Director of National Intelligence. https://assets.documentcloud.org/documents/3254237/Russia-Hack-Report.pdf (accessed January 2017).

US Office of Management and Budget. 2017. "2016 United States Budget." Washington, DC: US Office of Management and Budget. http://federal-budget.insidegov.com/l/119/2016 (accessed February 2017).

US Social Security Administration. 2009. "The Disappearing Defined Benefit Pension and Its Potential Impact on the Retirement Incomes of Baby Boomers." *Social Security Bulletin* 69: 3. Washington, DC: US Social Security Administration. https://www.ssa.gov/policy/docs/ssb/v69n3/v69n3p1.html (accessed May 2017).

————. 2013. "Effects of Unauthorized Immigration on the Actuarial Status of the Social Security Trust Funds." Actuarial Note, number 151, April. Baltimore: US Social Security Administration, Office of the Chief Actuary. https://www.ssa.gov/oact/NOTES/pdf_notes/note151.pdf (accessed July 2017).

Useem, Michael. 1984. *The Inner Circle*. New York: Oxford University Press.

Valverde, Miriam. 2016. "Pants on Fire! Trump Says Clinton Would Let 650 Million People Into the U.S., In One Week." *PolitiFact*, October 31. http://www.politifact.com/truth-o-meter/statements/2016/oct/31/donald-trump-says-clinton-would-bring-650-million-people-/ (accessed February 2017).

Vance, J. D. 2016. *Hillbilly Elegy*. New York: Harper Collins.

VanDerWerff, Todd. 2015. "Donald Trump's Secret Political Weapon Is His Mastery of Reality TV." *Vox*, August 14. http://www.vox.com/2015/8/14/9151251/donald-trump-apprentice-president (accessed January 2017).

Vine, David. 2015. "The United States Probably Has More Foreign Military Bases Than Any Other People, Nation, or Empire in History." *The Nation*, September 14. https://www.thenation.com/article/the-united-states-probably-has-more-foreign-military-bases-than-any-other-people-nation-or-empire-in-history/ (accessed January 2017).

Waldman, Michael. 2016. *The Fight to Vote*. New York: Simon and Schuster.

Warhurst, Chris. 2016. "Accidental Tourists: Brexit and Its Toxic Employment Underpinnings." *Socio-Economic Review* 14(4): 819–825.

Washington Post. 2015. "Full Text: Donald Trump Announces a Presidential Bid." June 16. https://www.washingtonpost.com/news/post-politics/wp/2015/06/16/full-text-donald-trump-announces-a-presidential-bid/?utm_term=.d88f564f46be (accessed March 2017).

Weigel, David. 2015. "In Michigan, Trump Attacks China, Critiques Auto Bailout, and Judges Bernie Sanders 'Weak.'" *Washington Post*, August 11. https://www.washingtonpost.com/news/post-politics/wp/2015/08/11/in-michigan-trump-attacks-china-critiques-auto-bailout-and-judges-bernie-sanders-weak/?utm_term=.83270a6e4122 (accessed February 2017).

Weiss, Linda. 2014. *America Inc.?* Ithaca, NY: Cornell University Press.

Western, Bruce. 1997. *Between Class and Market*. Princeton, NJ: Princeton University Press.

Western, Bruce and Katherine Beckett. 1999. "How Unregulated is the U.S. Labor Market? The Penal System as a Labor Market Institution." *American Journal of Sociology* 104: 1030–1060.

Wheeler, Russell. 2016. "The Growing Specter of Vacant Judgeships." Brookings Institution, April 12. https://www.brookings.edu/blog/fixgov/2016/04/12/the-growing-specter-of-vacant-federal-judgeships/ (accessed May 2017).

Whitford, Josh. 2005. *The New Old Economy*. New York: Oxford University Press.

Wilhelm, Heather. 2016. "Reminder: Hillary Clinton Lost Because She's Hillary Clinton." *National Review*, November 11. http://www.nationalreview.com/article/442063/hillary-clinton-lost-because-shes-hillary-clinton (accessed March 2017).

Wilkinson, Richard, and Kate Pickett. 2009. *The Spirit Level*. New York: Bloomsbury Press.

Williams, Joan C. 2016. "What So Many People Don't Get About the U.S. Working Class." *Harvard Business Review*, November 10. https://hbr.org/2016/11/what-so-many-people-dont-get-about-the-u-s-working-class (accessed May 2017).

Wilmers, Nathan. 2017. "Wage Stagnation and Economic Governance: How Buyer-Supplier Relations Affect U.S. Workers' Wages, 1978–2014." Unpublished manuscript, Department of Sociology, Harvard University.

Wilson, William Julius. 1987. *The Truly Disadvantaged*. Chicago, IL: University of Chicago Press.

———. 1997. *When Work Disappears*. New York: Knopf.

———. 2009. *More Than Just Race*. New York: Norton.

Wines, Michael. 2016. "All This Talk of Voter Fraud? Across U.S., Officials Found Next to None." *New York Times*, December 18. https://www.nytimes.com/2016/12/18/us/voter-fraud.html (accessed January 2017).

Wojdyla, Ben. 2011. "The Top Automotive Engineering Failures: The Ford Pinto Fuel Tanks." *Popular Mechanics*, May 20. http://www.popularmechanics.com/cars/a6700/top-automotive-engineering-failures-ford-pinto-fuel-tanks/ (accessed April 2017).

Wood, Geoffrey, and Mike Wright. 2016. "What Brexit Tells us about Institutions and Social Action." *Socio-Economic Review* 14(4): 832–836.

Wood, Thomas. 2017. "Racism Motivated Trump Voters More Than Authoritarianism." *Washington Post*, April 17. https://www.washingtonpost.com/news/monkey-cage/wp/2017/04/17/racism-motivated-trump-voters-more-than-authoritarianism-or-income-inequality/?utm_term=.6d848a1d4231&wpisrc=nl_most-draw8&wpmm=1 (accessed May 2017).

Yates, Elizabeth. 2016. "How the Tea Party Learned to Love Donald Trump." *Washington Post*, December 1. https://www.washingtonpost.com/news/monkey-cage/wp/2016/12/01/how-the-tea-party-learned-to-love-donald-trump/?utm_term=.d9cc04919f12 (accessed April 2017).

Yee, Vivian. 2016. "Donald Trump's Math Takes His Towers to Greater Heights." *New York Times*, November 1. https://www.nytimes.com/2016/11/02/nyregion/donald-trump-tower-heights.html?_r=0 (accessed February 2017).

Yonay, Yuval P. 1998. *The Struggle Over the Soul of Economics*. Princeton, NJ: Princeton University Press.

YouTube. 2012. "Sara Palin—Obama Is a Socialist . . . Socialism Leads to Communism." December 4. https://www.youtube.com/watch?v=ODATXu_2m-c (accessed February 2017).

Zengerle, Jason. 2017. "Is North Carolina the Future of American Politics?" *New York Times*, June 20. https://www.nytimes.com/2017/06/20/magazine/is-north-carolina-the-future-of-american-politics.html?rref=collection%2Ftimestopic%2FNorth%20Carolina&action=click&contentCollection=us&region=stream&module=stream_unit&version=latest&contentPlacement=3&pgtype=collection (accessed June 2017).

Zinn, Howard. 2003. *A People's History of the United States, 1492–Present*. New York: Harper Perennial.

INDEX

Note: Page numbers followed by the letter *f* or *t* indicate material found in figures or tables.

National Association of Manufacturers, 40
National Center for Policy Analysis, 83
National Commission on Fiscal
    Responsibility and Reform, 88
National Front (France), 154–55, 158–59
nationalism, 16, 21, 152, 156, 157
National Labor Relations Board (NLRB),
    27, 40–41
National Public Radio (NPR), 126
National Review, 6, 120
National Security Agency (NSA), 4
"National Threat Assessment for Domestic
    Extremism" (FBI report), 75
national/US debt, 9, 24, 82, 88, 113, 125–26,
    137, 160–62. *See also* debt
Native Americans, 58
neoliberalism
    assumptions of, 82
    corporate lobbying for, 83–84
    economic factors and, 17–18, 123, 162
    financial crisis/Great Recession
        and, 160–61
    free trade and, 153
    historical record of, 89–90
    ideological trends/labels and, 104, 108,
        116, 166–67
    immigration and, 97
    legislative mandates and, 134
    Reagan years and, 150
    rise of, 9, 12*f*, 13, 78, 81–87, 110, 125
    shift from Keynesianism, 85–86, 131
    think tanks and, 83
    Trump's economic plan and, 98, 101–2
Netherlands, 154
New Deal/New Deal Democrats, 13, 59,
    110, 167
New Democrats, 110–11
New Hampshire, xiii, 33, 41, 119, 132
New York Times, xvii, xviii
New York University School of Law, 118
9/11 attacks, 14, 57, 75–77, 116, 127, 141
Nixon, Richard M., 13, 29, 41, 58, 68, 81,
    109–10, 112, 115–16
North American Free Trade Agreement
    (NAFTA), 34, 53, 87, 90, 96–97, 111,
    149, 153, 161–62
North Atlantic Treaty Organization
    (NATO), 1, 23, 153, 162–63
North Carolina, 61, 118–19, 136
North Korea, 161, 163
Norwegian Progress Party, 155

Obama, Barack
    approval ratings of, 125
    budget fights and, 168
    DNC address (2004), 77
    election of, 127–30
    executive orders and, 139
    financial crisis/Great Recession and, 2,
        14, 130–33
    gender gap and, 114
    gridlock and, 123–25, 138, 142
    health care reform and, 133–38
    minority vote for, 60
    opinions on, 146*t*
    presidential campaign of, 49
    Romney loss to, 5
    talk radio/television lambasting of, 85
    Tea Party Movement and, 109, 167
    Trump on, xi, 19, 61
    US as world power under, 161
    working class hatred/skepticism and, 149
Obamacare, xii, 133, 140–41. *See also*
    Affordable Care Act (ACA)
Occupational Safety and Health
    Administration (OSHA), 112
Occupy Wall Street movement, 10, 12*f*, 132
Office of Management and Budget
    (OMB), 89
Office of the Inspector General, 5
Ohio, 27, 30, 33, 57, 149, 152, 166
oil, access to, 24
Olin Foundation, 83
O'Neill, Tip, 167
One Nation After Trump (Dionne, Ornstein
    and Mann), 9
O'Reilly, Bill, 85
Organisation for Economic Cooperation and
    Development (OECD), 44
Organization of Arab Petroleum Exporting
    Countries (OPEC), 32, 82
organized labor, 13, 27, 39–41, 111–13
Ornstein, Norman, 9, 124
The Other America (Harrington), 26
outsourcing, 34, 36–38, 43, 51, 53, 111

Palin, Sarah, 134, 164
Parton, Dolly, 25
Party for Freedom (Netherlands), 154
pattern bargaining, 41
Paulson, Henry, 127
Pearlstein, Steve, 38
Pence, Mike, 101